MEDIEVALIA ET HUMANISTICA

MEDIEVALIA ET HUMANISTICA

New Series
Edited by Paul Maurice Clogan

Number 1: In Honor of S. Harrison Thomson

Number 2: Medieval and Renaissance Studies in Review

Number 3: Social Dimensions in Medieval and Renaissance Studies

Number 4: Medieval and Renaissance Spirituality

Number 5: Medieval Historiography

MEDIEVALIA ET HUMANISTICA

STUDIES IN MEDIEVAL & RENAISSANCE CULTURE

FOUNDED IN 1943
BY S. HARRISON THOMSON

NEW SERIES: NUMBER 6

Medieval Hagiography and Romance

EDITED BY PAUL MAURICE CLOGAN

NORTH TEXAS STATE UNIVERSITY

1975

CAMBRIDGE UNIVERSITY PRESS

CAMBRIDGE

LONDON · NEW YORK · MELBOURNE

Published by the Syndics of the Cambridge University Press
The Pitt Building, Trumpington Street, Cambridge CB2 1RP
Bentley House, 200 Euston Road, London NW1 2DB
32 East 57th Street, New York, NY 10022, USA
296 Beaconsfield Parade, Middle Park, Melbourne 3206, Australia

© The Medieval and Renaissance Society 1975

Library of Congress Catalogue Card Number: 75–16872

ISBN 0 521 20999 4
ISSN 0076 6127

First published 1975

Typeset and printed in the United States of America by
Vail-Ballou Press, Inc, Binghamton, New York

Contents

Editorial Note	vii
Preface	ix
Two Types of Opposition and the Structure of Latin Saints' Lives Charles F. Altman, *Cornell University*	1
Hagiography and Romance in Medieval Ireland Ludwig Bieler, *University College, Dublin*	13
Irish Saints' Lives, Romance, and Cultural History William W. Heist, *Michigan State University*	25
Anglo-Norman Hagiography and the Romances M. Dominica Legge, *Oxford, England*	41
French Medievalists and the Saint's Play: A Problem for American Scholarship E. Catherine Dunn, *The Catholic University of America*	51
An Analysis of the Narrative Motifs in the Legend of St. Eustace Thomas J. Heffernan, *Emmanuel College, Cambridge*	63
The *Joseph of Arimathie:* English Hagiography in Transition Valerie M. Lagorio, *University of Iowa*	91
Didacticism and Drama in *Guy of Warwick* David N. Klausner, *University of Toronto*	103
John Capgrave's *Life of St. Katharine* and Popular Romance Style Derek Pearsall, *University of York*	121
Malory and the Ballad "King Arthur's Death" Robert H. Wilson, *University of Texas at Austin*	139

bi lag mon: A Crux in *Sir Gawayn and the Grene Knyȝt*   151
    William Matthews, *University of California at Los Angeles*

Isolt's Trial in Béroul and *La Folie Tristan d'Oxford*   157
    Ernest C. York, *University of Alabama*

The Heavenly Letter in Medieval England   163
    W. R. Jones, *University of New Hampshire*

William of Malmesbury and Some Other Western Writers on Islam   179
    Rodney M. Thomson, *University of Tasmania*

Literary Criticism in William Godwin's *Life of Chaucer*   189
    Paul M. Clogan, *North Texas State University*

REVIEW ARTICLES

Collected Works of Erasmus: Volume One   199
    Douglas Bush, *Harvard University*

Some Oblique Light: Three Studies in Reformation History   203
    Arthur J. Slavin, *University of Louisville*

Political and Social Thought in Fourteenth-Century England:
Two Recent Studies   208
    Michael Altschul, *Case Western Reserve University*

Toronto Medieval Latin Texts: Three New Editions   211
    Daniel J. Sheerin, *University of North Carolina at Chapel Hill*

REVIEW NOTICES   214

James J. Murphy, *Rhetoric in the Middle Ages* (Ernest Gallo)
Robert Chazan, *Medieval Jewry in Northern France*
(Thomas N. Bisson)
Edward A. Armstrong, *Saint Francis, Nature Mystic*
(Duane V. Lapsanski)
Marcelle Thiébaux, *The Stag of Love* (Paul E. Beichner, C.S.C.)

Books received   220

Editorial Note

Medievalia et Humanistica, founded in 1943 by S. Harrison Thomson, achieved national and international recognition as the first American scholarly publication devoted solely to the study of the Middle Ages and Renaissance. The new interdisciplinary series, begun in 1970 and edited by an international board of distinguished scholars and critics, publishes in annual hardbound volumes significant scholarship, criticism, and reviews covering all areas of medieval and Renaissance culture: literature, history, art, science, philosophy, law, music, architecture, social and economic institutions. *Medievalia et Humanistica* encourages the individual scholar to examine the relationship of his discipline to other disciplines and to relate his study in a theoretical or practical way to its cultural and historical context. The new annual series seeks to integrate the study of medieval and Renaissance culture by considering important topics of common interest from different perspectives and by indicating current trends and new directions in humanistic scholarship. The series encourages cooperation between scholars in various disciplines and provides a forum for the exchange of ideas and information of general interest to medieval and Renaissance scholars and critics. Review articles examine significant recent publications and major areas of current concern within specific fields, and contributing editors report on the progress of medieval and Renaissance studies in North America and Europe.

Medievalia et Humanistica is sponsored by the Comparative Studies in Medieval Literature Section of the Modern Language Association of America, and publication in the series is open to contributions from all sources. The editorial board welcomes interdisciplinary critical and historical studies by young or established scholars and urges contributors to communicate in an attractive, clear, and concise style the larger implications in addition to the precise material of their research, with documentation held to a minimum. Texts, maps, illustrations, and diagrams will be published only when they are essential to the argument of the article.

Individuals, institutions, and libraries may enter standing orders for the new series. Future volumes will be sent to them automatically. Such standing orders may, of course, be canceled at any time. Inquiries regarding single or standing orders for the new series and Numbers 1–3 should be addressed to the Publisher, Cambridge University Press, at 32 East 57th Street, New York, New York 10022, or at Bentley House, 200 Euston Road, London NW1 2DB.

Preface

Hagiography and romance share a good deal of common ground, and the close relationship of the two kinds of *matières* reveals essential tendencies and problems regarding medieval narrative art. The rich collections of early Christian saints' legends contain a great variety of styles of presentation, and many of these narratives follow the conventional pattern of romance. Both kinds of writing employ narrative, normally with a single protagonist as hero, and both celebrate an ideal and liberated experience, disengaged and disencumbered from the demands of reality. The vagueness of the term legend, which is an inheritance from the Middle Ages, and the diversity and pervasiveness of romance make definition of these two forms of writing difficult. Modern scholars have been aware of the problem of distinguishing the essential characteristics of romance and legend as types of narrative, so that today one studies not the definition but the genre of hagiography and romance. Yet the relationship of these two narrative forms has been somewhat complicated by the influence and imitation of the style and mode of one on the other. As Derek Pearsall remarks in his important study of the influence of popular romance style in the *Life of St. Katharine of Alexandria,* "the blurring of form which so perplexes the modern scholar, preoccupied with matters of generic definition, is the precise goal of these writers, whether they be entertainers with a touch of piety or hagiographers with an eye for their audience." By the time the vernacular languages began to emerge in Western Europe, hagiography had already established a long and popular tradition. At the end of the ninth century alone, six hundred Lives had been written. Many of the earliest and important texts written in the vernacular languages were, of course, accounts of saints' lives. By bringing hagiography and romance together in a symposium of original articles for this sixth volume in the new series of *Medievalia et Humanistica,* we hope to explore the boundaries and borderlands of two important kinds of medieval writing and to shed some new light on medieval narrative art in general.

Charles F. Altman, whose field is narratology, identifies the characteristics of medieval narrative by dividing hagiographical accounts into *passiones* or legends of the martyr saints and *vitae* or biographies of confessor saints, giving the distinction proper structural definition. Ludwig Bieler, the foremost expert on the subject, shows how Irish hagiography inherited from Christian antiquity not only the form of aretalogy but also many details of a romantic character common in pagan narrative literature which had been absorbed in such works as the apocryphal Acts of the Apostles and other biblical apocrypha current in Christian Ireland. William W. Heiss examines Irish saints' Lives from both classical background and Celtic background and poses valuable questions regarding the influence of religious foundations, dominant classes, and the reform of the Irish Church in the eleventh and twelfth centuries. M. Dominica Legge, the distinguished scholar of Anglo-Norman literature, points out that the *Voyage of St. Brendan*, the earliest Anglo-Norman text, written in 1106, contains elements which later became characteristic of romances. "Saints' Lives were written as counterblasts to romances and to provide the Laity with more elevating literature." Professor Legge's conclusion that the resemblances between hagiography and romance are accounted for by the social conditions of the time should interest scholars concerned with the question of audience and public and the extent and nature of literacy. Though the medieval miracle play on the life of a saint has long been regarded as the last form of Latin religious drama composed in the twelfth century, E. Catherine Dunn argues that the saint's play may well be the earliest form of medieval drama, antedating the "Quem quaeritis" texts of Easter Sunday in the tenth century. Thomas J. Heffernan analyzes the three main narrative units – conversion, sufferings, and martyrdom – of the popular legend of St. Eustace in three Middle English versions, revealing the presence of familiar structural motifs and showing that hagiographers relied on their listeners' familarity with verbal reminiscences of earlier texts. The close alliance of hagiography and romance is examined by Valerie M. Lagorio in the legendary *vita* of Joseph of Arimathea, who in French Arthurian romances became the Grail keeper and evangelizer of Britain. David N. Klausner studies the differences between an English romance – immensely popular from the thirteenth to the sixteenth centuries – and the legend of St. Alexis, and emphasizes the tenuous border between romance and legend, showing how writers in each genre borrow from one another. With a knowledge of medieval law, Ernest C. York offers an interesting interpretation of the problem of some of the transmissions of the legend of Tristan and Isolt. William Matthews undertakes a philological inquiry terminating in the illumination of a textual crux in a famous fourteenth-century English romance, which will doubtless find its way into later editions of the text. Finally, Robert H. Wilson identifies as late sixteenth century the ballad "King Arthur's Death," hitherto considered a medieval work.

In addition to the symposium on hagiography and romance, W. R. Jones contributes a fascinating study of the history and popularity of the Christ-letter, which circulated widely through eastern and western Christendom from late antiquity to the modern period, and places his study in the larger context of popular religious invective and millenarianism, a subject which is of special interest today, when considerable attention is being given to popular religion and prophecy in the late Middle Ages. Rodney M. Thomson makes an important contribution by examining the knowledge and attitudes regarding Islam among western Christian writers of the Middle Ages, and in particular the English monk William of Malmesbury, who is one of the earliest westerners to demonstrate an accurate knowledge of Islam's origins and nature. Moreover, this volume also contains four review articles and four review notices of significant recent publications. The next volume in the new series of *Medievalia et Humanistica* will explore from different perspectives the topics of science and poetics and will also include articles on varied subjects. Review articles will evaluate significant recent publications and major areas of current concern within specific fields, and contributing editors will report on the progress of medieval and Renaissance studies in North America and Europe.

P.M.C.

October 1975

MEDIEVALIA ET HUMANISTICA

Paul Maurice Clogan, EDITOR
North Texas State University

EDITORIAL BOARD

Articles for Future Volumes Are Invited

Original typescripts (not photocopies or carbons) should be presented on good quality, standard 8½ x 11 inch paper, doubled-spaced with ample margins. They should be accompanied by a stamped, self-addressed manuscript envelope, addressed to the Editor, *Medievalia et Humanistica*, P. O. Box 13348, North Texas Station, Denton, Texas 76203. The length of the article depends upon the material. Brief footnotes, prepared according to the second edition of the *MLA Style Sheet* or the twelfth edition of the Chicago *Manual of Style*, should be double-spaced, numbered consecutively, and placed at the end of the article. All quotations, citations, and references should be carefully verified before submission. Books for review and inquiries regarding *Fasciculi* I–XVII of the original series should be addressed to the Editor.

Authors outside the United States and Canada may submit original typescripts in English to the nearest or most appropriate editor for consideration. A prospective author is encouraged to contact his editor at the earliest opportunity to obtain a copy of the style sheet and to receive any necessary advice. The addresses and fields of the editors outside the United States and Canada are:

Professor Giuseppe Billanovich, Via Giovanni Rusca 15, Padova 35100, Italia (Medieval and Humanistic Philology)

Dr. Derek Brewer, Emmanuel College, Cambridge CB2 3AP, England (Medieval Literature)

Mr. Peter Dronke, Clare Hall, Cambridge CB3 9DA, England (Medieval Latin Poetry and Thought)

Professor J. R. Hale, Department of Italian, University College London, Gower Street, London WC1E 6BT, England (Renaissance History)

Professor Denys Hay, Department of History, University of Edinburgh, William Robertson Building, George Square, Edinburgh EH8 9JY, Scotland (Renaissance History)

Professor Dr. Heinz Liebing, Ernst-Lemmer-Str. 10, D – 3550 Marburg/Lahn 6, West Germany (Church History)

Professor Ian D. McFarlane, Wadham College, Oxford OX1 3NA, England (Renaissance French and Neo-Latin Literature)

Professor Jean-Claude Margolin, 75 Bld Richard-Lenoir, 75011 Paris, France (Humanism, Renaissance Philosophy and Neo-Latin)

Professor Dr. Heiko Oberman, 7400 Tübingen, Hölderlinstr. 17, West Germany (Church History, Late Medieval Theology and Reformation)

Professor Dr. Paul G. Schmidt, Seminar für Klassische Philologie der Universität, 34 Göttingen, Nikolausberger Weg 9c, West Germany (Medieval Latin Philology)

Two Types of Opposition
and the Structure
of Latin Saints' Lives

CHARLES F. ALTMAN

I will begin by distinguishing two different types of contrast common in medieval texts. When an author or artist opposes virtue to vice he employs what I will call *diametrical* opposition. Augustine aptly summarizes this style and the world view it implies as he introduces the opposition of earthly and heavenly cities in the eleventh book of *De Civitate Dei*:

Sicut ergo ista contraria contrariis opposita sermonis pulchritudinem reddunt; ita quadam non verborum, sed rerum eloquentia contrariorum oppositione saeculi pulchritudo componitur. Apertissime hoc positum est in libro Ecclesiastico, hoc modo: "Contra malum bonum est, et contra mortem vita: sic contra pium peccator. Et sic intuere in omnia opera Altissimi, bina et bina, unum contra unum."[1]

The second type of contrast I will term *gradational* opposition. Thus, Gregory the Great's celebrated distinction between action and contemplation is clearly a gradation, and not a diametrical opposition.[2] Action is not bad, like vice, it is simply not *as* good as contemplation. Instead of treating the secular as opposed to the spiritual, this second system treats the secular as a stop on the way to the spiritual, or perhaps I should say *step*, for the new metaphor is clearly the ladder, with its implied continuity between less and more value.

This simple distinction is one of the most important we have for defining the style of medieval authors. In this essay I will exemplify the characteristics of narrative texts organized according to each type of contrast. In so doing I will claim that hagiographical accounts are best divided into two groups. In the first group are the *passiones*, or legends of the martyr saints; these, like the medieval epic, operate according to the principles of diametrical opposition. In the second we have the *vitae*, or biographies of confessor saints; these grow slowly away from the diametrical configuration of the *passio*, eventually adopting fully the gradational form of romance.

The distinction between *vita* and *passio* is one which has often been made, by Delehaye and others,[3] but it has never been given proper structural definition. The principal elements of the early martyr legends, whether in Latin or Greek, are three, each defined according to the basic diametrical opposition of martyrs to persecutors:

1. dialogue in which a government representative attempts to induce a Christian to recant his beliefs or to sacrifice to the pagan gods; this dialogue serves to identify the values of the *passio* not with the individuals portrayed, but with the groups and religions they represent
2. persecution and actual martyrdom, involving the exemplification of virtue and vice through the opposition of the two parties
3. a support system for each side, including a deity and a sympathetic group

The author clearly belongs to one of these groups and thus narrates not in the third-person but in the first-person plural.

The major function of the *passio* is thus to play up the discontinuity between the two groups. Miracles, for example, serve to differentiate the persecuted from the persecutor, to distinguish positive from negative value. In the *Martyrdom of Polycarp*, one of our earliest accounts of the persecutions, the miracle's role is clearly demonstrated. Polycarp is bound and a fire lit around him, but the flames belly out like a ship's sail in the wind, thus protecting him from harm. When he is stabbed by an official, we are told that such a large quantity of blood came out that the flames were extinguished, "and even the crowd marvelled that there should be such a difference between the unbelievers and the elect."[4]

The *passio* plot operates by the removal of all those who represent exceptions to the dominant ideology. This aspect of the martyr legend is elegantly exemplified by the most important model for all subsequent *passiones, Passio Sanctarum Perpetuae et Felicitatis.*[5] The words and actions of the Romans testify to their view that Christians are unwelcome exceptions to the law requiring everyone to sacrifice for the welfare of the emperor. From the Roman point of view, the governor's sentence and the subsequent martyrdom of Perpetua and her friends serve to purge the world of all those who refuse to obey the law. From the point of view of Perpetua's vision, however, the situation is reversed: she imagines herself led into the arena opposite the Devil dressed as an Egyptian. This imaginary combat, which Perpetua soon wins with supernatural help, contrasts vividly with the quite real slaughter which follows. Here, then, is a further dichotomy, which explains the Christians' hope in the face of bloodthirsty persecution: there are, it would seem, two stories, one overlaying the other. One concerns the real world, seen from the Roman point of view; the other is apocalyptic, portraying the end of time from the Christian point of view. The real arena may represent the Mediterranean world, which can support only one religion at a time, and thus must eliminate all exceptions, but the visionary arena represents the Last Judgment, where once again only the true believers will survive. Though many martyr legends make no explicit reference to Christianity's ultimate victory over its persecutors, the notion is clearly everywhere implicit.[6] The two overlapping points of view in the *Martyrdom of Perpetua and Felicitas* may be diametrically opposed, but each solves its problems by the same method – all those who diverge from the pertinent norm are simply eliminated.

We find in these short *passiones* many of the attributes characteristic of the medieval epic, indeed of all narrative organized according to the principle of diametrical opposition. To choose a variety of well-known texts, Augustine's *City of God*, Prudentius' *Psychomachia*, *Beowulf*, *Waltharii poesis*, the *Song of Roland*, and the Last Judgment typanum at Conques all share the following attributes of the *passio*: scenes involving alternation between two diametrically opposed forces, subordination of the individual to the group's goal, a plot which proceeds by the removal of exception and re-creation of unity, definition of virtue by opposition to vice, and identification of the narrator with the text's positively valued group. By no means do all of the medieval texts which we have come to call epics conform perfectly to this system, but in its abstract form this expansion of the basic diametrical configuration clearly represents one of the fundamental poles of medieval narrative.

The fourth century begins hagiography's long evolution away from the diametrical form. Some reasons for this movement, such as Constantine's conversion and the resultant tolerance of Christianity, are obvious, but there are other less obvious reasons as well. Thus, in the second half of the fourth century, the church fathers began to write the life stories of those monks who had successfully attempted a solitary life of prayer and asceticism in the Egyptian desert. The most widely and consistently influential of these, Athanasius' *Life of Anthony*, almost immediately adapted in Latin by Evagrius, will serve us here as an example.[7] The Athanasius-Evagrius *Life* borrows many of its thematic motifs from the *passio*. The desert, like the arena, is seen as a limited space which cannot be inhabited by the Devil and the man of God alike. There is therefore much strife reminiscent of the martyrs' suffering. In a like manner, internal divisions within the church cause Anthony to speak out against the Arian heresy, thus supporting one of Athanasius' major causes. Such concerns occupy a large portion of the text, as they will in other saints' Lives written during the early and difficult years of the church.

The overall arrangement of the text, however, is by no means that of the martyr legend. Instead of relating a string of diametrical oppositions, one martyr after the other going to his death as in so many *passiones*, the story of Anthony is arranged as a *vita*, the narrative being structured by the events of Anthony's life, rather than by an ongoing *theomachia* or religious war. This arrangement calls for many new motifs. For example, it requires a motivation for Anthony's departure to the desert; this is pro-

vided through a device which will later become a hagiographical commonplace: the scriptures kindle in him the desire to rise above this worldly
life. Whether, like Hilarion, the budding saint has heard about the exploits
of a previous hermit, been inspired by the scriptures like Guthlac, or been
moved by a marvelous tale like Brendan, the *vita* will often begin with
the birth of what René Girard has called *triangular desire*.[8]

The saint's desire is rarely, however, of the diametrical type; he seeks
not to destroy his opponents but to transcend secular cares. Thus saints
will follow Anthony's example in giving all their worldly goods to the
poor; in so doing they affirm not only the higher status of their spiritual
goal, but they also underline the fact that worldly goods are not useless,
they are simply inferior to spiritual values.[9] This first act clearly defines
the eremitic occupation and the *vita*'s structure as one of gradation. It
also exemplifies the major plot motif of the *vita*, the identification and
glorification of the individual who stands out from the crowd, the man of
exceptional spirituality who paradoxically stands as an *exemplum* for all
others. The hermit's progress is thus constantly measured in terms of distance from the human norm. He begins, like us, by solving the problem
of his physical needs, but goes on to concentrate on spiritual cares; at first,
he performs feats within the bounds of natural law, but then God grants
him the power to perform miracles. As the solitary servant of God achieves
new understanding of the spirit, he passes this knowledge on to those who
have not yet risen as high on the spiritual scale. Anthony's long address
to the monks is the archetype for the instructional motif, but as the *vita*
form matures, the saint's teachings tend to be spread out among his various
miracles.

The Athanasius-Evagrius *Life of Anthony*, along with Jerome's various
biographies of hermits,[10] provided an important formal example for the
centuries to come. A proper history of the Latin *vita* would show how the
thematic material of hagiographical texts is slowly adapted to the gradational nature of their biographical form. Influential texts like the *Navigatio
Sancti Brendani*[11] and Gregory's *Life of Benedict*[12] give increased attention to the saint as an exceptional figure whose example is to be imitated;
at the same time they reduce the emphasis on his role of opponent to
devils or heretics. Where the Church is less well rooted, however, this
process takes longer. Those Lives which imitate the altar-smashing of
Sulpicius Severus' Saint Martin,[13] for example, retain a significant propor-
tion of the *passio*'s diametrical opposition.[14] But the basic pattern is clearly
reversed: miracles no longer demonstrate the difference between martyr
and persecutor, between God and the Devil; instead they identify the
exceptional characteristics of a single man and the extent to which he has
progressed along the continuum stretching from the cares of the world to
those of the spirit. One clear indication of the *vita*'s divergence from the
passio tradition can be found in the evolution of the concept of "imita-

tion." In *passio* and *vita* alike, the saint claims to be imitating Christ, but in each case a different aspect of Christ's life is imitated, the *passio* choosing the most diametrical aspects, the *vita* turning more and more to gradational elements in Christ's life.

We find a first culmination of the *vita's* gradational approach in eighth-century Northumbria, which produced many saints' Lives of high literary quality.[15] Among these, three are devoted to the life of Saint Cuthbert.[16] The composer of the last two, the Venerable Bede, was in an excellent position to consolidate the advances made by four centuries of *vitae:* he knew all the important earlier Lives, he had the Lindisfarne anonymous *Vita S. Cuthberti* as source and model, and he was extremely familiar with, and sympathetic to, the gradational theology of Gregory the Great.

Bede's prose *Life of Cuthbert* is particularly interesting for its treatment of Cuthbert as an exceptional individual and for the parallel which it establishes between the opposition of the group to the exception and the contrast between worldly and spiritual values. In almost every chapter these two oppositions coincide, elegantly demonstrating the *vita's* twin emphases on the individual and on his progression toward greater spiritual value. The establishment of Cuthbert's exceptionality is carried out in four major ways: First, he is constantly singled out from the group which he is with, either by his own action, the group's recognition, or divine intervention. While others sleep Cuthbert prays by the sea, when those around him throw water on a phantom fire he prays for it to cease, when the doctors can find no cure for a sickness Cuthbert employs his own spiritual methods. Second, he regularly differs from the established norm, visiting towns which previous bishops never reached, living on an island previously thought uninhabitable, and so forth. Third, he is frequently beset by temptations, his reaction differing radically from that of a normal man in a similar situation. Thus, when Cuthbert is hungry and miraculously receives food through the roof while he is praying, we sense the continuation of his prayer as an exception, because we know that we would have devoured the food immediately. Likewise, the commonplace whereby the saint is called to be bishop is a test requiring him to turn down the honor at first, thus diverging from the behavior we expect from the common run of man. Finally, throughout the text, Cuthbert's dwelling places are chosen according to a strict principle of geographical exception: when he is at Lindisfarne he lives on the edge of the monastery, in a detached cell, then he proceeds to the island of Farne, which stands out from the English mainland as Cuthbert does from those around him.[17] In short, Bede has turned the initial impetus of the anchorite life, departure from the world of men into the desert, into a coherent method of structuring his entire text. Earlier authors, *state* that they are writing about a saint because of his exceptional nature, but Bede succeeds in demonstrating the relationship between the saint's exceptionality and the text's existence.

While visiting Coldingham, Cuthbert leaves his bed in the dead of night. This uncommon behavior arouses the curiosity of one of the young monks, who follows Cuthbert down to the sea (ch. 10). There he witnesses an unexpected scene: after having stood for hours in the deep water, praying constantly, Cuthbert is dried off and warmed up by two otters. The young monk, obviously expecting something of a more scurrilous nature, quickly confesses his presumption and promises not to reveal the purpose of the saint's nightly vigils before Cuthbert's death. In this simple tale we have an elegant figure for the composition of a saint's life. Many events no doubt took place on that same night in Coldingham, but we hear none of those, for none were sufficiently abnormal to capture the attention of a potential narrator. Cuthbert's actions, on the other hand, are unusual, and thus arouse the eventual narrator's curiosity, without which Cuthbert's affair with the otters would never have been known.

Having sketched some of Cuthbert's exceptional characteristics, we can now proceed to show how the concept of exception informs the text's plot structure. Like other saints, Cuthbert is first represented in secular life. When he first separates himself from worldly life, he enters a monastery. Next, he then abandons life with other monks in favor of a solitary existence on the island of Farne, but later returns to the mainland as bishop. This simple progression, more or less parallelled in a very large number of *vitae*, aptly represents the form's basic structure. The saint begins as part of a group;[18] as the text advances he progressively separates himself from that group until he is eventually proven to be utterly exceptional. At this point he returns to the group, but instead of becoming reintegrated into it, the original group now redefines itself around the saint. This return to the group is usually carried out in one of three ways: the saint, like Anthony, opens his doors long enough to share his new knowledge with the world; or, like Gregory and Martin, he is called back to the world as bishop; or he may simply return to the community in the form of relics, thus often lending his name to the church where he lies at rest. In all of these cases, the plot structure is the same: the saint diverges from the norm, then draws others to his exceptional level, as if he were climbing a ladder then turning back to help those climbing behind him. The exception is stated, emphasized, then generalized. This pattern contrasts remarkably with the configuration previously noted in the *passio,* where the plot also begins with the presence of exception, but ends with its eradication. Here, on the contrary, the plot begins with exception, but ends with its apotheosis.

An important demonstration of the status of exception in the *vita* is provided by Bede's treatment of the miracle, the exceptional event that lies at the very heart of the form. Most chapters in the *Life of Cuthbert* reveal a simple but significant structure. Bede presents the group or the established norm, then he shows how Cuthbert's variation from that norm proves salutary; finally, lest anyone doubt his story, he demonstrates its authenticity or probability. Each chapter, therefore, leads from the presentation to the authentification of miraculous events. The text as a whole mirrors this structure in a most creative manner. At first the miracles stand by themselves, inspiring the awe and admiration of witnesses and reader alike. As Cuthbert progresses in saintliness, however, the narrator introduces a clever twist; suddenly miraculous events are seen as a new norm rather than as exceptions: "Qui enim auctori omnium creaturarum fideliter et integro corde famulatur, non est mirandum si eius imperiis ac votis omnis creatura deserviat."[19] This paradox, that a miracle *non est mirandum*, serves two specific functions within the text.[20] First, it redefines the exception as the new rule, and second, it recreates continuity between the life of the saint and that of the ordinary man. Bede continues: "At nos plerunque iccirco subiectae nobis creaturae dominium perdimus, quia Domino et creatori omnium ipsi servire negligimus."[21] The implied conclusion of this statement is that the common man, if only he will imitate the saint's faith, can in fact become just like the saint. This reaffirmation of gradational opposition justifies the *vita*'s tendency to make the exception to the old rule into the new rule. If diametrical opposition and the elimination of exception represent a conservative approach devoted to maintaining the old order, the *vita*'s gradational opposition clearly celebrates the ascension to a new order through the affirmation of exception.

The saint is of course not the only one meant to ascend to a higher level. His return to the world, whether as high official, teacher, or holy relic, occasions the conversion or rededication of those around him, whether by example, precept, or miracle of healing. When the common man changes his life by imitating the saint, he of course imitates the saint's pattern of exceptionality as well. Like the saint he lifts himself above himself, *se super se* as Bede puts it, following Gregory the Great.[22] This transformation is symbolically represented in Gregory's *Life of Benedict* by the exchange which takes place at the end of Chapter 1. The men who come to visit the holy man in his cave bring gifts of food; in return they take away the spiritual rewards which Benedict bestows upon them. In his prologue, Bede clearly spells out the role which the text itself can play in this process. He exhorts the congregation on Lindisfarne to reread his *Vita S. Cuthberti* so that "pia sanctissimi patris memoria vestros animos ad desideria regni coelestis ardentius attollitis."[23] This is, of course, the role which hagiographical texts are always expected to fulfill, whether they are full-fledged *vitae* or short *legenda* meant to be read aloud in church.

This sketchy analysis hardly does justice to Bede's text, let alone to a century rich in Northumbrian hagiography. Not all the eighth-century *vitae*, however, conform to the gradational model. Eddius Stephanus' *Vita S. Wilfridi*[24] is built throughout according to the diametrical model, with those who support Roman views on the date of Easter, led by Wilfrid, attempting to eliminate those who follow the Celtic model. Here there is no apotheosis of exception but instead constant appeals to unity and attempts, sometimes quite violent, to create it. That the *Life of Wilfrid* belongs to a type quite distant from the standard *vita* form is quite visible from the stated purpose of Wilfrid's miracles which, we are told, are performed to avenge the wrongs done to him. Like the *passio*, Eddius' text is narrated in the first-person plural, it depends on the establishment of diametrically opposed groups, and it culminates in Wilfrid's victory and a subsequent return to unity. In a very real sense, the *Life of Wilfrid* is not a *vita*, but a hagiographical epic. To understand the vast gulf separating the formal traditions of Wilfrid's and Cuthbert's *Lives*, we have only to note that Cuthbert is in fact one of the victims of Wilfrid's politicking – he and his Abbot Eata are expelled from Ripon when Wilfrid gains control over that abbey – yet Bede never so much as mentions this fundamental conflict which was the *cause célèbre* of the era.[25] Instead, he organizes his *Life* around Cuthbert's personal quest for spiritual knowledge, thus celebrating the exceptional rather than eliminating it.

To summarize my conclusions about the general form of the *vita* I will repeat only the basic contentions:

1. The actions of the saint are both inspired by a story, that of Christ or a previous saint, and end with a story, that of the new saint, who was led to new heights by the desire to imitate a man of holy character.
2. The saint is defined as an exception to the old norm or group; the new norm which his exceptionality represents is opposed to the old norm gradationally, not diametrically.
3. The saint's return to the group represents not a return to the old norm but a redefinition of the group according to the saint's new norm.

It would be a simple matter to show how these structural characteristics become an important part in the organization of vernacular romance. More central to our present concerns, however, is the fact that vernacular saints' lives very quickly adapt their structure to the norm represented by Bede's *Cuthbert*. A single example must suffice.

The eleventh-century *Vie de Saint Alexis*,[26] one of the earliest and most influential of continental vernacular *vitae*, in every way conforms to the model which I have sketched above. Alexis is a model youth, from a secular point of view at least: he is a good student, he serves the emperor well, he comes from a rich family, and marries a noble wife. All around him he finds love and honor – but not "parfit' amor" (v. 68) or "durable honur" (v. 69) according to Alexis. The biblical language which he uses to exhort his wife to take a more worthy spouse clearly identifies the source of his inspiration and his desire. Soon after Alexis deserts the family group he gives all his possessions to the poor. When he returns home to die beneath the staircase he is not simply reintegrated into the group, for a heavenly voice identifies him as the man of God. Final identification is facilitated by the autobiography which Alexis has written. Once he has been recognized, the community begins to reorient itself around his concerns. His wife is the first to turn to imitation of the saint, claiming:

> ja mais hume n'avrai an tute terre.
> Deu servirei, le rei ki tot guvernet
> (vv. 493–4).

Soon the rulers, the people, and finally Alexis' own family will follow the wife's lead.

The gradational nature of *Alexis* is clearly proclaimed by the relationship between the parents and their son. The first section of the text is devoted to the couple's desire for a son; the birth of Alexis is thus treated as a source of great joy. When Alexis returns after his voyage, however, the father takes him into the house not because Alexis is his natural son, but as an act of charity. To share one's home with natural children is good, but welcoming a stranger "por amor Deu" (v. 223) is better still. Just as Alexis "plus aimet Deu que trestut sun linage" (v. 250), his family learns to put divine concerns above human ones. Like Anthony and Cuthbert, Alexis diverges from the norm and isolates himself from the group only in order to climb the ladder of spirituality, and then to draw the others up the ladder behind him.

NOTES

1. *De Civitate Dei*, XI, 18; PL 41:332. The quotation is from Ecclesiasticus 33: 15. An earlier version of this article was presented at the Medieval Section of the Eighty-Ninth Annual Convention of the MLA, New York, 28 December 1974.
2. For the action/contemplation distinction, see *Homilies on Ezechiel*, especially II, ii; PL 76:948–58. For the relationship of Gregory's gradational theology to Benedictine monasticism, see Cuthbert Butler, *Benedictine Monachism* (Cambridge, England: Speculum Historiale, 1961; 2nd ed.), pp. 82–6, 93–110, 400–3.
3. For the *vita/passio* distinction, see Hippolyte Delehaye, *The Legends of the Saints: An Introduction to Hagiography*, trans. V. M. Crawford (Notre Dame, Ind.: University of Notre Dame Press, 1961; orig. Brussels, 1907), pp. 92–8. See also Delehaye, *Sanctus, essai sur le culte des saints dans l'antiquité* (Paris: Société des Bollandistes, 1927), and René Aigrain, *L'Hagiographie: ses sources, ses méthodes, son histoire* (Paris: Bloud & Gay, 1953), pp. 132–76.
4. καὶ θαυμάσαι πάντα τὸν ὄχλον, εἰ τοσαύτη τις διαφορὰ μεταξὺ τῶν τε ἀπίστων καὶ τῶν ἐκλεκτῶν. *The Martyrdom of St. Polycarp*, trans. and ed. Herbert Musurillo, in *The Acts of the Christian Martyrs: Introduction, Texts, and Translations* (Oxford: Clarendon Press, 1972), p. 15.
5. In Musurillo, *Acts*, pp. 106ff. The same volume also contains, pp. 194ff., *Passio Sanctorum Mariani et Iacobi* and *Passio Montani et Lucii*, both in

all probability directly modeled on the *Passio Sanctarum Perpetuae et Felicitatis*. On the latter text and its influence see Musurillo, *Symbolism and the Christian Imagination* (Baltimore, Md.: Helicon Press, 1962), pp. 47–50.

6. The relationship between Roman persecution and the Day of Judgment is clearly stated by Tertullian in *De spectaculis* XXX; PL 1:660–2. On the relationship between Tertullian's theology and that of the early martyrs, see W. H. C. Frend, *Martyrdom and Persecution in the Early Church* (1965; rpt. New York: Doubleday Anchor, 1967), pp. 254–84. Following many other critics, Frend suggests that Tertullian may have edited *Passio Sanctarum Perpetuae et Felicitatis*.

7. Both the Greek and the Latin texts are included in PG 26:835–978. For critical apparatus see St. Athanasius, *The Life of Saint Anthony*, trans. and ed. Robert T. Meyer (Westminster, Md.: Newman Press, 1950).

8. In *Mensonge romantique et vérité romanesque* (Paris: Grasset, 1961).

9. See Possidius' *Vita S. Augustini*, PL 32:35, Sulpicius Severus' *Vita S. Martini Episcopi*, PL 20:162, and *Felix's Life of Saint Guthlac* (Cambridge, England: Cambridge University Press, 1956), ch. 19, for other well-known examples of this motif.

10. For Jerome's *vitae* of St. Paul of Thebes, Hilarion, and Malchus, see PL 23:13–60.

11. *Navigatio Sancti Brendani Abbatis*, ed. Carl Selmer, Univ. of Notre Dame Pub. in Med. Stud. 16 (Notre Dame, Ind.: University of Notre Dame Press, 1959).

12. Gregory the Great's *Life of Benedict* constitutes the second of his *Dialogorum libri quatuor*, PL 66:125–204; more recently edited by Umberto Moricca, *Gregorii Magni Dialogi* (Rome, 1924).

13. The most recent edition of the *Vita S. Martini Episcopi* is *Vie de St-Martin*, ed. Jacques Fontaine (Paris: Cerf, 1967–1969). On Sulpicius Severus see Delehaye, "Saint Martin et Sulpice Sévère," *Analecta Bollandiana* 38 (1920), 10ff.; also Nora K. Chadwick, *Poetry and Letters in Early Christian Gaul* (London: Bowes & Bowes, 1955).

14. The same is true of *vitae* which emphasize a saint's antiheretical activities, like Possidius' *Life of Augustine*, PL 32:33–60; more recently edited by Herbert T. Weiskotten as *Sancti Augustini Vita Scripta a Possidio Episcopo* (Princton, N.J.: Princeton University Press, 1919).

15. On eighth-century English hagiography, see Theodor Wolpers, *Die Englische Heiligenlegende des Mittelalters* (Tübingen: Max Niemeyer Verlag, 1964); Charles W. Jones, *Saints' Lives and Chronicles in Early England* (Ithaca, N.Y.: Cornell University Press, 1947); Bertram Colgrave, "The Earliest Saints' Lives in England," *Proceedings of the British Academy* 44 (1958), 35–60; Benjamin P. Kurtz, *From St. Antony to St. Guthlac*, Univ. of California Pub. in Mod. Phil., No. 12 (Berkeley: University of California Press, 1926); James W. Earl, *Literary Problems in Early Medieval Hagiography*, DAI 32 (1972), 6926A (Cornell).

16. For the two prose Cuthbert *vitae*, see Colgrave, *Two Lives of Saint Cuthbert* (Cambridge, England: Cambridge University Press, 1940). On Bede's versions of the Cuthbert story, see Colgrave, "Bede's Miracle Stories," in *Bede, Life, Times and Writings*, ed. A. H. Thompson (Oxford: Clarendon, 1935), pp. 201–29.

17. For other examples of geographical exception, see the *Lives* of Anthony, Martin, and Guthlac cited above.

18. The group with which the saint is associated varies from text to text:

Martin is a soldier, Benedict a student, Augustine a teacher, and so forth.

19. Colgrave, *Two Lives*, p. 224.

20. This motif, extremely common in Jerome's *vitae* (see, e.g., PL 23: 21, 24, 43), is repeated many times in Bede's prose *Life* (e.g. *Two Lives*, pp. 158, 160, 178).

21. *Two Lives*, p. 224.

22. For Bede's use of this expression, borrowed from Lamentations 3: 28, see *Two Lives*, p. 154; for Gregory's use of this concept and expression see, *inter alia*, *Homilies on Ezechiel* II, v, 8–9 (PL 76:989–90).

23. *Two Lives*, pp. 144–46.

24. *The Life of Bishop Wilfrid*, ed. Bertram Colgrave (Cambridge, England: Cambridge University Press, 1927).

25. There is of course good reason for Bede's silence on this issue: he himself supported the Roman cause on the Easter question.

26. *La Vie de Saint Alexis*, ed. Christopher Storey (Geneva: Droz, 1968).

Hagiography and Romance in Medieval Ireland

LUDWIG BIELER

The student of hagiography as a literary *genre* cannot ignore the rôle which popular tales have played in it since an early time. The accounts of the trials of Christian martyrs of the primitive church are, of course, almost entirely free not only of contamination with secular stories but of the miraculous element in general. Even after the horrors of the persecution under Diocletian had left their mark on the *Passiones* of martyrs, dwelling as they do on the atrocities they had to suffer, and miracles began to be given more room in this context, the authors of these accounts would rather tend to keep to biblical models. It was the official recognition of Christianity in the ancient world, its becoming the religion of the emperors and the ruling classes that made the "martyr," who had been the Christian hero *par excellence*, give way to the "confessor" (the two words, literally, mean the same), who is "heroic" in that he displays "heroic virtue" – not only moral virtue practised in a heroic degree (the *virtus heroica* of the schoolmen) but also, and above all, by giving proof of *virtus* in the sense of supernatural power, as a practitioner of "white magic."

The term *virtutes*, Greek *aretaí*, was given by the ancients to the extraordinary and memorable deeds, often miraculous, of gods and heroes, and was taken over by those who wrote about their Christian counterparts. The Greek word *aretalogus*, in a derogatory sense, meaning "a teller of tall stories," "a jester," was made a loanword in Latin;[1] the Greek *aretalogía* was, in a neutral sense, introduced as a technical term for the account of the miraculous deeds of a religious hero by Richard Reitzenstein[2] and has become generally accepted. Aretalogy opened the door to the influx of all sorts of secular stories either *in toto* or of selected motifs of pagan or generally superstitious character. Lives of saints, however, were not the first production of Christian literature to resort to such borrowing. It pervades the apocryphal books of the Old and New Testament, in particular the apocryphal Acts of the Apostles,[3] and has its place also in Jewish (rabbinical) tradition. Needless to say, stories and motifs of this kind comprise a number of different types: myth, legend, saga, *Märchen*, and the wide range of popular superstition; not a few are "romances" in the more specific meaning of the term. In the present article the term "romance" will be used to cover them all.

When Ireland became Christian during the fifth and sixth centuries, the western church – like that of the east – had already in her hagiographical literature thoroughly amalgamated those elements and integrated them into the pattern of a literary *genre*. Some of its characteristic specimens, e.g., the Life of St. Martin of Tours by Sulpicius Severus or the *Dialogi* of Gregory the Great, as well as some biblical *apocrypha*,[4] soon found their way into Ireland. Such stories did not fail to appeal to Irish converts. The background was similar, as the syncretism of late antiquity contained as many popular beliefs and stories in which they played a part as did Celtic religion, folklore, and native stories in Ireland. Acceptance of Christianity, which might be prompted by all sorts of motives, would not necessarily close the mind against these popular beliefs, even under the pressure of dogmatic orthodoxy. In Ireland especially, where, as a rule, the conversion of a chieftain was followed by the mass conversion of his people, it was natural that ideas that did not openly contradict the main tenets of Christianity should persist. Thus, native saga, which was not an element of pagan religion (unlike Graeco-Roman mythology), would be perfectly acceptable. As a matter of fact, the monasteries played an important rôle in preserving secular literature, which at least orally, thanks to the privileged class of the *filid*, had attained to a high degree of perfection at an early time, although the oldest manuscripts in which it is now preserved, *Lebor na hUidre* ("The Book of the Dun Cow")[5] and the Book of Leinster,[6] date of the beginning of the eleventh and the second half of the twelfth century respectively. In later tradition St. Patrick himself made Cainte, a Miraculous survivor of the *Finn*, tell him the ancient stories and caused them to be written down.[7]

Relations between secular or non-Christian stories and Christian ones vary considerably. There must have been a fair amount of unconscious popular blending of saga themes and hagiographical themes.[8] Not always is the Christian story the imitation of a secular one.[9] There is also the possibility – too often overlooked – of spontaneous creation of identical or near-identical incidents that has its basis in universal thought patterns of the popular mind.[10] Such a possibility may make it impossible to decide where priority lies. Sometimes it even happens that a hagiographical motif is imitated in a nonhagiographical tale – as, for instance, the Life of Apollonius of Tyana by Philostratus[11] was intended to be a pagan counterpart to the Gospel stories. Rev. Félim O'Briain[12] gives some interesting examples from the hagiography of early Ireland. Within hagiographical tradition he claims origin in Ireland[13] for St. Brigit's miraculous hanging of her wet cloak on a sunbeam to dry. This miracle has come to be transferred to some saints of Brittany and of the diocese of Clermont; a miracle of this type would originally be told of a saint who had, as was the case of Brigit, taken over some features of a sun-goddess. Conversely, borrowing from secular tales is assumed by Charles Plummer for the story of the birth of St. Declan, which was "bodily" taken over from such sagas as the "Expulsion of the Deisi," the "Death of Medb" and "Medb's Three Husbands";[14] the birth-stories of Aed Slane and of Molaisse of Devenish are borrowed from the story of the birth of Fiacha Muillethan "merely with a change of name,"[15] and the meeting on the sea of SS. Bairre and Scuithin is "an ecclesiastical version of the meeting of Bran and Mannanan mac Lir."[16]

On the following pages I shall discuss briefly a selected number of "romance themes" (in the wide meaning of the term as defined above) that are found in Irish hagiographical literature. In doing so I shall follow not the chronology of the saints concerned, whose dates are not always beyond dispute, but that of their Lives, which are on the whole more accurately dateable; it is, after all, in these literary productions that the phenomenon which I am studying presents itself.

I begin with the early Life of St. Samson of Dol, an emigrant from Wales to Brittany who died *c.* 565. This Life I date, with the Abbé Duine and F. Lot against R. Fawtier,[17] to 610–615. In spite of his Welsh origin, Samson has links with Ireland: he lived for some time as a hermit on the Hill of Howth (*arx Etri*, Ir. *Dún Étair*).[18] Two incidents of this Life have an interesting secular background. Anna, the future mother of our saint, and her husband Amon, unhappy about Anna's apparent sterility, hear of a wise *librarius* (later called *magister*) far away in the north and decide to go there and consult him (c. 2). When they arrive, this wise man, even before he is told what troubles them, foretells Amon that his wife will give birth to a son if he offers *pro anima illius* a silver rod (*virgam argenteam*) "equaling his wife" (*coaequantem uxori tuae*), and Amon, overjoyed, promises to give three silver rods equal to one another. In the following night, for which the wise man invites them to his place after their strenuous journey, an angel appears to Anna in a vision, confirms the magister's prophecy and tells her to give the child, who is to be a great saint, the name Samson (c. 4). The "equality" of the silver rod to Anna is not specified; it may be either by weight or by size, as in a number of parallels (e.g., four rods of silver and one of gold equaling the stature of a penitent as an offering to St. Richarius for having offended him, or by weight on several occasions in the *Mabinogion*).[19] Both stature and thickness are implied in the Laws of Hywel Da:[20] for certain *iniuriae* to the king compensation is to be made by rendering a "virga argentea eiusdem altitudinis cum rege sedente in cathedra sua usque ad os eius et eiusdem grossitudinis cum digito eius medico" (the third or "leech" finger).[21] In a situation similar to Anna's, the mother of St. Briocius[22] is told to offer three rods, two of silver for herself and her husband, and one of gold for the future saint (c. 4). In an early paper[23] I have argued that metal rods or tapers of wax as offerings are probably primitive representations of the person who gives them, and were later understood as representing units of weight or money (cf. *aes grave*).

The background of the second episode is more complex. Samson, passing through a large forest on the way to his ailing father, meets a horrid woman, who describes herself as a *theomacha*. She is not allowed to go away from that forest because her husband had died there, but she has a mother and eight sisters still living in a forest even more remote. After she has rejected the saint's admonitions to mend her ways, she drops dead at his prayers (c. 26f.). It has long been seen[24] that the savage woman and her eight sisters are the nine witches of Gloucester, a locality which is consistent with the setting of that episode. The description of herself as *theomacha*, however, is classical (Euripides, *Bacchae* 45f., 1255f. of Pentheus) and Christian (Acts v. 39).[25]

Something about the Lives of St. Brigit has already been said in the general introduction. Two details, however, call for a fuller discussion. Cogitosus, who wrote his *Life* of the saint about the middle of the seventh century, tells (c. 28) of a lecherous man who has designs on a certain gentlewoman, but she refuses him. He then resorts to a ruse: he gives her a brooch (*sentis*)[26] for safekeeping, then steals it from her and throws it into the sea. Afterwards he demands of her to return it, and when she cannot produce the brooch, he threatens to make her his slave; as her master he could force her to submit. The woman asks St. Brigit to intercede for her, and at once a fisherman comes along with a fish freshly caught, in whose inside the brooch is found. A very similar incident is included in the Irish saga *Táin Bó Fraích:* Froech loves Findabair, the daughter of king Ailill and queen Medb, and as a token of her love she gives him a precious ring, a gift from her father. Ailill, who disapproves of their union, steals the ring while Froech is bathing and throws it into the water. He then demands of Findabair to produce it and threatens to put her to death if she cannot do so. But a salmon is caught and served at table, and the ring is found inside it. Froech's courtship is accepted, and he becomes an ally of Findabair's parents in the *Táin Bó Cuailnge.* James Carney assumed[27] that the episode in Cogitosus was the source of that in the *Táin* as it was the source of the story of Rhydderch's ring in the *Vita s. Kentigerni.* However, this is a *Wandermotiv* found with variations in stories all over the world, and a comparison of details, so far from establishing a special connection between the two versions, rather seems to tell against it.[28]

The second detail is not found in Cogitosus, who apparently took exception to the implied pagan background of his heroine. It is found in the *Vita Prima* (Colgan's *Third Life*), which in its present form dates from c. 800, but is a reworking of an earlier text of either Aileran or Ultan, who both belong to the second half of the seventh century. Dubthach, Brigit's father, has an affair with his slave-woman Broisech, and she becomes pregnant. One day, riding in Dubthach's chariot, they pass a druid's place, and the druid sends his servants out to see who is in it: "currus enim sub rege sonat." The servants report that it is only Dubthach in the chariot; but the druid replies: "It is not he that I have in mind, but the woman behind him" (who, as a person of no social rank, had not been mentioned by his servants). He asks whether she is pregnant, and Broicsech declares her master to be the father of the child she is bearing. The druid prophesies that she will give birth to a daughter, "que lucebit in mundo sicut sol in vertice celi (c. 2)." The sentence "currus enim sub rege sonat" is almost literally repeated in the account of the same incident in the *Vita metrica* of the saint by the ninth-century bishop Donatus of Fiesole (v. 165f.).

Similar stories are told about several other Irish saints[29] and all of them contain the characteristic sentence either literally or in a slight variation, even where the prophesying person is not a druid but a bishop[30] or a saint.[31] This phrase, as Professor D. A. Binchy has pointed out to me, recalls a detail in the story *De Sil Chonaire Móir* ("Of the Seed," i.e., the offspring, "of Conare Mór").[32] In this tale one of the tests which a claimant to the throne of Tara has to undergo is that the *Fal*, a phallic symbol of stone, make a strident sound when it comes in contact with the axle of the future king's chariot. This is quite literally "currus sub rege sonat." Here we clearly have a pagan idea taken over into a Christian context, and, as far as I can see, only into this particular one; I have not found it anywhere else in Hiberno-Latin literature. Its pagan origin is evident from the fact that in the earlier instances the speaker is always a druid. To make this statement has become a hagiographical formula.[33] Part of this formula is possibly also the prophecy that the unborn child, who is called *rex*, is compared to the sun, but this question must be left open.[34]

Tírechán and Muirchú, the earliest "biographers" of St. Patrick, both wrote in the second half of the seventh century, but all attempts at dating their works more accurately or at establishing a chronological relation between them are inconclusive. Tírechán in his *Collectanea*[35] tells the story of a giant whom Patrick restores to life. The giant refers to the pains he is suffering, is baptized and, having revealed his name and how he was killed, is buried again (c. 40).[36] A comparison with similar stories in the Lives of St. Cainnech (c. 9)[37] and St. Cronan (c. 4)[38] (which is to a certain extent modeled on Tírechán), shows that the companions of the saint would, in the basic form of the story, have expected the resurrected man to tell them something about the other world as does, e.g., king Echu, who is temporarily resurrected by Patrick (*Vita III* c. 66, *Vita Tripartita* r 2098ff). This is, of course, one of the main themes of the stories of St. Patrick's Purgatory and its antecedents.[39] The people of St. Cainnech say that the dead man whose head they have found, could, if he were still alive, tell them stories of old, and this is done rudimentarily by Tírechán's giant. It is, however, of peripheral importance only.[40] In the fight of two brothers over the possession of their dead father's hereditary land (ch. 32), the arms of the fighters are made immovable by the prayer of St. Patrick. When the saint restores them to their normal functions, the fighting brothers repent and grant Patrick the object of their quarrel for the building of a church. Tírechán is clearly under the influence of Sulpicius Severus, *Dialogi* II.3, but the motif is one of the commonest in hagiography.

The most elaborate "romantic" story in Tírechán's work, although entirely Christian in concept, is that of the conversion and death of the daughters of king Loiguire (c. 26). The two young maidens, Ethne and Fedelm, are being brought up by druids in Mayo. One morning, when they go to the well of Clebach to wash themselves, they see Patrick and his clergy sitting there, and, impressed by their strange appearance and attire, they wonder who they are. The girls are inclined to see in them either elves (*viri síde* "the people of the site") or divinities of the earth, or some spóok. They ask them who they are and from where they have come. Patrick remarks: "It would be better to profess our true God than to ask about our home." The elder of the two girls at once wishes to satisfy her curiosity by asking all sorts of questions about how Patrick's God compares with the nature gods in whom the Irish believe. Patrick instructs them in solemn, almost hieratic language, reminiscent of the Gallican liturgy, about the persons of the Trinity. He adds that he would want to join these young daughters of an earthly king to the son of the heavenly king whom he preaches, and they tell him how eager they are to enter into this bond. After they have answered some formal baptismal questions, Patrick baptises them; but they cannot yet see their bridegroom face to face before they have received the Eucharist and have tasted death (*nisi mortem gustaveritis*). The girls ask for both, and their wish is fulfilled. They are buried beside the well. Based on a combination of several hagiographical motifs, this is in structure and language by far the finest story in the *Collectanea;* its charm flows mainly from the sustained *Stimmung* by which it is pervaded. This episode surpasses so greatly the narrative art which Tírechán displays elsewhere that it is almost certain that he had before him a literary source of more than average quality.[41]

Tírechán (c. 8) and Muirchú (c. 1. 15–22) concur in telling the story of Patrick's fight with Loiguire's druids at Tara, but they do not place equal emphasis on the same details. Both, it would seem, depend on a primitive *vita*, to which Tírechán refers (ch. 1, 7) as "plana illius historia." Muirchú develops dramatically the coincidence of the paschal vigil and the pagan spring festival at Tara, of the paschal fire and the new fire which is to be kindled in the king's palace and before which any other new fire in sight of Tara, pain of death, must not be raised.[42] Tírechán introduces his account almost incidentally. Having enumerated the churches founded by Patrick in the plain of Brega, he adds that the last one in this list, Argetbor, was entrusted to bishop Kannanus, whom Patrick had ordained in the night of his first Easter in Ireland, and to whom he gave the first blessed candles to carry to Tara "to light the blessed fumes before the eyes and the nostrils of the pagans and king Loiguire and his druids"; the paganism of the Irish is literally to be "smoked out." There follows Patrick's and Benignus' fight with the druids of Loiguire, who himself, however, does not, as in Muirchú's account, take an active part. The death of either druid is told in inverse order, which might have been the sequence of the earlier source. After the death of Lochru, Patrick proclaims that "in this hour paganism in Ireland has been entirely destroyed"; but Muirchú preferred to make this spectacular incident, the burning of the druid, his final climax. In the second death, that of the blaspheming druid Lochletheneus (Muirchú's Lucet Máel), who is raised into the air and then falls to his death, the words of Patrick's prayer in Tírechán, "Domine, iece (i.e., "eice") a me canem, qui oblatrat faciem tuam et me; eat in mortem," sound more like the primitive text of his source than the formal prayer substituted by Muirchú. The stone on which the falling druid was smashed, Tírechán says, was seen by him with his own eyes – a typically "aetiological" legend. Tírechán entirely omits the encounter of Patrick with Loiguire at the place of the Easter fire, the miraculous destruction of the king's armed men, the feigned invitation of Patrick to Tara, and the folkloristic motif (also widely taken up in hagiography)[43] that Patrick and his companions were not seen by the men lying in ambush for them because they appeared to them as so many deer. Muirchú's Loiguire, in spite of granting Patrick permission to preach, does not accept the faith; Tírechán (c. 12, 1) explains this by making Loiguire declare that his father Niall forbade him to believe and ordered him to have himself buried in full armour in the hills above Tara, facing the site where Tara's traditional enemies, the sons of Dúnlang (the dynasty of Leinster) are buried. This detail may or may not be historical, and the sceptic would seem to have the better case; but Tírechán has introduced here to good effect a pagan concept and a custom which reflects it.

Tírechán says nothing of the "test" for establishing the respective power of Christianity and druidism which precedes the final (and for the druid, fatal) "proof" by burning. The king suggests that both should throw their sacred books into the water and those which are not drowned should decide the superiority of one set of beliefs over the other. Patrick accepts this, but the druid objects on the grounds that Patrick worships the water as a deity (which Muirchú interprets as a reference to baptism). Then the king proposes burning of the books as an alternative; again Patrick is willing to do so, but the druid, on much flimsier grounds, again opposes him. Now Patrick suggests the final, crucial test to which the druid himself and Patrick's disciple Benignus are to submit (I.20, 8ff.). This contest has been adapted in a strange way by the author of the Life of St. Fintan (Munnu; c. 27).[44] In a dispute with the abbot Lasrean about the date of Easter the saint offers his opponent a choice of "proofs," among others that a book of the old (Celtic) computus and of the new (Roman) one should be thrown into the fire and the true one be vindicated by not being burnt; or two monks, one of his and one of Lasrean's, should undergo the test of burning. Lasrean, however, would not accept this, with the plausible argument that Fintan is so holy that God would do for him whatever he may ask for. They then settle their dispute amicably.[45]

In the supplement to Muirchú and Tírechán in the Book of Armagh (III.5, c. 55), we are told that two "hostes" (war bands) contending for the possession of the body of St. Patrick went to war, but "corpus in grabato duo hostes viderunt apud se et non pugnaverunt." This statement is elucidated by the account of Muirchú (A II.14) that the Airgialla of Armagh and their overlords, the Uí Néill, fought with Ulaid for possession of the saint's body and had already penetrated to Downpatrick when they saw two oxen with the body on a cart moving in their direction and followed it; but as they came to the river Cabcenne (unidentified, probably marking the border of Down and Armagh) the body disappeared, and this *felix fallacia* caused them to desist from fighting. In *Vita III* (c. 91) and *Vita Tripartita* (r 3018–20) each of the warring parties sees a cart with the saint's body and follows it, the one to Armagh, the other to Downpatrick, but only the latter turns out to be real. Irish hagiographers were rather fond of this motif and elaborated it in various ways. In *Vita s. Abbani* (cc. 50–2)[46] it is the people of North Leinster and South Leinster who claim the saint's body, and to each appear two oxen with the body on a cart and are followed. Moyarney in South Leinster, where Abban had died, of course wins. Here the detail is added that the oxen on both sides, their service done, disappear in nearby rivers – clearly a mythological concept. Similar duplication or even triplication of holy bodies is found in the Lives of St. Enda (c. 11)[47] (the body is that of his sister Faenche) and of St. Darerca or Monenna (Conchubranus III.11)[48] and in the *Lectiones de S. Baldredo* in the Breviary of Aberdeen,[49] *Lectio* 6.[50]

Also in the second half of the seventh century Adamnán wrote his Life of St. Colum-cille. It was certainly written before a visit to king Aldfrid of Northumbria in 688/9, to which II.46 alludes; it possibly gave Muirchú the idea of dividing his *Life* of St. Patrick (as I think he did in his second recension) into three books. Adamnán is a great story-teller, not only in the *Vita Columbae*, but also in the hagiographical sections of his *De locis sanctis*; his story of a knight's bargaining with the *confessor* Georgius of Diospolis (III.4) compares in humor with Muirchú's *Gratzacham* story (A I.24 = B II.6). The miracles of Columba are told in a vivid style, but few go in their contents outside the ecclesiastical frame. This is true even about the story of Libranus (II.39), which in structure has all the elements of "romance." Cormac, on his third attempt to find a "hermitage" in the northern sea (II.41), sails "ultra humani excursus modum" and penetrates into districts where his coracle is assailed by strange and unknown beasts; but Columba "though absent in body but present in the spirit," by his prayers turns the southern wind, which for a fortnight has driven Cormac farther and farther north, into a north wind which brings him home. Here we have an anticipation of motifs which dominate the Voyage of St. Brendan. The finest chapter in Adamnán's work is certainly his account of the saint's last days and his death (III.23). The detail of the monastery's horse, which sheds tears into the saint's lap, sensing his imminent death, takes up a well-known motif that is at least as old as the horse Xanthos in Homer which foretells Achilles that he is soon to die.[51]

The *Vita Tripartita* (soon after 901?) has retold at least two incidents of the Patrick legend in sagalike fashion: the petitions which Patrick is granted on the top of Mount Cruachu (Croaghpatrick)[52] are transformed into a great scene of bargaining with an angel about greater and greater spiritual privileges, and the story of Ende, son of Amolngid, and his brothers (Tírechán cc. 14f., 42) is similarly developed.[53]

The Voyage of St. Brendan has probably developed from the experiences of Irish monks in search of solitary islands in the northern seas.[54] In its elaboration, however, it is in the tradition of the Irish *imrama* (seafaring tales), as well as in those of classical and later antiquity, e.g., Lucian's *Vera historia* and the *Physiologus*. Brendan's search for the "Land of Promise" (*Tír tairngire*) is the Christian counterpart of the *Tír na nÓg* and of the *insulae fortunatae* of the ancients. Here is a link also with the visits to the other world, both pagan and Christian (Vergil's *Aeneid* VI, biblical *apocrypha* and such Irish visionary literature as the *Fís Adamnáin*).[55] The Island of the Birds (c. 22) combines the typical *Märchenmotiv* of the "Paradise of Birds" with Christian imagination: these birds, who join Brendan and his monks in chanting the holy office, have, without sinning, become involved in Lucifer's fall. Christian speculation underlies also the fanciful "grace" accorded to Judas, whom they meet on one of the islands which they pass on their journey (c. 25): he is released on Sunday from hell to this place, wind-swept and lashed by high seas, with his demon torturers at bay, but waiting until he will be at their mercy again.

This brings us to the last class of literary productions which might be mentioned here, although they are hagiographical only in so far as most of them are associated with the name of some saint: visions of heaven and hell. To this literature also Ireland made some notable contributions: the visions of St. Fursa, known already to Bede (*Hist. eccl.* III.19), the tenth- or eleventh-century Vision of Adamnán,[56] and St. Patrick's Purgatory, famous all over the world thanks to Henry of Saltrey's account of the visions seen there by the knight Owen in 1153.[57] The material on which these Christian romances draw is most varied; pagan and Christian antiquity and the ancient orient as assimilated in late-antique syncretism are the main contributors. Sometimes the author's purpose is rather topical: the vision seen in Cork by Tundalus in 1148 and written up by a monk named Marcus at Ratisbon in the following year introduces meetings with persons recently deceased who had played an important role in the Irish ecclesiastical reform which centered around St. Malachy.[58] To deal adequately with the problems of this class of literature would require a paper of its own.[59]

NOTES

1. Iuvenal, *Sat.* xv. 16; Suetonius, *Aug.* 74.
2. *Hellenistische Wundererzählungen* (Leipzig, 1906), p. 8ff.
3. R. A. Lipsius and M. Bonnet, *Acta Apostolorum Apocrypha*, vols. I–III (Leipzig, 1891–1903); E. I. Hennecke, *New Testament Apocrypha*, ed. W. Schneemelcher, Engl. transl. ed. R. MacL. Wilson, II (London, 1965).
4. Muirchú compares (by implication) St. Patrick's prayer for the destruction of the blasphemous druid Lochru (*Vita s. Patricii* I.17) with the episode in the *Actus Petri cum Simone* in which the illusive ascension of Simon Magus leads to his downfall by the prayers of St. Peter (Lipsius-Bonnet I, p. 83; Hennecke, II, p. 315f.); that his Monesan (A I.27–B II.1) reasons from the creation to the creator "following the example of Abraham" seems to be derived from some apocryphal text (cf. R. H. Charles, *The Book of Jubilees or the Little Genesis*, XI. 16f.), probably *via* St. Jerome; and the explanation of the Diaspora of the Jews after 70 A.D. as a divine punishment in the *Vita Quarta* of St. Patrick (c.1) is clearly an echo of the *Vindicta Salvatoris* (*Evangelia Apocrypha*, ed. C. Tischendorf, 2nd. ed., Hildesheim, 1966, pp. 471–86).
5. MS Royal Ir. Acad. 23 E 25, ed. R. I. Best and O. Bergin, 1929.
6. MS Trinity College Dublin H.2.18, ed. R. I. Best and M. A. O'Brien, 5 vols. (Dublin, 1954–1967).
7. *Acallamh na Senórach* ("Dialogue of Ancient Men"), ed. W. Stokes, in *Irische Texte*, 4. Serie Heft 1 (Leipzig, 1900), lines 2464–7; cf. R. Thurneysen, *Die irische Helden- und Königssage* (Halle, 1921), p. 48.
8. Félim O'Briain, "Saga Themes in Irish Hagiography" (see note 9), p. 35.
9. Cf. Ch. Plummer, *Vitae Sanctorum Hiberniae* (Oxford, 1910), I, p. cxxix f., and three other articles by Félim O'Briain: "Miracles in the Lives of Irish Saints," in *Irish Eccles. Record*, 5.ser., 66 (1945), 331–42; "Saga Themes in Irish Hagiography," in *Féil-Sgríbhinn Thorna* (Cork, 1947), pp. 33–42; "The Hagiography of Leinster,' in *Féil-Sgríbhinn Eóin Mhic Neill* (Dublin, 1940), pp. 454–64. Cases in point referred to by O'Briain are: St. Brigit (Cogitosus c. 26; *Vita I* c. 110) heals Lugiud of his excessive appetite, just as Ossian, last survivor of the giant Fianna, is healed of his by a scholar – who, however, invokes Brigit ("Saga Themes," p. 36f.). The milking of a cow three times in one day in the *Lives* of Brigit has a parallel in the Irish stories about Bláthnait (*ibid.*, p. 38f.). Her healing of a "flat-faced" boy (i.e., one who was born without eyes, nose and mouth), whom his father wants to kill (*Vita I*, c. 102) has a close parallel in the story "The collar of Morann son of Man" (see W. Stokes and E. Windisch, *Irische Texte* III 1, Leipzig, 1891, pp. 88–90) without being necessarily

derived from it (*ibid.*, p. 40f.). To the *genre littéraire* of hagiography as well as to popular tales belong numerous miracles which introduce animals ("Miracles," p. 339); However, the story of the tame fox in Cogitosus (c. 23) seems to me typically hagiographical in character. On the story of the stolen brooch (Cogitosus c. 28) see below. The Irish *imrama* (seafaring tales) of Maeldun, Bran and others and the *Navigatio s. Brendani* show a very similar mixture of pagan and Christian elements ("Saga Themes," p. 35).

10. See my *Theîos Anér. Das Bild des 'göttlichen Menschen' in Spätantike und Frühchristentum* I (Vienna, 1935), p. 146.

11. Ed. K. L. Kayser II (Leipzig, 1871).

12. E.g. "Saga Themes," p. 39f.

13. "Miracles," p. 336.

14. Plummer, *loc. cit.*, p. lxii.

15. *Ibid.*, p. cxxxii.

16. *Ibid.*

17. See J. F. Kenney, *The Sources for the Early History of Ireland*, I (Columbia University Press, 1929), p. 174.

18. R. I. Best, see F. Lot in *Revue celtique*, 35 (1914), 288.

19. See R. Fawtier, *La Vie de Saint Samson* (Paris, 1912), p. 37, n.3.

20. MS Peniarth 28, see H. D. Emanuel, *The Latin Texts of the Welsh Laws* (Cardiff, 1967), pp. 110, 194.

21. Note that the instances quoted from the *Mabinogion* also refer to compensation.

22. See his *Vita*, in *Anal. Bollandiana* 2 (1883), pp. 162ff., which in this detail is possibly modeled on that of St. Samson.

23. "Silberstäbe als Weihgeschenk," in *Anzeiger der Akademie der Wissenschaften in Wien*, phil.-hist. Kl. 1931, pp. 1–12.

24. Fawtier, *op. cit.*, p. 45f.; F. C. Burkitt, in *Journ. Theol. Stud.*, 27 (1925), 46f.

25. For the term and the idea behind it, cf. O. Weinreich, *Tübinger Beiträge zur Altertumswissenschaft* 5 (1929), pp. 334ff.

26. Explained as *spina*, i.e., *fibula* (cf. French *épingle*) by P. Grosjean, *Bulletin Du Cange* 17 (1942), 73–7.

27. *Studies in Irish Literature and History* (Dublin, 1955), pp. 53–6.

28. See my review of Carney's book in *Deutsche Literaturzeitung* 78, Heft 1, January, 1957.

29. See my paper "Zur Interpretation hagiographischer Parallelen," in *Sitzungsberichte der Heidelberger Akademie der Wissenschaften*, phil.-hist. Kl., Jahrgang 1974, pp. 8–10.

30. *Vita s. Comgalli* c. 5.

31. E.g., St. Ita in *Vita s. Mochoemog* c. 5.

32. Ed., with introduction and commentary, by L. Gwynn, in *Eiru* 6 (1912), pp. 130–43.

33. I use this term after the analogy of *Märchenformel*.

34. See "Hagiog. Parallelen," p. 9f.

35. Ed. by E. Hogan in *Anal. Boll.* 1 (1882), pp. 531–85; 2 (1883), pp. 35–68, 213–38. A new edition by me, with introduction and commentary, to be published in the Dublin Institute for Advanced Studies series, *Scriptores Latini Hiberniae*, is in preparation. On *Collectanea*, see my paper "Tírechán als Erzähler," in *Bayerische Akademie der Wissenschaften. Sitzungsberichte*, phil.-hist. Kl., Jahrgang 1974, Heft 6, p. 4 with n. 1.

36. The suggestion, first put forward by Robin Flower, *The Irish Tradition*

(Oxford, 1947), pp. 6–8, and further developed by J. Szövérffy (*Zeitschrift f. celt. Philologie* 25, 1955, 184–96) and James Carney (*The Problem of St. Patrick*, Dublin, 1961, pp. 142–52) that Tírechán cs. 40 and 41 (and a parallel of the latter in Muirchú A II.2) were modelled on the Trajan episode of the Whitby Life of St. Gregory the Great is being questioned by me in a forthcoming article in *Forma Futuri, Studi in onore del Cardinale Michele Pellegrino* (Turin, 1975).

37. Plummer, *Vitae Sanctorum Hiberniae* I, p. 155f.
38. *Ibid.*, II, p. 23.
39. See below, p. 21.
40. The man in the *Vita Cainnici* tells *multas fabulas, quas propter brevitatem non possumus narrare*.
41. This "source" need not have referred originally to the daughters of king Loiguire; the tomb at Clebach may have contained the bodies of two unnamed maidens. However, I am very doubtful whether J. Carney's (*Problem of St. Patrick*, pp. 125ff.) reconstruction of a common source for Tírechán's Clebach story and Muirchú's story of the conversion and death of the British princess Monesan (B II.1) has sufficient probability to be accepted: see my discussion in "Tírechán als Erzähler," pp. 16–22.
42. The confrontation is meaningful here, where it forms the starting point of the decisive victory of Christianity over paganism (at the end of the contest Loiguire grants Patrick protection for preaching throughout his territory). A similar incident in the life of St. Gerald of Mayo, c. 9 (Plummer, *Vitae Sanctorum Hib.* II, p. 111f.) lacks this motivation.
43. See H. Günter, *Psychologie der Legende* (Freiburg, 1949), pp. 30, 160, 177, 231, 250.
44. Plummer, *op. cit.*, II, p. 102f.
45. For this whole section, see my "Hagiogr. Parallelen," p. 18f.
46. Plummer, *op. cit.*, I, p. 31f.
47. *Ibid.*, II, p. 64f.
48. M. Esposito, *Proceedings R.I.A.* XXVIII C 12 (1910), p. 236f.
49. Edinburgh, 1510.
50. See "Hagiogr. Parallelen," pp. 12–4.
51. *Iliad* 19, 404–23.
52. Cf. Tírechán c. 38; III.2, c. 52 with *Vita Tripartita* r 1310ff.
53. See Eóin MacNeill, *St. Patrick* 2 (1964), pp. 170–73, 176f.
54. See above about Cormac.
55. Carl Selmer, *Navigatio s. Brendani abbatis* (Notre Dame, 1959), pp. xx–xxv.
56. See J. F. Kenney, *Sources for the Early History of Ireland*, I (Columbia University Press, 1929), p. 444f.
57. See Kenney, *op. cit.*, pp. 354–56, with bibliography up to 1929; St. John D. Seymour, *St. Patrick's Purgatory* (Dundalk, 1918), includes the accounts of visions seen there by numerous famous pilgrims throughout the Middle Ages. Those of George of Grisophan (ed. L. L. Hammerich, Copenhagen, 1931) are of special interest.
58. See Kenney, *op. cit.*, p. 741f.
59. See the survey in H. L. D. Ward, *Catalogue of Romances in the Department of Manuscripts in the British Museum*, II (1893), pp. 397–557.

Irish Saints' Lives, Romance, and Cultural History

WILLIAM W. HEIST

One connection between the ecclesiastical and secular documents of early Ireland is that all are the products of a privileged learned class, a fact perhaps sufficient to account for the celebrated tolerance of secular literature by the Irish clergy. Ireland is of course not the only country whose aristocracy supplied the leadership of both churchmen and laymen in the days of the Church's highest prestige, but it offers rather extreme examples. In few countries, surely, might a man be at the same time king and abbot of one or more monasteries, or the office of abbot and bishop descend from father to son through several generations, or monasteries not only ally themselves in war with secular armies but even initiate war against one another.

These facts of history, which Kathleen Hughes has documented very clearly,[1] throw an eerie light on the popular title "Ireland of the Saints." Among other things, they indicate that secular learning and literature and those of the Church are alike not merely in being the property of privileged classes: both are apparently the learning and literature of the *same* privileged class. We may accordingly find it profitable to look for similarities in the functions, as well as in the forms and genres, of the literatures of both the secular and the ecclesiastical establishments.

Though the saint's Life is a genre little studied in our university curricula, it has received some scholarly attention; and it is no novelty to call it a type of romance. It has been so called by Ludwig Bieler,[2] perhaps echoing Charles Plummer's use of "religious romance,"[3] or Hippolyte Delehaye's term *"romans hagiographiques."*[4] It has also of course been treated as biography, the hagiographers commonly being blamed for not anticipating the tastes of the modern reader, and the depth of disparagement generally in inverse ratio to the time-depth of the writer's scholarship.[5] These Lives have also been classified as "the beginnings of the 'novel with a purpose,'"[6] "mountain of legend and molehill of history,"[7] "pseudo-sagas,"[8] and "aretalogies."[9]

Those who have devoted most attention to defining the genre and to tracing its development are Father Delehaye and Professor Bieler, both of whom begin with Classical traditions. Father Delehaye distinguishes three fundamental *acta* of saints according to the subject matter: Passions of the martyrs, Acts of the apostles, and Lives of the saints, of which only the last occur in Irish tradition. He classes texts that share more than one of the three as hybrids: Life and Martyrdom, Life and Acts, Life and Acts and Miracles.

Bieler sees the Celtic, and specifically the Irish, Lives as modeled on the distinctive form and style of Latin hagiography that had evolved by the end of the sixth century, when an interest in Irish hagiography is first attested. As he puts it, "The primitive acts of martyrs and stories about the Desert Fathers – Christian counterparts to the *Facta et Dicta* type of ancient literature – had given way to more elaborate compositions which embedded those elements in a frame of double ancestry: ancient biography and aretalogy. To . . . *vita et conversatio* . . . is added an ever stronger ingredient . . . *virtutes et miracula.*"[10]

Bieler is perfectly right in taking the earliest Lives of saints of Irish origin to be self-conscious literary efforts of a certain ambition, whose authors were well aware of imitating established models of a highly developed form. This much had been seen by earlier readers; and indeed, the clue had been supplied by Muirchú, author of the first full-scale Life of Patrick, whose preface says (by the usual interpretation) that his is the first Life of an Irish saint except that of Brigit written by his father Cogitosus. This clearly implies awareness of lives of other saints who were *not* Irish. And for what it is worth, the Book of Armagh, in which Muirchú's *Life of St. Patrick* along with other Patrician material is preserved, also contains the *Life of St. Martin of Tours* by Sulpicius Severus, thus certainly known to Ferdomnach, the scribe of this manuscript.

The Lives by Muirchú and Cogitosus, the latter of which also survives (along with that of the Welsh-Breton St. Samson of Dol, probably the oldest Life of any Celtic saint), have been studied thoroughly. Agreement has been noted not only in general construction but in actual wording, evidently too close to have occurred by chance. Bieler, with most modern scholars, agrees that this probably results from the authors' all having followed some handbook of hagiographical writing current in the sixth and seventh centuries. He also emphasizes that these early Lives continue a literary form, the aretalogy, that derives from Classical models in which the *aretai*, or *virtutes* – the wonders of the god, and later the saint – are narrated (pp. 243–4). The interest here is twofold: we identify an additional strand that went into the making of the early Christian Lives; and this lends some weight to the argument that the Irish Lives have a mainly literary ancestry – one, we may add, in which visions and marvels were likely to play a prominent part from the very fact that the Irish had no real martyrs among their early saints and so needed something other than the details of martyrdom to provide narrative interest.

I have no quarrel with this paper of Bieler's, which I find illuminating and wholly admirable. But I wish to examine the Irish Lives not so much for their foreign models and sources as for the possible elements of native literature that they contain and the native or naturalized forms that may have shaped them. And I should like to consider what forces in Irish history may have affected the Lives at various stages in the development of the genre, and what function they fulfilled in the culture of successive periods during the time in which they were produced. Very little of what I have to say is original, of course, and I must depend completely on others for my notions of Irish history, whether social, political, or religious.

Our first testimony to the existence of an Irish hagiographical document comes from the *Tripartite Life of St. Patrick*, where we are told that Columcille (died A. D. 597) first recorded the miracles of St. Patrick. Bieler says that the fact that such a collection was made proves an interest in hagiography just at a time when it might be expected (p. 244). He means, if I read him correctly, that this is the period immediately after that of the founders of the great monasteries – indeed, *during* the time of some of them, like Columcille himself – and hence a time when we might expect an interest within the monasteries in their founders as symbols of their corporate identity. The aretalogical collections were soon to assume the form, or at least the name, of *Vitae* – Lives – and the models of these, as we have seen, were already established.

The first Lives from Ireland are in Latin, and presumably so were the first deliberately collected materials for such Lives, like those that Columcille compiled. They were intended for use in the monasteries. It is possible that some adaptation of these Lives or collections of miracles might be presented to the laity in the form of homilies, as was certainly done later. The *Tripartite Life of St. Patrick*, for instance, is so called because it is arranged in the form of homilies to be read on the three successive days on which St. Patrick's feast was celebrated at Armagh. It is mostly in Irish, but about 10 percent is in Latin, presumably because it was originally written in that language and the Irish began as an interlinear gloss that was never completed. So full a gloss seems unlikely to have been added for clerics reading the Life for their own instruction or amusement; but it could be very useful for anybody who had to translate it aloud and at sight, as for a lay audience. But a collection like Columcille's, which may have been one source of the *Tripartite Life*, would not normally have been translated, I imagine. It would rather have been regarded as raw material to work into homilies, whether for delivery in Latin or in Irish.

There is general agreement on the central function of these early Lives and related materials. They promoted and documented the claims of the various monasteries in which they were written to territorial hegemony, including especially the collection of dues, based either on original foundation by the saint being celebrated or on cession of rights by a given church or monastery to the claimant's founder. This same motive would apply to writing in later periods, up to the severe Viking invasions beginning in 832, and despite the ascetic reformation of the late eighth and early ninth centuries; it would apply again in the tenth and eleventh centuries, when the Vikings had become Christians.

To this motive we can trace many a detail in the Lives, as where one saint, having founded a monastery, is made to cede it to another, not always a contemporary or even a near one. Or, when such an anachronism would seem too blatant, the founder may be told in a vision or by an angelic messenger or a prophetic contemporary that the spot on which he has built is reserved for some future saint. And as Bieler points out, not only does the *Book of the Angel,* which is preserved in the Book of Armagh, list the prerogatives of Armagh as delivered to Patrick by an angel, but the last two paragraphs – a sort of epilogue – clearly indicate that an arrangement between Armagh and Kildare had been reached (pp. 252-3). The last paragraph reads: "The holy man therefore said to the Christian virgin: O my Brigit, your *paruchia* in your province will be reckoned unto you for your monarchy; but in the eastern and western part it will be in my domination." (Kathleen Hughes tr.) Neither Cogitosus nor Muirchú, incidentally, shows any knowledge of contact between Patrick and Brigit. But the association of these two "pillars of the Irish," to whom was added Columcille as the third thaumaturge, has persisted.

In at least one instance this motive of laying claim to a *paruchia* – the group of churches and monasteries that owed obedience to a mother institution personified in its founding saint – has gone beyond fixing the content and has determined the actual form of a hagiographical document. This is the work known as *Tírechán's Memoir,* preserved in the Book of Armagh. It is not strictly a Life of Patrick, but a record of his missionary activity in Ireland as Tírechán was able to collect it. The places Patrick visited and the churches he founded are carefully named; and the organization of the *Memoir* is geographical, taking Patrick on a veritable tour of Ireland, in accord with Tírechán's fundamental purpose. Since the *Memoir* was drawn upon in compiling the *Tripartite Life,* this organization survived into that Life, and others in turn derived from it.

From Bieler's point of view, the high point of Irish hagiography is represented by Muirchú's *Life of Patrick,* also preserved in the Book of Armagh (see p. 255). It is based upon earlier writings, certainly, and possibly upon oral traditions, but it achieves the kind of coherence and realization of character in action that justify Bieler's judgement, which despite the breadth and depth of his scholarship is, like that of most of us, that of a post-Renaissance man brought up on that sort of standard. How valid this would seem to Muirchú's contemporaries and to his medieval successors is another question. Muirchú's *Life* survived not because of its literary qualities, but because it was copied into the Book of Armagh, which was preserved not so much for the Patrician documents for which we chiefly value it, nor for the *Life of St. Martin of Tours* which ends it, but for its middle content, a complete text of the New Testament, valued throughout most of its existence as a precious relic believed to be the work of Patrick's own hand.

To return to some of the other early Lives that I have mentioned, the *Life of St. Brigit* by Cogitosus is the earliest saint's Life by an Irish author whom we can identify. It is generally agreed, however, that Cogitosus made use of earlier Lives of this saint – the names given of earlier writers on Brigit are Ultán and Aileran the Wise (*a n-écnai, Sapiens*). The seventeenth-century editor Colgan, in his *Trias Thaumaturga*, attributes the one now known as "Colgan's Third Life" to Ultán. Nora K. Chadwick, in the Riddell Memorial Lecture of 1960, says it is probably the work of Aileran, while others have thought it probably Ultán's as revised by Aileran. It seems, like Muirchú's *Life of St. Patrick*, to have been written to enhance the prestige and the territorial claims of the monastery.

But apparently there was less record of Brigit than of Patrick or, especially, of Columcille, and the *Life* consists mainly of miracles of a spectacular and not always edifying kind. Charles Plummer, evidently influenced by the solar mythologists of the last century, found much in the lives of Irish saints, Brigit among them, to suggest that their qualities were often derived from those of sun or water deities, if they were not in fact euhemerized gods. But as Bieler remarks, Brigit is the only one for whom such a pagan origin can be convincingly argued (p. 264). A plausible explanation of how this may have happened was published by R. A. S. Macalister.[11]

Since Cogitosus says nothing of any connection between Patrick and Brigit, the life seems not to point to any formal division of territory with Armagh, like that of the *Book of the Angel*, though glorification of the saint and hence of Kildare was certainly its function. Looking at its place in the literary culture of the time, we may ask ourselves what secular literature in the native tradition might have been familiar to either a monastic or a lay audience in the seventh century. As it happens, we have some evidence on that point, since the *Cín Droma Snechtaí*, a little book copied at the monastery of Drumsnat in that century, was the earliest book in Irish whose contents we know. It contained stories and poems about the otherworld king Midir, who carried off the queen Étain, of the prehistoric king Eochaid; about the voyage of Bran to the Land of Promise; about the sea god Mannanán mac Lír and how he became the father of Mongán, a historical king in Antrim in the seventh century. As Gerard Murphy has shown, these traditions must have been in oral circulation during the seventh century; and it was the monks who copied them down, as some centuries later they did the stories of the Red

Branch and other heathen literature, most of which must have circulated, in written or oral form, since before Christianity. There is evidence that the longest and best-known tale of the Ulster cycle, the *Táin Bó Cualnge*, was also written down in the seventh century. The story of Mongán's paternity, however, attaching a rich body of supernatural tradition to a historical, and indeed very recent, king, seems a specially strong indication of a kind of culture in which the magic attached to a historical Brigit with characteristics recalling the goddess of the same name would fit quite naturally.

Adamnán's *Life of St. Columba* is remarkable for its scholarly and literary background. Adamnán, ninth abbot of Iona in succession to the patron, had both written records and relatively reliable and abundant oral testimony from which to work. The form of the *Life*, as Bieler says (p. 249), is that of an aretalogy flanked by a brief introduction on Columcille's birth and a longer narrative at the end detailing his death and the period just before and after it. It is arranged in three books, each dealing with one class of wonders as Adamnán conceived them: Book I, Prophecies; Book II, Miracles; and Book III, Visions. Mrs Chadwick observes that this arrangement was already old-fashioned when Adamnán wrote, for the writing of continuous narrative biographies had already spread to Celtic lands. I am unable to agree with this statement entirely, so far as Ireland is concerned; for, in fact, the simple plan of Birth, Deeds, and Death, with the Deeds mostly miracles, continues to the end of Irish hagiography, old-fashioned or not. The ending, on Columcille's death, where the narrative becomes chronological, has been much admired, perhaps especially the story of the old white horse weeping with its head on the saint's bosom, foreseeing his death. This recalls the Gray of Macha laying his head on Cú Chulainn's breast as he sagged from his pillar in death – a floating motif in traditional Irish story.[12]

Let me emphasize that there is no doubt of the basically literary quality of Adamnán's work, nor of his dependence upon foreign models. But besides following these models he did, according to his own testimony, collect accounts of the life of Columcille from informants, some of whom he names and whose sources he partly specifies. Some of those sources were men who actually knew Columcille, and all of them were religious, mostly monks from the Columban monasteries. One would expect of them greater intelligence, sophistication, and responsibility, and hence accuracy, than one would of a random batch of informants, largely uneducated, such as generally supply folklore collectors with tales.

Nevertheless, we find a fair number of familiar folktale motifs among these accounts, and one item recurs several times. This is the tale of a prophecy or vision imparted by Columcille to a single monk sworn to keep the matter secret so long as the saint lived. Perhaps Columcille was indeed so modest as to wish to discourage tales of his miraculous powers from circulating, as these tales are meant to imply. But one is bound to wonder whether such a spate of these postmortem revelations of special attention to the teller by the saint may not have stemmed equally from natural vanity in these informants. Perhaps anybody who *was* anybody in Iona or Derry or Durrow in the years after 597 felt obliged to produce some such evidence of closeness to the patron.

None of this is very surprising if we visualize an Irish monastery of the seventh century as the very simple and primitive affair that both the unintentional records of the lyrics occasionally produced in it and the archeological remains suggest. What was a scriptorium? The suggestion, both in Lives of Irish saints and in the lyrics (though the lyrics and most of the Lives are of later date), is that it might have been a single monk writing in a tiny hut, or sometimes without even the hut:

> A hedge of trees surrounds me,
> A blackbird's lay sings to me,
> Above my lined booklet
> The trilling birds chant to me.
>
> In a gray mantle from the top of bushes
> The cuckoo sings:
> Verily – may the Lord shield me –
> Well do I write under the greenwood.

"This," remarks Mrs Chadwick, "is how an Irish scribe looked upon his task of writing, as he described it in a little poem written in the margin of Priscian's Latin grammar, in the first half of the ninth century."[13] And she makes point that we do not know much of their libraries, except that books were certainly in short supply. As she says: "In our study of the early Celtic Church it is easy to overlook the enormous wealth of oral tradition current in Ireland at this time. The amount of knowledge which the monks derived by listening to native learning, oral history, poetry, stories of magic and the heathen gods was infinitely greater than what they learned from Latin Books."[14] Her emphasis is not excessive.

We ought, however, to include among these accounts tales of magic and the gods, the aristocratic class of stories about the heroes of the Ulster cycle and the legendary history of kings, both of which Gerard Murphy considers to have circulated in oral form in the seventh and later centuries – as long as the courts of the Irish kings, where such tales would be welcome, were maintained.[15] The abbots of Iona, from the founder Columcille through his biographer Adamnán, were with one possible exception members of the royal family of the Uí Néill, and Columcille was remembered as the friend and patron of poets – broadly speaking, of all who were the custodians of native tradition. And up until the Anglo-Norman reform movement it seems to have remained normal for leading families to supply not only kings but abbots and bishops, sometimes all three in the same person. So we can assume that the sense of literary form and content, in both the producers and the consumers of Lives of saints during this entire period, was partly formed by such native learning. The other chief formative element, was the learning brought in by the Church.

We cannot expect more than rather faint signs of native heroic narrative to appear in saints' lives. The only possible central character, the saint himself, was already fixed in hagiographical writing in a way impossible to reconcile with that of a traditional Irish hero. But we do find a good deal of correspondence of the genre to tales of the gods (myth) and to folktales (Märchen), with their emphasis on magic and wonder, and to the closely related tales of romantic adventure, some of which, according to surviving lists, were part of the required repertory of the *filidh* who performed for the aristocracy.

One class of these adventure stories comprises the *immrama*, of interest for themselves, as a type, and for their relationship to other types of narrative. The *immram*, or voyage, is obviously paralleled by other voyage literature from many cultures. The earliest of them, the *Voyage of Bran*, is of the eighth century and wholly pagan except for some probably interpolated verses. But in the following century Christianized specimens appear describing wonderful islands – originally, no doubt, the pagan otherworld – visited by monks and penitents. Murphy thinks that one of these Christianized *immrama*, the *Voyage of Máel Dúin*, of the ninth century, became the model for the late-ninth- or early-tenth-century Latin *Navigatio Brendani*, a story of the historical St. Brendan of Clonfert, which was translated into many languages and had a quite remarkable influence upon European literature.[16] It was incorporated into most versions of the *Life of St. Brendan*, and either in that form or by itself made Brendan perhaps the best-known Irish saint in Europe in the later Middle Ages, or second only to Patrick, whose fame was likewise spread by a popular romantic piece, the vision called *St. Patrick's Purgatory*.

Now Gerard Murphy, in his chapters in *Early Irish Literature*, discusses the *immrama* and the closely related *echtra*, or "adventure-journey," as literature of the historic period under the title of "Saga and Myth of Ancient Ireland." I prefer to class them with the romantic tales discussed in his second chapter, along with the Ossianic lore, even though this results in some blurring of the lines between the successive periods to which Murphy relates the genres. This blurring seems to me to be a historical fact, no matter what basis one uses for distinguishing periods. Murphy himself makes the point that simple folk had all along had their magically-controlled tales, which they apparently preferred to the aristocratically-conditioned tales of gods, heroes, and kings told in kings' palaces and royal *óenaige* (fairgrounds) in ninth- and tenth-century Ireland; but that after the Anglo-Norman invasion of 1175, when the old kingly Ireland rapidly decayed, the romantic tales of Finn came to the top, even among the *filidh*, while the aristocratic tales lost their vitality and remained only as they were preserved in manuscripts.

What Murphy is in fact demonstrating is that such folk literature as the Fenian tales were well enough known and can hardly have been kept secret from the aristocracy. Though they played no important role in the qualifications of a *fili*, bits and pieces of short narrative belonging to this lower-class literature do appear among the learned writings of the eighth to tenth centuries. I suggest that the audiences for stories in this period were not so sharply segregated as the official lists of tales a *fili* should know imply; and that the upper classes, including the clergy, enjoyed the alternative ranges of literature available to them: popular romantic tales, the traditional *filidh-eacht*, and, at least for the clerics, Latin writings as well.

Thus the cultural change that ultimately replaced Cú Chulainn with Finn mac Cumhail may have begun before the Anglo-Norman conquest and was perhaps not dependent upon it. Kathleen Hughes depicts a growing worldliness in the monastic churches in the ninth and tenth centuries, when the Vikings had destroyed the old balance of power and left the churches dependent on allied kings for their survival. She notes that earlier sources had reported the boons which Patrick had obtained of God, but that the *Tripartite Life* is the first to include a demand for "nine companions' load of gold to be given to the Gael for believing." The *Tripartite Life* similarly alters Tírechán's description of how Patrick, remaining forty days and forty nights on Crúach Pátraic, is permitted to see the fruits of his labors, to a long account of a contest on the mountain between the saint and an angel, Patrick refusing to leave the mountain until his excessive demands are granted. And she adds another occasion, when Patrick urges a young woman about to marry to become a nun, her father agreeing to it "if heaven were given to him in exchange, and if he himself were not compelled to be baptized." Patrick "promised these two things, although it was difficult for him." Here she comments, "The hagiographer obviously felt uneasy about the theological implications of the tale, and adds a postscript describing how Patrick resurrected the man after his death and baptized him. The hagiographer's object is to prove Patrick's power, and if God is belittled in the process, or Christian doctrine made ridiculous, it does not seem to matter."[17]

Of course, the greater popular appeal aimed at in the *Tripartite Life* could be detected immediately by the fact that it is in Irish, not Latin. There is also an Old Irish *Life of Brigit*, which Michael O'Brien dates to the late eighth century and which is likewise, perhaps, a translation originating in an interlinear gloss. Is the use of Irish in this *Life of Brigit* due to the fact that Kildare was a double monastery? Were the nuns less well trained in Latin than the monks, so that they needed a translation? Or was it, too, for a lay audience? The *Life* seems to reflect the same tradition that Cogitosus used, indicating that some Latin *Life of Brigit* existed earlier, despite Muirchú's statement of Cogitosus' priority. And Bieler thinks the Old Irish *Life* cannot be far removed from the *vita primitiva*. But despite the popularity of the intended audience implied by the use of Irish, the content is not greatly different from that of Cogitosus, nor is the emphasis on Brigit's wonder-working powers and also on her extreme and sometimes embarrassing generosity, as when she gives away Bishop Conlaed's vestments, lacking other garments for charity. I should guess that these Lives were prepared for a restricted community, that of the religious of Kildare; but the large church that Cogitosus describes as newly built in his time had three sections, one for the laity, so that the first Life may have been intended also as a persuasion to donations; and if so, this would constitute a strong motive for making an Irish version that the laity could understand.

To return to the Lives of Patrick: the function of the *Tripartite Life* seems clear. The glorification of the patron remains, but it is now bidding for a broader and more popular audience. This is evident not only in the content that Miss Hughes emphasizes and in the language, but in the external form itself. Though it is a series of three homilies, no care has been taken to fit all three into an appropriate shape: only the first part bears the full homiletic form; the others have each only a brief introduction followed by a string of miracles. And there is an appendix of additional miracles to be inserted at will, which leads Bieler to think that the final stage of the legend was never reached, though the *Tripartite Life* was near it. To prepare in full three separate homilies, each a whole yet part of a larger whole, seems to have been beyond the hagiographer's architectonic skill.

But the change from the earlier function of hagiographical tradition seems clear. Mrs Chadwick has described the Age of the Saints of the sixth century as one which "had no need to formulate its beliefs, its rules, and its penitential system, or to write its saintly biographies. These things were all a matter of received discipline, of common knowledge, and general acceptance."[18] And she would ascribe the great output of religious literature in the seventh and eighth centuries to reaction against the challenge of those then urging conformity to Roman organization and practice. "A new situation had arisen as a result of the Roman challenge. A 'literature of the subject' was needed by the 'case for the defence,' both for the information of the adherents of their own party, and also for propaganda against the Romanizing party, which was felt to be threatening cherished traditional usages with annihilation."[19] It was not, she emphasizes, an age of reformation, but of formulation, containing nothing not derived directly from the Age of the Saints.

It was in this age, in the 630s perhaps, that according to Muirchú

Cogitosus wrote down the first Life of an Irish Saint; and it was in the last third of the same century that Tírechán's *Memoir* and Muirchú's *Life of Patrick* and Adamnán's *Life of Columba* were written. All, of course, operate to glorify the saints they celebrate, and hence their churches; but they seem to be intended for the monastic society itself and not for outsiders, not even for the Irish Christian laity. Their chief function, if Mrs Chadwick is right, is to give the Irish monasteries a sense of certainty of their own cohesiveness, founded on a firm and holy tradition, as a stiffener of their own backbones in the face of external opposition.

In the latter part of this period, but more notably in the ninth century, the Viking raids posed a new threat to the monasteries, and one against which arguments and holy tradition were no defence. The monasteries had earlier put armies of a sort into the field against one another or against petty Irish kings – even against the king of Cashel. But neither the monasteries nor these kings were strong enough to withstand the Vikings without alliances among themselves, and they seem to have been unable to form such alliances. As Kathleen Hughes describes the situation, the repeated lootings, killings, and destruction seem to have left the monasteries that had already been the strongest even stronger compared to their rivals, since they were the ones with the greatest resources for recovery. Armagh, in particular, and Kildare, along with several other monasteries, emerged very strong after the Norse had become permanent settlers, had been converted to Christianity, and had begun to intermarry with the Irish.

The *Tripartite Life of Patrick*, written in the closing years of the ninth century and remaining in full or abridged form as the practically complete legend of Patrick, represents as we have seen an extension of the narrative to appeal to a wider public, the laity, and is correspondingly cruder and coarser. The function is no doubt to impress the hearer with the wonder of it all, to include him in the saint's company but at a greater distance than that implied for the audiences of the earlier lives, especially that of Adamnán's *Life of Columba*.

The eleventh and twelfth centuries appear to be the time during which the bulk of the extant Latin Lives of saints were written in Ireland. A certain stability seems to have been reestablished in the tenth century, so that the churches were increasingly able to exist without overwhelming fear of physical attack. At least, through their secular alliances they were more capable than before of taking vengeance and exacting reparations. The attacks that did continue were not now from foreign heathen, but from native Christians, mostly Irish. Meanwhile contact with England, the Continent, and the Papacy greatly increased, and with this contact the pressure to conform not merely on the old points of paschal computation and the shape of the tonsure, but in the episcopal organization of the whole Church and in the rejection of laymen and married clergy from their dominant positions in it. Beginning in the eleventh century, the Irish Church came more and more to conform in its organization to episcopal rather than abbatial rule, and its monasteries to reform themselves on the Benedictine model, which was rapidly becoming the usual one in the Irish monasteries on the Continent. In the twelfth century this reform was completed, or virtually so, and such Continental orders as the Augustinian canons and the Cistercians had been naturalized in Ireland.

Despite the large numbers of Lives of Irish saints produced in these centuries, I have not thus far been able to satisfy myself very completely about their function. What we have is a sort of machine-made product, mostly anonymous. One cannot be sure to what extent these are new productions or, supposing them to be simple reworkings of earlier records now lost, what the dates and the form of such records may have been – simple notes, poems, full-dress Lives, annals, or what – since most of them are too unhistorical to yield useful clues. In Kenney's opinion, most of those we have are simply the latest in a series of recensions.[20]

Even the Lives that show more individuality and apparent historicity may prove ambiguous. For example, an Irish word *gall-cherd* survives in the Latin *Life of St. Cainnech* in the Codex Kilkenniensis. This suggests a date during the Viking invasions of the ninth century, since Plummer's gloss "foreign art" appears to be correct, and since the *gaill* were normally the Norse invaders. The term refers to tossing children into the air and catching them on points of spears, a practice attested for the Vikings. Plummer considers the corresponding Codex Salmanticensis reading *gíal-cherd* an error, translating it "hostageship."[21] But Kenney renders it "treatment of hostages,"[22] which seems closer to the meaning, literally "hostage art." And this could suggest an earlier date than the ninth century, since it eliminates the need to posit Vikings in Ireland and points to a more savage period of Irish society. We have no other record of this precise practice among the Irish, but hostages were of course taken so that they might on occasion be tortured, mutilated, or slain. So the matter remains uncertain, even when evidence is so striking as this.

I suggest that something like Murphy's explanation of the change in the secular literature that took place at this time – eleventh and twelfth centuries – would account for much in the surviving Lives of saints. This is the time in which the monastic scribes recorded a great deal of early literature – the Book of Invasions and three great miscellanies containing much of the secular literature of early Ireland: the *Book of the Dun Cow*, the *Book of Leinster*, and Bodleian MS. Rawlinson B. 502. But this collecting was done in what seems to have been an antiquarian spirit, while the poets and storytellers now turned to developing literary forms of the tales of Finn and other stories of the folk.

So, perhaps, with the saints' Lives, but with Latin Lives representing the old literature of the elite, Lives in Irish those still living and developing – though very few Irish lives are recorded so early. And we must add a qualification concerning the Latin Lives. They were certainly reworked for homiletic purposes or for lectionaries, both at this time and later, in the thirteenth and fourteenth centuries, as is evident from their form, from their arrangement in collections according to the calendar, and in at least one case from the direct testimony of the writer. But I suspect that, in the form we possess, the Latin Lives still existed chiefly for those who understood Latin, even though they may sometimes have been translated in homilies addressed to the laity, like some other works that long existed only in Latin (e.g., the *Gesta Romanorum* during the first century and a half of its existence).

As a result of early Irish missions on the Continent and in England some Irish saints' Lives were written or rewritten by foreigners quite early. Thus the Italian monk Jonas wrote the *Life of St. Columbanus* at the saint's monastery at Bobbio in the seventh century; the first Life of St. Fursa was written, probably at Péronne, in the seventh century, and Bede summarizes it in his *Historia Ecclesiastica*, doubtless because Fursa's first foreign mission was at Cnoberesburgh (now Burgh Castle, Suffolk). These Lives continued to be reworked both in Ireland and abroad in the eleventh and twelfth centuries. To the twelfth century, too, we can assign the writing of Lives of Irish saints by foreigners with the evident purpose of absorbing these saints into the general Roman tradition. Thus Lawrence, a monk of Durham, wrote a *Life of St. Brigit,* and Jocelin of Furnes, a monk of Furnes abbey in Lancashire, after writing a *Life of St. Kentigern,* was installed at Downpatrick, apparently to write new Lives of Patrick, Columcille, and Brigit. We have that of Patrick and possibly that of Brigit, none of Columcille. As Bieler points out, his *Life of Patrick* is in fact a piece of propaganda for the new order, of which by clever implication he makes Patrick a champion, the intention being to make the reformers appear to be the direct inheritors and continuators of the Ireland of the Saints and, if we may call it so, the Irish Primitive Church. This policy is also evident in the writing of Lives of two of the new order's staunchest protectors among Irishmen, St. Malachy (Máel-Máedóc Úa Morgair), by St. Bernard of Clairvaux; and Laurence O'Toole (Lorcán Úa Tuathail) of Dublin, whose several Lives were written by canons of Eu, in Normandy, where he died.

Most of the texts of these Lives of the eleventh and twelfth centuries are known to us in three great collections made in the fourteenth century, the Codices Kilkenniensis, Insulensis, and Salmanticensis, all written in Ireland. The Salmanticensis gives some evidence of compilation in a house where Irish was not known, hence Anglo-Norman or English. Copies for some of its Lives came from at least one Irish-speaking establishment, however; and one Life, that of St. Cuanna or Cuannatheus, appears to have been translated from Irish to Latin by the lenders expressly for this compilation.

These collections represent, in a way, the last stage at which we can speak of Lives of Irish saints in exclusively national terms. That they are intentionally national is clear from the fact that they contain almost exclusively Lives of Irish saints: the Kilkenniensis has otherwise lives of Louis of Toulouse and Anthony of Padua, the Salmanticensis a life of St. Catherine, and the Insulensis one of St. David, doubtless due to his many associations with Irish saints.

The function of these collections would seem to be mixed: no doubt they served somewhat that of a Dictionary of National Biography, but they must also have been intended as inspirational, devotional, and austerely entertaining. The Codex Insulensis, as Plummer has shown, is represented by two fourteenth-century Rawlinson MSS., of which the younger is a close copy of the elder, but with the Lives rearranged in the order of the calendar – no doubt for convenience of reading in choir or refectory. This younger manuscript is larger than the elder, as if for reading on a lectern, as is the Codex Salmanticensis. So the Lives of these collections seem to have functioned in a quasiliturgical way as well as for private entertainment or devotions.

It would not be safe, of course, to say that meanwhile the Lives composed in Irish went their own way entirely unaffected by the Latin Lives that the clergy were reading. No doubt a good deal of tradition from dubiously Christian and dubiously historical sources was incorporated into the popular Lives – more even than into the Latin Lives, to judge from the surviving specimens – and passed on by one layman to another, like other folktales. But the people of course learned from the clergy: one thinks of the Franciscans, of whose baneful influence on the people FitzRalph, the fourteenth-century Archbishop of Armagh, complains so bitterly. The Codex Kilkenniensis seems to have been compiled in a Franciscan house, and hence probably the presence in it of the two Lives of foreigners, both of whom were Franciscans. Still, we must be slow to blame the clergy for all excesses: we learn even in modern times that what people *think* a priest has told them might astonish the priest, if his profession had not taught him to be surprised at nothing. J. T. Fowler, in his edition of Adamnán's *Life of Columcille*, records the following:

On Aug. 4, 1893, the editor was told the following by the widow Keelan, aged 74, at Tara: "St. Columcille never had a father. The way it was was this: St. Bridget was walkin' wid St. Paathrick an' a ball fell from heavin, an' it was that swate she et it all up, an' it made her prignant with Columcille, an' that's what a praste towld me, an' it's thrue. St. Bridget, and St. Paathrick, an' St. Columcille, all lays in one grave in Downpaathrick, so you can put that down." (*Adamnani Vita S. Columbae* [Oxford, 1894], p. lvi, n. 1.)

This miraculous conception reminds one somewhat of that of the Virgin Mary, but a good deal more of the conception of a queen of Ulster who swallowed Étain of the Tuatha Dé Danann when the latter in the form of an insect came down through the smokehole and fell into her drink, later to be born in a mortal incarnation.[28] Here we seem to see the lore of the saints indeed succeeding to the lore of the gods, magical history still making itself at home in the mouths of the storytellers to supply a part of the permanent frame of reference of a particular society in a particular part of the world. This function is no doubt being lost very rapidly; and if the lore remains, it will do so in some other function. But at least persists in that conservative society down to our own time.

NOTES

1. *The Church in Early Irish Society* (London: Methuen, 1966), passim.
2. "The Lives of St. Patrick and the Book of Armagh," in *Saint Patrick*, ed. John Ryan (Dublin: Radio Eireann, 1958), p. 53.
3. *Vitae sanctorum Hiberniae* (Oxford, 1910), I, xcv, n. 3, alluding to Réginald Biron's French translation (Paris, 1905) of Dom Suitbert Bäumer's *Geschichte des Breviers* (Freiburg, 1895). Biron (I, 398, n. 3) speaks of "légendes, embelliés d'une façon poétique et romanesque" serving as a diversion for the pious reader.
4. In *Les Passions des martyrs et les genres littéraires* (Brussels: Société des Bollandistes, 1921), esp. Ch. IV.
5. Some of the more appreciative scholars are Waldo H. Dunn, *English Biography* (London: Dent, 1916), Introd. and ch. I, passim; C. H. Talbot, *The Anglo-Saxon Missionaries in Germany* (London; Sheed & Ward, 1954), pp. vi–xvii; and John A. Garraty, *The Nature of Biography* (New York: Knopf, 1957), pp. 59–62. Belletristic writers such as Harold Nicolson, *The Development of English Biography* (London: Hogarth, 1959), pp. 9–18, or Frank O'Connor, *The Backward Look* (London: Macmillan, 1967), pp. 56–8, are apt to be myopically severe in their censure.
6. Dunn, op. cit., pp. 36–7.
7. Daphne Pochin Mould, *The Irish Saints* (Dublin: Clonmore & Reynolds, 1964), p. 304.
8. Frank O'Connor, op. cit., p. 57.
9. Ludwig Bieler, "The Celtic Hagiographer," *Studia Patristica*, 5 (1962), *Texte und Untersuchungen zur Geschichte der altchristlichen Literatur*, 80 (for 1959), 243–65, passim. Subsequent references to Bieler will be to this work.
10. "The Celtic Hagiographer," pp. 243–4. On the origin and development of aretalogy and its transformation into Christian legend, see Moses Hadas, *Hellenistic Culture: Fusion and Diffusion* (New York: Columbia University Press, 1959), pp. 170–81. Hadas also relates aretalogy to Hellenistic romance, as origin, the opposite of the relation I see between religious and secular narrative in Ireland. The connection between aretalogy and Christian narrative seems to have been first suggested by Richard Reitzenstein, *Hellenistische Wundererzählungen* (Leipzig, 1906), to whom both Hadas and Bieler refer. Hadas, p. 307, n. XIII, 20.
11. *Proceedings of the Royal Irish Academy*, 34C (1919), 340–1.
12. Motif B149.1.2 in the Stith Thompson *Motif-Index* (rev. ed., Bloomington: Indiana University Press, 1966); see also T. P. Cross, *Motif-Index of Early Irish Literature* (Bloomington: Indiana University Press, 1952).
13. N. K. Chadwick, *The Age of the Saints in the Early Celtic Church* (London: Oxford University Press, 1961), p. 160.
14. Ibid., p. 158.

15. Eleanor Knott and Gerard Murphy, *Early Irish Literature*, ed. James Carney (London: Routledge & Kegan Paul, 1966), p. 142.
16. Ibid., p. 113. The other *immrama* also played a considerable part in the development of Arthurian romance: see Roger S. Loomis, "Irish Imrama in the Conte del Graal," *Romania*, 59 (1933), 557–64.
17. Op. cit., pp. 224–5.
18. Op. cit., pp. 141–2.
19. Ibid., p. 142.
20. *The Sources for the Early History of Ireland*, Vol. I: Ecclesiastical (New York: Columbia University Press, 1929), p. 295.
21. Op. cit., I, xxii, n. 4.
22. Op. cit., p. 395.
23. This is Thompson Motif T511.5.2; the T511 series has many parallels, but no specific number has been assigned the widow Keelan's story.

Anglo-Norman Hagiography and the Romances

M. DOMINICA LEGGE

Anglo-Norman hagiography begins with the earliest text extant in that dialect, written about 1106. This is not a Life, although it is so described in the manuscripts, but might well be labeled a romance in its own right. This is the *Voyage of St. Brendan*[1] by Benedeit, perhaps a Westminster monk.[2] The story was extremely popular and occurs in many languages, and no wonder. Whether it has as a main source an Irish *imram*, or whether it is itself simply an *imram*, is immaterial for our present purpose. The voyages of the historic Brendan may account for the legend, but these were confined to places within easy reach of Ireland, such as Kibrandon in Argyll. A Latin *Navigatio* existed at least as far back as the ninth century, and it used to be thought that the Anglo-Norman poem was a translation of it, with certain discrepancies. This, however, is based upon a misinterpretation of the word "letre." In fact at the behest of Queen Maud, Benedeit had already written a new version of the legend in Latin, which, again for Queen Maud, he put into French. The Latin has disappeared, presumably because it did not conform to a version already well known. Yet the popularity of the French poem was such that not only was it copied at least once, in Picard, on the Continent, but was twice retranslated into Latin, first in prose and then in verse. In what follows, parallels will be drawn between certain parts of the *Voyage* and romances, some of which may indicate that the writer of the romance knew the *Voyage*.

ll.71–122. Before his voyage Brendan visits a hermit, who gives him advice. In the *Navigatio* it is the hermit who visits Brendan. The reversal of roles at once suggests a parallel with Tristan's visits to Ogrin in Beroul,[3] ll.1360–422 and ll.2279–448. Hermits continued to appear in Arthurian romance, their function becoming more and more mechanical.[4]

ll.163–4. Here again there is an alteration from the *Navigatio* account, where the embarkation is said to have taken place from the "sedes Brendani." For reasons explained by Waters, Benedeit substituted a rock from which the monks could lead into the boat, "saltus Brendani" in

41

the Latin retranslation. We are all familiar with Lover's Leaps and the Soldier's Leap at Killiecrankie. Leaps are part of folklore. Waters quotes the "Salt Malatous" from the *Bataille Loquifer*, where "salt" is not in rhyme, but points out that Beroul echoes almost word for word the lines of Benedeit when he describes Tristan's escape from the chapel:

Brendan ll. 163–4.

> Vint al roceit que li vilain
> Or apelent le Salt Brandan.

Beroul ll. 953–4.

> Encor claiment Corneualen
> Cele pierre le Saut Tristran.

It is dangerous to assume direct influence in the case of rhyming octo-syllabic couplets treating the same theme. It has misled some critics into thinking that Thomas pillaged Marie de France – but the resemblance here is striking.

ll.185–202. Brendan, having chosen fourteen companions, reluctantly accepts three pier-head jumpers, foretelling that two would fall victim to Satan and the third would be sorely tempted. The first of these intruding monks steals a goblet, is pardoned by Brendan, dies at once but goes to Paradise as a repentant sinner. On account, of past sins, the second jumps ashore on Hecla and is seen by Brendan to be dragged to hell by a hundred devils. In spite of Brendan's prophesy, the third "softly and sud-denly vanished away," no explanation being vouchsafed to the pilgrims or anyone else. The parallel here is not close, but the three felon barons of Beroul come to mind. Disregarding the slaying by Governal of an anonymous felon (ll.1708–11) – a slip about which far too much has been made – two are killed by Tristan (ll. 4040, 4472). The manuscript breaks off before the fate of the third is mentioned, so it is unknown whether he too was killed.

ll.435–80. A favorite legend in the Middle Ages was that of the sea-creature mistaken for an island by sailors who lit a fire on its back. The story was probably invented about a sea-turtle[5] and, indeed, a shell-backed creature fits well into the account of the delayed action of the fire. In the *Brendan* it is the greatest of sea-fish upon whose back the pilgrims prepare their Easter feast. In the earliest Old French Bestiary written by Benedeit's compatriot and contemporary Philippe de Thaon,[6] soon after 1121, the creature on whose back "notonniers" light a fire occurs under the rubric "Cetus" gallice "balains" (ll.1915–40). It is described as a beast, not a fish. This is immaterial, the confusion between a whale and a fish being tradi-tional in the case of Jonah. The transformation of the sea-turtle into a fish or whale is probably due to a knowledge in the West of the story of

Sindbad the Sailor, in which case there is here an influence of romance upon hagiography. Other extraordinary creatures, serpents, monsters, a griffin and a dragon (in this case all marine or aerial) are commonplaces which occur in romances, from *Yvain* and *Fergus* down to *Fouke Fitz-Warin*.

ll.481–580. The Paradise of Birds. A tree covered with singing birds is not, as some writers seem to forget, unknown in Nature. Nevertheless it is reasonable to suppose a literary tradition here, starting from the famous musical-box at Constantinople described by Liutprand, who saw it in 949.[7] The glories of the Imperial Palace and the wonders of the bronze statues and automata of the Hippodrome were reflected in many *chansons de geste* and romances. In the case of the tree a direct influence of the *Brendan* upon *Yvain*[8] may be suspected. "The trees," says R. L. G. Ritchie, "overhanging the fountain are obscured by a flock of birds which sing in harmony and have, demonstrably, flown out of the French text of the *Navigatio Sancti Brendani*."[9] "Demonstrably" because Calogrenant says:

> 'S'ecoutai tant qu'il orent fet
> Lor servise trestot a tret.'
> (11.471–2)

There was no point in making the birds at Barenton sing a religious service if the birds in the *Brendan* had not sung a prayer, vespers, compline with the proper psalms and matins. True, Crestien might have known the *Navigatio*, but the account of the episode there is much more diffuse.

ll.781–822. The pilgrims reduced to a state of hunger and thirst come across an intoxicating spring, and in spite of Brendan's warnings, drink too much of it and fall into a drunken slumber. Magic springs occur in lais and romances. In this class the spring of Barenton must be excluded, for this really exists, *experto crede*. There is a spring in *Fergus*[10] (100–4; 101–20) which cures the hero of madness.

ll.791–4. The monks strive to make headway against a coagulated sea. This is, as Waters points out in a note, the "Mer Betee" of epic and romance. This is usually, like the "Arbre Sec," mentioned as marking the bounds of the civilized world. It is so used in *Fergus* 74–10, the *Dit de Guillaume*,[11] the Burgundian jongleur version of *Guillaume d'Angleterre*, improbably attributed to Crestien de Troyes, the *Renart*[12] and in the *Roman du Comte de Poitiers*.[13] It is curious that in the *Brendan* (and in the *Navigatio*) the explanation of the sluggishness of the sea is no more clearly explained than it was by Pytheus, who first described it, yet in the north of Europe Vikings, fishermen and whalers were well acquainted with ice. In *Fouke Fitz-Warin*[14] the hero sails far north beyond the

Orkneys and is forced to turn back when "la nef en la mer pur la gelee ne poeit avant passer" (p. 63). This must be independent of the tradition of the Mer Betee. Yet so strong was this tradition that it accounts for a variant in the *Charette*. In the description of the river which flows under the Pont de l'Epee, the Guiot copy[15] says that anything which fell into it is carried away as if it had fallen into the "mer betee." This is a variant for "salee." The whole point of a "mer betee" is that it does not move. On the other hand, "salee" seems feeble, and it is just possible that "mer betee" is here used of an accursed sea. However, the Guiot variants are often unsatisfactory.

ll.825–96. A recapitulation of the wonders of the First Voyage. The only surprise is that the cauldron abandoned on the fish's back is recovered, and the fish, now given a proper name based on an Irish word, is called Jacoine. After feasting in safety the monks are kindly transported by Jacoine to their next port of call. This operation on the part of the traditional sea-monster possibly is unique.

ll.1641–1808. Paradise at last. Amongst the sources for the description is the Apocalypse, but also Claudian, unmentioned by Waters. Claudian is one of the sources for many gardens, including that in the *Roman de la Rose*.[16]

The influence of the *Brendan* upon any romances cannot be proved, but there is a suspicion that both Beroul and Crestien de Troyes were acquainted with it. In any case, it has been shown that the *Voyage* and the romances have much in common.

Ailred of Rievaulx's well-known reference to a novice, supposed to be himself, formerly moved by tales of a certain Arthur, when read in the light of Walter Daniel's account of Ailred's visit to Walter Espec, raises once again the question of whether the tales come out of Geoffrey of Monmouth. For the talk at Helmsley ranged widely, and in the speech attributed by Ailred to Walter Espec before the Battle of the Standard, reference is made to Walter's knowledge of old tales, and it is known that he possessed a copy of Geoffrey sent to him by Robert of Gloucester, one of Geoffrey's patrons.[17] Was there perhaps reading aloud, or singing or talk about the exciting legends woven into a book by the Canon of St. George's?

Whether Ailred or one of his pupils was the novice who turned away from idle tales to more pious reading, writers of Saints' Lives liked to advertise their wares by contemning other works of fiction. Denis Pyramus's[18] condemnation of secular works – the *Partenopeus* and Marie de France's *Lais* – is often quoted in a vain attempt to date works. All that can be established is the obvious fact that Denis was writing after the

Partenopeus and the *Lais*. The association of the *Partenopeus*, a treatment of the fairy-mistress theme, with the *Lais* leads to the supposition that Denis had in mind *Guigemar* and *Lanval* in particular. The *Lais*, "qui ne sunt del tut verais," are said to be popular amongst counts, barons, and knights, and it is added that kings, princes, courtiers, counts, barons, and vavasours all love tales, songs, and fables. Denis, a court poet in youth, he tells us, was still writing for the same courtly public, and it was his intention to provide them with a "deduit," a pleasure which would not only delight but improve the hearers. The story of St. Edmund was not only true according to the monks, but entertaining indeed. Today it is nearly as hard to swallow the legend of the king's head discovered after his martyrdom – zealously guarded by a wolf, and detected because it was giving the hunting cry of "Here, here" in English as well as Latin or French in order to give an air of authenticity – as it is to believe in fairies.

Less known is the reaction of Chardri to secular literature. Chardri, who belongs probably to about 1200, has never been identified, and the recent suggestion that the name is an anagram of Richard does no more than make it less eccentric.[19] In his *Josaphaz*, Chardri says in his epilogue that we hear about Roland, Oliver, and the battles of the Twelve Peers rather than about the Passion (ll.3934–8). This is remarkable, for Johannes de Grocheo, writing about 1300, classed saints' Lives and epics together as exempla, each a "cantus gestualis."[20] In the prologue to his *Set Dormanz* which follows *Josaphaz* and is edited with it,[21] Chardri gives a list of what he has not studied and of which we shall not speak – the fables of Ovid, and Tristram, Galerun, Renart, and Hersent. The mention of Tristan l'Amerus in the same breath as the adulterous Renart was calculated to make a courtly audience wince.[22]

Except, possibly, in the case of the *Brendan*, which is not the biography of the saint and has mythical features, there seems no evidence that the subject matter of the saint's Life influenced the romances. True, the romance often deals with the adventures of a hero, but his amatory and military exploits have little in common with the pious works of a saint. What is clear is that romance influenced romance and saint's Life influenced saint's Life. It is, however, quite otherwise in the case of poetic form. Considering the opinion of Johannes de Grocheo quoted above, some may think it surprising that few hagiographers employed the form of the *chansons de geste*. There are in Anglo-Norman two poems in alexandrines associated with Edward the Confessor. One, a fragment dealing with the miracle of St. Wulfstan's crozier, based on Ailred's Life, can only be reconstructed in part from the prose *Livere de Reis de Engletere*,[23] of which it is the source for the episode. The alexandrines are not in laisses, but usually in pairs, though sequences of three or four lines rhyming together are not infrequent. Such sequences are not rare in Anglo-Norman. Whether this is an extract from a complete translation from Ailred cannot be determined. The second poem is an account of the miracle of St. Edward's Ring. This has no connection with the first, its source being an interpolation into the Life written by Osbert of Clare.[24] It is therefore probably complete as we have it. Two saints' Lives written on the Continent but popular in England are written in epic lines, but grouped in stanzas of five lines, probably in imitation of Latin hymns. They are the Life of St. Alexis in decasyllables and the Life of Thomas Becket by Guernes de Pont-Sainte-Maxence in alexandrines. More interesting is the case of Matthew Paris.[25] His Life of St. Alban is probably the earliest of his four saints' Lives, and the only one surviving in holograph. It is written in laisses of alexandrines, exactly like a late *chanson de geste*. The text is in two columns, and above it is a running set of miniatures in pairs. The rubrics to the pictures are in octosyllabic couplets. The other three Lives, Edward the Confessor, translated from Ailred, Thomas Becket, surviving only in fragments, and Edmund of Abingdon, are all in octosyllabic couplets. In the case of St. Edward and St. Thomas, the text is in three columns, but the pictures at the top of the pages are in pairs, not corresponding exactly to the columns. This rather clumsy arrangement seems to be a legacy of the lay-out of St. Alban, where it makes sense. St. Edmund, unfortunately, survives in a copy without the pictures. These were unnecessary in this manuscript, for although it belonged originally to a laywoman, it is part of the collection of saints' Lives given to the nunnery of Campsey for mealtime reading and may have been commissioned for that purpose. It is the only Life translated from a Latin Life by Matthew Paris himself, and the only one in which he names himself. He planned another illustrated book, which, if it was ever completed, has disappeared. The plan, sketched on a fly-leaf of the St. Alban MS., is that pictures of saints, arranged in pairs, were to be accompanied each by a lyric stanza of explanation, but not a complete Life.

What was to become the standard verse-form for both saints' Lives and romances, the octosyllabic couplet, was first used in the *Brendan*. True, the couplet had been used in the two tenth-century poems in the Clermont-Ferrand MS., the Passion and St. Leger, but these were written in the same form as the Latin originals, and the lines are in stanzas of four lines in the case of the Passion and if six in St. Leger. In the *Brendan* the lines run consecutively. Wace, at the beginning of his career in Normandy, used the couplet for his Lives of St. Nicholas and St. Margaret, and for his poem on the Assumption. The first person to use the couplet for a secular narrative was Gaimar. Although his chronicle is not a romance, it contains much fiction in the early part of the *Estoire des Engleis*,[26] and his lost *Brut* was based on Geoffrey of Monmouth. It has, besides, so many courtly features that Miss Pope used to say that Gaimar had some claim to be the earliest of the courtly writers of narrative. Wace, who may have known the work of Gaimar, used the couplet for his *Brut*[27] and for the later parts of his *Rou*.[28] With Crestien de Troyes and his successors, and with independents such as Hue de Roteland, the couplet becomes standard for romance.

For saints' Lives and the like there is, however, an important difference between Continental and Anglo-Norman technique. About fifteen saints' Lives and similar didactic and devotional poems written in lyric stanza form, mostly from the twelfth century, are listed by Vising. This list excludes short prayers and other devotional works for which the form is appropriate. The most important of the saints' Lives is that of Thomas Becket by Benet, a monk of St. Albans.[29] This is over 14,000 lines long, in tail-rhyme stanzas. No Anglo-Norman romance exists in this form, but later on it was used in the East Anglian group of Middle English romances, parodied by Chaucer in *Sir Thopas*. For some reason narrative writers in England, whether in French or English, seem to have had a predilection for stanzas, especially in tail-rhyme, which is particularly unsuitable. Derived from its use in Latin hymns, it is a mystery why it was adopted for narrative. On the Continent, it was used only for lyric poetry.

There is an obvious reason for the use of the couplet for both saints' Lives and romances; they were written for the same public. This is made clear by Denis Pyramus and Chardri, and the *Brendan* was written for a Queen, and as she herself was an accomplished Latinist, presumably for her less learned entourage. The laisses of the *chanson de geste*, and those of the Anglo-Norman romances like *Boeve de Haumtone*, were intended to be chanted or intoned before a large mixed audience in the Hall or market-place. They were easily heard and easy to learn by heart, and improvisation when memory failed was also easy. Some even of this class were read from a book, as Thomas, the author of *Horn*, tells us in his prologue.[30] But the octosyllabic couplet is almost as difficult to learn by heart as "So she went into the garden to cut a cabbage-leaf to make an apple-pie." The romances and other works in this form were meant to be read aloud in a small gathering in the "chambre," to lords, ladies, maids-in-waiting and pages. In *Yvain*, Crestien paints a delightful picture of family life (ll.5362–5374). A seventeen-year-old girl is reading a romance aloud to her aged parents who are resting on the grass in the garden. It has been suggested that the parents were too old to have been taught to read, and that their daughter belonged to a generation which had been taught, but reading a book aloud in a family circle continued to the end of the last century, and perhaps into this one. Crestien's principal patron was that great lady, Marie de Champagne. Matthew Paris wrote his Life of Edward the Confessor for Queen Eleanor of Provence, and his St. Edmund for Isabelle, Countess of Arundel, patroness of Wymondham, a cell of St. Albans. His picture book of saints was planned for a Countess of Winchester. The Life of St. Alban was probably written for some patron of the Abbey itself. In other cases of Lives of patron saints of monasteries the purpose may have been for entertaining laity at some Gaudy. This is very likely so for St. Modwenna, St. Osyth, Simon of Walsingham's St. Faith, and Denis Pyramus's St. Edmund. Sometimes a monastery seems to have had to go outside its walls and to commission work from a known writer. A Canon of Chichester ordered a Life of St. Richard of Chichester from Peter of Peckhan, Fetcham, or Abernon, whose *Secré de Secrez* and *Lumere as Lais* had presumably won fame. Sources for the Life of a patron saint were often Latin texts written in the same monastery as the translation, but, so far as is known, the only cases where the Latin was the work of the translator are the *Brendan* and Matthew Paris's St. Edmund.

Mention of Matthew Paris brings up again the question of how much private reading was done. Notes on a fly-leaf of the Life of St. Alban tell us that Isabelle, Countess of Arundel, had borrowed a book containing the Lives of St. Thomas and St. Edmund, which was to be lent next to the Countess of Cornwall until Whitsuntide. These Lives Matthew Paris had translated and illustrated himself, and the manuscript presumably followed the usual pattern of text below a running set of miniatures at the top of the pages. Did these ladies read the books to themselves, or did someone else read them aloud while the lady sat beside looking at the pictures? Or was the text read and the pictures looked at afterwards as a reminder? Today children will recite by heart the text of Beatrix Potter's books while looking at the pictures, fondly imagining that they are reading. Comparison between the laity of the Middle Ages and the children of today learning to read is not frivolous. The meaning of "read" is discussed by H. J. Chaytor in *From Script to Print.*[31] What did Gaimar mean when he said that his patroness, Dame Custance Fitz-Gilbert, had purchased for a silver mark, refined and weighed, David's song about Henry I written for Queen Adeliza of Louvain, and "En sa chambre sovent le lit"? (ll. 6481–92) It is not clear whether she read it herself or whether she had someone to read it to her. Presumably Custance had been at court before her marriage. The regularity of the Matthew Paris layout is rare in the case of romances, and is never as early. Often only the initial page is decorated at the top. The Anglo-Norman Apocalypses and the crude Continental copy now in the Cloisters at New York follow Matthew Paris's pattern, with the exception that the pictures were planned first, and only as much of the text was copied as would fill the bottom of the page. The Lives from St. Albans are therefore of great interest in considering the problem of how much the laity read to themselves.

It is social conditions, then, which account for most of the resemblances between Anglo-Norman Saints' Lives and romances.

NOTES

1. Ed. E. G. R. Waters (Oxford, 1928); R. L. G. Ritchie, "The Date of the Voyage of St Brendan," *Medium AEvum*, XIX (1950), 64–6; cf. and for subsequent texts M. D. Legge, *Anglo-Norman Literature and its Background* (Oxford, 1963).
2. M. D. Legge, "Les origines de l'anglo-normand littéraire," *Revue de Linguistique Romane*, XXXI (1967), 48.
3. Ed. A. Ewert (Oxford, 1939).
4. A. J. Kennedy, "The hermit's rôle in French Arthurian Romance," *Romania*, XCVI (1974), 54–83.
5. F. McCulloch, *Mediaeval Latin and French Bestiaries* (Chapel Hill, 1960), pp. 91–2.
6. Ed. E. Walberg (Lund and Paris, 1900).
7. S. Méjean, "A propos de l'arbe aux oiseaux dans Yvain," *Romania*, XCI (1970), 393–9.
8. Ed. T. B. W. Reid (Manchester, 1942).
9. *Chrétien de Troyes and Scotland* (Oxford, 1952).
10. Ed. E. Martin (Halle, 1872).
11. Ed. Francisque Michel, *Chroniques Anglo-Normandes* III (Rouen, 1840), p. 192.
12. Branches XII–XVII ed. M. Roques (Paris, 1960).
13. Ed. B. Malmberg (Lund and Copenhagen, 1946), l. 1263.
14. Ed. L. Brandin (Paris, 1930).
15. Ed. M. Roques (Paris, 1958), l. 3016.
16. C. S. Lewis, *The Allegory of Love* (Oxford, 1936), pp. 74–5, 129.
17. M. D. Legge, "Gautier Espec, Ailred de Rievaulx et la Matière de Bretagne," *Mélanges Frappier* (Geneva, 1970), pp. 619–21.
18. *La Vie S. Edmund le Rei*, ed. H. Kjellman (Goteborg, 1945), ll. 25–49.
19. *Le Petit Plet*, ed. B. S. Merrilees. Anglo-Norman Texts XX (Oxford, 1970), p. xxxi.
20. J. Wolf, *Die Musiklehre des Johannes de Grocheo*, Sammelbunde der Internationaler Musik-gesellschaft I (1899), p. 90.
21. Ed. J. Koch (Heilbronn, 1879).
22. M. D. Legge, "Quelques allusions littéraires," *Mélangez Le Gentil* (Paris, 1973).
23. Ed. J. Glover, Rolls Series XLII (1865).
24. Ed. H. J. Chaytor, *Miscellany Kastner* (Cambridge, 1930), pp. 124–7.
25. Cf. R. Vaughan, *Matthew Paris* (Cambridge, 1958).
26. Ed. A. Bell, Anglo-Norman Texts XIV–XVI (Oxford, 1960).
27. Ed. I. Arnold, Société des anciens textes français (1938, 1940).
28. Ed. A. J. Holden, Société des anciens textes français (1970, 1971, 1973).
29. Ed. B. Schlyter (Lund and Copenhagen, 1941).
30. Ed. M. K. Pope, Anglo-Norman Texts IX–X (Oxford, 1955).
31. (Cambridge, 1945) *passim*.

French Medievalists and the Saint's Play

A Problem for American Scholarship

E. CATHERINE DUNN

The origin of the miracle play on the life of a saint remains a major literary problem unsolved by medieval studies in our time. This type of religious drama is widely regarded as the *final* manifestation of Latin dramatic composition, occurring about two centuries after the Easter plays of the Carolingian era, and thus flowering as a phase of the twelfth-century Renaissance in Western Europe. Anglo-American scholarship has been largely content to follow the lead of G. R. Coffman and Karl Young, who assigned the Latin plays of St. Nicholas to the twelfth century and designated them as compositions freely but obscurely related to medieval Latin hymnody and lyric poetry of that period.[1] The only American who questioned these large generalizations was Professor Hardin Craig, who suggested twenty years ago that the miracle play might some day be revealed as a genre with the same liturgical origins as Easter and Christmas plays.[2] The problem has been largely dormant in American circles, perhaps because the saint's play has a very limited place in vernacular English drama, and is regarded rather as a phase of Continental literary history.[3] In a sense, this relegation is correct, because hagiographical drama *was* a flower of the French gardens. However, the tendency to avoid the generic question has impoverished American scholarly literature by insulating it against a rich tradition of French thought that is far more liberal on certain issues related to the miracle play, and raises fundamental questions about the very nature of medieval drama. Although my field is Middle English, I have nevertheless ventured into this Continental territory.

The dramatic performance of a saint's life on his festival day may be the oldest type of liturgical drama, older than the "Quem quaeritis" tropes of Easter Sunday that are now accepted as the original form. Such is the burden of my own thinking, and I have found in my French reading a general support for the explorations I have made into the Carolingian context of this genre. Although, to my knowledge, no one has formulated the thesis that I have adopted, I have developed it over a period of years in which I have studied a school of nineteenth-century historians freely associated with the École des Chartes. The implications for a radically interesting concept and chronology of saints' plays are present in their studies, and their insights into the liturgy seem more profound than any that I find in present day dramatic scholarship.

The most significant element in the French writing on medieval drama, virtually absent from other approaches, is a knowledge of the Gallican liturgy. This obscure rite, on which no definitive study yet exists,[4] prevailed in much of western Europe before the Carolingian era and the introduction of the Roman rite into Gaul and Catalonia. Certain features of Gallican ceremonial may well have been the seeds of liturgical drama already in the sixth and seventh centuries, and these very features seem to be the ones that clashed with the Roman forms introduced into the area about the middle of the eighth century. Moreover, Jacques Chailley has suggested that the whole "troping" movement and its resulting dramatic developments were a Gallican reaction against the austerity and classical grandeur of the official Roman texts, and that this Gallican resurgence was permitted by ecclesiastical authority in a compromise with the popular temperament and its prayer styles of a more "romantic" type.[5] Karl Young himself conceded that he was puzzled by an apparent contradiction at the heart of the Carolingian Renaissance – that this age witnessed the imposition of a classical Latin diction and a Roman style, while yet producing a form of verbal and musical embellishment in the paraliturgical tropes that overwhelmed the abstract and intellectualized prayer of the Gregorian chanting.[6]

French scholars vary in their assessment of this cultural conflict, but the story, insofar as it can be pieced together from fragmentary records, is the history of the troping movement and of the liturgical drama. The impact of the Roman rite seems to have been shattering both to the native Celtic population of Gaul and to the more recently established Franks,[7] although the Merovingian rulers and clergy made the historic decision. This extraordinary program, begun under Pepin and completed by Charlemagne, imposed an alien *style* upon a people, but style, as an expressive process, is rooted in ethos and temperament. The impact of the classically-oriented liturgy, expressive of the Mediterranean spirit, or rather, the Roman spirit, was a shock to both the Celtic and the Germanic ethos, that required a century or more of adjustment.

It is perilous to speak of *a* Gallican rite,[8] because local variations (e.g., at Lyons and Vienne) were considerable, and amounted to minor "uses."[9] By the sixth century, however, there was enough uniformity in practice to constitute a recognized rite. Historians still differ on the origins of this liturgy and its relationship to Roman usage and to Oriental customs, but the salient features are readily distinguishable from the sixth century and are generally recognized by commentators. One of these characteristics had special potential for dramatic development, for it was a particular way of celebrating a saint's festival and was deeply rooted in popular devotion. This was the custom of marking a saint's feast by public recitation of his *vita* at the Mass of his day. The crucial record occurs in a letter of St. Germain de Paris (576), supported by other more casual statements of Cesarius of Arles, Gregory of Tours, and Abbot Hildwin. Modern historians make St. Germain's account of the Gallican Mass lections the basic foundation of their comments on the cult of the saints at this time.

In order to understand the situation one must realize that the Gallican Mass included the reading of three lections, a prophetic one (from the Old Testament), an apostolic one (from the New Testament epistles), and an evangelical (Gospel) selection. The threefold reading had been an earlier custom in the Roman liturgy and was ultimately of Eastern origin, but it had been curtailed in the practice of Rome during the centuries contemporary with the Gallican prominence in western Europe.[10] The reading of a saint's Life, then, was a special practice, used only on a sanctoral feast, and was substituted for either the prophetic or the apostolic lection.[11]

St. Germain, after speaking of the three ordinary lections, makes note of two exceptions, for the Easter season and for saints' days:

Actus autem apostolorum vel Apocalypsis Johannis pro novitate gaudii Paschalis leguntur, servantes ordinem temporum sicut historia Testamenti Veteris in Quinquagesimo, vel gesta sanctorum confessorum ac martyrum in solemnitatibus eorum, ut populus intelligit [sic] quantum Christus amaverit famulum, dans ei virtutis indicium, quem devota plebicula suum postolat patronum.[12]

The Acts of the Apostles and the Apocalypse of St. John, then, were the special material for the Paschal season, and the Lives of the saints were assigned to their particular festivals with the intent of edifying the congregation, who would marvel at the power granted to one of the Lord's servants and would be encouraged to seek his intercession as patron.[13]

This practice of reading or chanting the saint's Life came into confrontation with the Roman rite when the latter was introduced. M. Raynouard, a nineteenth-century historian, provides the key to the story. In writing an introduction to troubadour poetry, he commented on some quasi-liturgical pieces that he regarded as underlying this secular poetry, one of these being a poem on the martyrdom of St. Stephen, which he dated rather vaguely in the late eleventh century. In accounting for this piece he traced its origin to the Gallican lections of the saint's life and indicated that it represents a survival of the practice in spite of general prohibition by Roman ritual canons: "L'ancien rit [sic] gallican ordonnait que les vies des saints seraient récitées à la messe du jour consacré à leur fête. Quand Pepin et Charlemagne introduisirent la liturgie romaine, il fut permis aux églises de France de conserver du rit gallican les usages qui ne contredisaient pas le rit romain."[14] He goes on to say that only readings from Holy Scripture were permitted in the Mass of the Roman rite and that the Gallican saint's lection was consequently removed from the Mass – except for the Life of St. Stephen. This reading (for December 26) was taken from the Acts of the Apostles and was therefore Scriptural.[15] He adds that Stephen's *vita*, as he edited it in his anthology, was a farced epistle, the Latin and the Romance parts being chanted alternately.

Whether or not Raynouard is correct in placing the farced epistle chronologically (and his timing is quite vague), his testimony to the ultimate origin of that genre in Gallican custom is important. Other French historians have added to this position details about the use of the saint's Life as a quasiliturgical feature, outside of the Mass itself. As only the St. Stephen text was kept in the Mass,[16] the others were assigned to the nocturns of the Matins Office, or were sung outside of the church edifice altogether.[17] (This transfer from Mass to Matins probably set the pattern for the transfer of the Easter trope from the Introit of the Mass to the hour of Matins, but that is a separate story.)

Chanted hagiography as a paraliturgical form of the Matins lection on a saint's day is supported by much French literary history, and is assigned to tenth-century origins. This date makes it contemporary with the Easter plays, which are now accepted as the earliest form of liturgical drama, with the play in the *Regularis concordia* of c. 975 surviving as the earliest text we have, and certain semidramatic texts from the Continent dating from the earlier half of the century. Raynouard himself had indicated that once the Roman prohibition against extra-Scriptural readings in the Mass was enforced, "ces vies [des saints] ne furent plus lues que pendant l'office de la nuit."[18] Marius Sepet, whose general theories on the origin of medieval drama focused upon the Matins *lectiones* as the essential framework for that drama, expressed the opinion that the miracle play owed its inception to dialogued lections in the night office of Matins on a saint's day, developed gradually from about the middle of the ninth century.[19] Amadée Gastoué has spoken of saints' Lives sung in church as part of the nocturnal office (preceding or following the authorized liturgy),[20] and Prosper Alfaric writes of *La Chanson de sainte Foy* as a vernacular version of a Latin Passion of the saint, read at Matins in both forms, the vernacular one "comme un nouveau Nocturne," "un sorte de reprise laïque."[21] Finally, Paul Zumthor, citing Jacques Chailley, says that melodic tropes of the Matins *lectiones* "se développèrent, au xe s., en particulier sous forme de cantiques hagiographiques."[22]

The chanted saint's Life was also detached from the Matins liturgy and recited outside of the church edifice. This second kind of "l'hagiographie chantée" seems to have been a later development than the troped lections of the Matins office, i.e., generally an eleventh-century phenomenon rather than a tenth. The chronological development, however, cannot be precisely determined, because the surviving examples of the genre are few and cannot be accurately dated. Both Gaston Paris and Edmond Faral see the saint's Life as a clerical composition, originally recited to a devout congregation within a church and later delivered separately from any church service, this second stage drawing the *chanson* into the repertory of the secular jongleurs.[23] Both Amadée Gastoué and Dominica Legge regard the surviving texts of the St. Léger legend and those of St. Eulalia, St. Alexis, and St. Foy as pieces to be sung either in or out of the church and composed in the vernacular language for a popular audience.[24]

Edmond Faral, whose study of the medieval jongleurs has become a classic of cultural history, places the vernacular saint's legend in the context of the *chanson de geste* and regards the two types of compositions as virtually identical in meaning and style.[25] He observes that public performers who recited either of these two kinds of narrative were excepted from the Church's frequent condemnations of the jongleurs. Thomas de Cabham's *Penitential,* explicitly freeing such performers from censure, designates them as "joculatores qui cantant gesta principum et vitas sanctorum."[26] Faral, quoting this well-known phrase (p. 44) says that Cabham's view was not an isolated one but was the general medieval position of church authorities. This close association of hagiographical legend and *chanson de geste*, observed also by Paul Zumthor, and more recently by Karl Uitti,[27] raises important questions about the methods of performance, the literary sophistication of the narratives, and the kind of musical accompaniment involved. It is precisely here that my own interest in the genre becomes most intense, because the interrelation of this recitative with drama is at stake.

The older French historians had pointed toward the merging of narratory and dramatic form in the *chanson de geste* tradition, and more recent ones generally accept it without debate, as, e.g., Jean Rychner.[28] That the precise relationship of drama to narrative in the medieval context still causes some problems, however, is indicated by Professor Roy, of the Université de Montréal. Just last April (1974) he found it necessary to argue vigorously that our conception of medieval drama should be flexible enough to include the so-called "elegiac comedies" of the twelfth century, and, indeed, should be broad enough to embrace all of our modern "performing arts."[29]

Such a broad and flexible view of medieval drama directly opposes the strict limitations delineated in the work of Karl Young, who refused to recognize the presence of drama unless a text contained rubrics calling explicitly for costume and action.[30] Even Edmond Faral, who accepted the continuity of the jongleur tradition with that of the ancient Mediterranean mimes, had been cautious about identifying the jongleurs as actors.[31] The basic question is whether there is *mimesis* here (in the Aristotelian sense), the imitation of an action. The saint's legend was a narrative of heroic virtue handled in a basically nonrepresentational style, abstracting from the biographical details an idealized portrait of perfection that transcended historical accuracy and rose to the level of a poetic construct, an imagined, perhaps "mythic" composition (as Karl Uitti puts it).[32] Such an idealized narrative lent itself to symbolic action[33] that could be rendered in rhythmic gesture of pantomimic or dance stylization without the necessity of representational detail, as long as the plot line itself was handled by the narrator or chanter. I should like to consider briefly three structural features of the saint's legend that point toward recitative accompanied by symbolic action, while I recognize that no one except myself has been willing to call this performance a saint's play. These three features are: strophic pattern, secular melody, and sacred dance.

The strophic form of the saint's Life gave it structural integrity as a heroic poem, and constituted a kind of troping that must be kept distinct from the line-by-line embellishment given to the Latin liturgical texts of the Mass. Gastoué writes that the life of St. Stephen, which he regards as contemporary with the *Chanson de Roland*, "forme moins une paraphrase du texte sacré, qu'une vraie Passion, dont toutes les strophes se suivent avec un sens achevé."[34] This narrative integrity is observable even in the quite early vernacular texts like the St. Eulalia, St. Leger, and St. Foy, which are really *cantilenae*, paralleling and "doubling" the Latin prose lection, as Alfaric says (p. 70), and thus detachable as a unit from the liturgical context.

This stanzaic pattern led to a second feature of the legend, i.e., a musical structure different from that of the Gregorian chant. We are told that the composers turned to popular melody as a resource. Indeed, it is possible that folk song had been used already in the Gallican saint's lection antedating the introduction of the Roman rite. The French historian who goes furthest in this direction is F. J. Fétis, who puts the troping of epistles as early as the seventh century, and considers that the music, even at this early time, was popular melody.[35] (The language of the farced, i.e., troped material, according to his judgment, was Latin from the seventh to the ninth century, but Romance vernacular from that time on.)[36] Widespread theorizing has occurred on the use of popular music in the entire troping movement, but the dearth of manuscripts to support such theories is a handicap to their acceptance.[37] The use of popular or folk song at least in the liturgical sequences is tenable, according to P. Wagner.[38] This possibility is full of implications for the chanted hagiography, because the origin of the saints' legends has been associated with sequence melodies: "The French saints' Lives seem to have begun as translations of the legend versified to fit the tune of the proper sequence, which could be sung in church or outside it for the benefit of the illiterate. This explains the peculiar forms of the *Eulalia*, the Passion [of Christ], *St. Leger,* and *St. Alexis.*"[39]

Gastoué's term for this secular music used in saints' legends is *cantilena vulgaris*, a phrase he used to distinguish this type of music from liturgical music (*cantilena romana*). Writing as late as 1924, he still claims a genuine originality in grasping the nature of strophic saints' Lives: "Je ne crois pas qu'aucun historien ou musicologue du chant religieux l'ait fait ressortir: les farces en langue vulgaire ne sont point autre chose que des couplets de cantilènes, interpolant le texte sacré."[40] This use of secular melody does not, of itself, mean that the saints' Lives were directed to illiterate audiences, an inference sometimes made all too easily. Pierre Aubry has suggested that even members of religious orders, who might be relatively well educated, enjoyed the vernacular language and the secular melodies of troped compositions because they recalled to memory the emotional associations of childhood faith and family life.[41]

The third element in the sung legends is perhaps the most controversial one, but also the most important for their dramatic nature – the accompaniment by sacred dance. It is here that imitation of action becomes involved and the passage from narrative to theatrical art is conclusive. It seems that in Western European culture few groups have readily accepted the appropriateness of dance movement in religious worship. Efforts in our day to revive the custom, as a feature of the ecclesiastical renewal following the second Vatican Council, have generally produced shock and disapproval in American circles. The tradition of liturgical dance, however, is especially strong and continuous in Spanish religious life,[42] where the medieval records are the most conclusive and the most valuable, but the French can also trace the custom and can associate it rather closely with the celebration of saints' days. I plan a separate essay for the very complicated problems involved here, but a precis of them can be given here.

E. K. Chambers, whose first volume of *The Mediaeval Stage*[43] was devoted to the backgrounds of the drama in folk ritual and festival, has written about the psychological nature of dance rhythm as imitating either a state of soul or an external activity of human life such as ploughing, sowing, or harvesting. Dance may be an exterior expression of joy, for example, or it may reproduce the events that create joy and satisfaction in the daily life of a people. Citing Du Méril,[44] he discussed this mimetic character of dance and the close association between the psychic and the physical phenomena.

Historically, the expression of emotion in mimetic rhythm has taken two major forms, one frenetic and the other highly disciplined. The pagan mystery cults had a "Dionysiac" element which frequently associated ritual dance with orgies that invited disapproval even in the ancient Mediterranean world.[45] This quality evoked the censures of Greek and Roman ecclesiastical writers in the Patristic era and of church councils for centuries.[46] However, dance could also be highly structured, and when it imitated religious experience it could be ordered into a reverential expression of awe and adoration. It was then far removed from the frenetic ecstasy and was allied with the ordered beauty of procession, genuflection, and kneeling in prayer – a liturgical action. Such is the case that Alfaric makes for the performance of the Life of St. Foy.[47]

Religious dance never achieved an official status in the Church as a whole, but local church authority tolerated it from time to time without encouraging it.[48] Individual clerics arranged and supervised this activity, especially in conjunction with Christmastide celebrations, and records of its occurrence at Easter, Ascension, and Pentecost also survive. The three days beginning with St. Stephen's feast itself (December 26) and extending through the successive days of sanctoral celebration, John the Evangelist, and the Holy Innocents, were a time of revelry throughout medieval Europe, and dancing is explicitly mentioned in the practices that were permitted. The revelry was referred to as the *tripudia*, the word itself (in the singular, *tripudium*) originally a Roman designation for a stately dance,[49] and by extension a general term for celebration and merry-making,[50] not limited to dance but including it as a component.

The feast of St. Stephen on December 26 thus became the focus for a whole cluster of practices that can be traced back into the Gallican recitation of his life during the Mass and that survive in some of the oldest farced epistles. The custom of religious dance in the December *tripudia* is discussed as a general practice by well-known medieval liturgical writers like John Belethus and Durandus of Mende.[51] There are also specific records of it in individual churches, the most significant one being found in the Cathedral of St. Stephen at Sens, an account extracted by Jacques Chailley from the precentor's book at this church.[52] In the full-scale study of these records that I am making, the customs present in the religious dancing of St. Stephen's day should support the theory that recitative, accompanied by pantomimic dance activity, was here a form of drama, related in some sense to ancient Roman theater, and a stage in the history of the miracle play.

The controversy over the continuity of pagan dramatic traditions throughout the Middle Ages has been a long and acrimonious battle in European scholarship, with little participation by American writers. It seems unnecessary to repeat the skirmishes over the conciliar condemnations of the mimes as evidence either for the continuity of ancient theatrical activity or for the disappearance of it. This kind of evidence has been threshed out and beaten to shreds too many times. It is likely that a more fruitful study can be made of ecclesiastical techniques and practices, having their origin in pagan antiquity but divorced from the secular stage itself, and drawn upon by clerical ingenuity in the Gallican and Carolingian eras as methods of public recitation, adaptable into the total construct of the liturgy and capable of sacralization in this context. Richard Axton has begun this type of study in a new book on medieval drama, without, however, considering the saint's play.[53] The *earliest* form of this adaptation bids fair to be the saint's Life, and the earliest form of liturgical drama to be the miracle play. The French scholarship of the past century and a half has laid the groundwork for this study without making full use of the potential it contains for historical reconstruction of the medieval drama. The two features of this scholarship which pose great challenges to American study of the saint's play are, in the final analysis, the use of the Gallican liturgy and a liberal attitude toward the definition of medieval recitative as a form of genuine drama.

NOTES

1. Karl Young, *The Drama of the Medieval Church* (Oxford: Clarendon Press, 1933), II, 309ff; G. R. Coffman, *A New Theory Concerning the Origin of the Miracle Play* (Menasha, Wisc., 1914).

2. *English Religious Drama of the Middle Ages* (Oxford: Clarendon Press, 1955), p. 83 and p. 323.

3. Dr. Mary del Villar's recent doctoral thesis surveys the development of the saint's play, beginning with twelfth-century origins, and without challenging the basic assumptions of British and American scholars. ("The Saint's Play in Medieval England," Diss. Univ. of Arizona, 1970). See my article, "The Origin of the Saint's Play: the Question Reopened," in *Medieval Drama: A Collection of Festival Papers*, ed., William A. Selz (Vermillion: University of South Dakota, 1968), pp. 46–54.

4. Johannes Quasten, "Gallican Rites," *New Catholic Encyclopedia* (New York: Harcourt, 1967), VI, 258.

5. I suggested the general lines of this argument as part of a recent article, "Popular Devotion in the Vernacular Drama of Medieval England," *Medievalia et Humanistica*, N. S. 4 (1973), 55–68, Chailley, *L'école musicale de Saint Martial de Limoges jusqu' à la fin du XIe siècle* (Paris: Les Livres Essentiels, 1960), pp. 186ff.

6. Young, I, 180–2.

7. Joseph Jungmann, *The Mass of the Roman Rite: Its Origins and Development*, trans. Francis Brunner, rev. Charles K. Riepe (New York: Benziger Bros., 1951), p. 58; François J. Fétis, *Histoire générale de la musique* (Paris: Firmine Didot, 1869–76), V, 107.

8. Quasten, pp. 258–61.

9. "Gallicane (Liturgie)" in Fernand Cabrol and Henri Leclercq, *Dictionnaire d'archéologie chrétienne et de liturgie* (Paris: Librairie Letouzey et Ané, 1913–53), Vol. 6, cols. 473–593. (Hereafter referred to as *DACL*.)

10. J. Quasten, "Oriental Influence in the Gallican Liturgy," *Traditio*, 1 (1943), 64–5. The three readings have been restored as a general practice in the vernacular liturgies established after the Second Vatican Council of the 1960s.

11. A full account of the Mass for a saint's day as it would be celebrated for pilgrims to his shrine is given by A. Marignan, *Le Culte des saints sous les Mérovingiens* (Paris: Émile Bouillon, 1899), pp. 107–25. Msgr. Louis Duchesne says that the saint's Life was a lection in the Ambrosian rite at least until the eleventh century. (*Origines du culte chrétien* [Paris: Ernest

Thorin, 1889], p. 186, n. 2.) H. Netzer quotes not only St. Germain but also Hildwin, Abbot of Saint-Denys, on the tradition of reading the saints' lives. (*L'Introduction de la Messe romaine en France sous les Carolingiens* (Paris: Alphonse Picard, 1910), pp. 5–6.

12. Sancti Germani Parisiensis Episcopi, 'Expositio Brevis Antiquae Liturgiae Gallicanae in Duas Epistolas Digesta," in Migne, *Patrologia, Series Latina* (Paris: Garnier, 1878), 72, cols. 90–1. The attribution to St. Germain was first made by E. Martène in the eighteenth century, according to O. M. Dalton, ed. Gregory of Tours' *History of the Franks* (Oxford: Clarendon Press, 1927), I, 336.

13. Jean-Baptiste Thibaut, *L'Ancienne liturgie gallicane* (Paris: Maison de la Bonne Presse, 1929), discusses this passage of the "Expositio" in pp. 35–6.

14. M. Raynouard, *Choix des poésies originales des troubadours* (1816–21; rpt. Osnabrück: Biblio-Verlag, 1966), II, cxlvi.

15. Raynouard, pp. cxlvi–cxlviii.

16. Raynouard's is the only explicit statement that I found on this point. H. Netzer does not mention it. Although Raynouard has carefully collated his manuscript texts, he has not documented his large historical generalizations here.

17. See notes 23–33.

18. Raynouard, p. cxlvii.

19. Sepet, *Origines catholiques du théâtre moderne* (Paris: P. Lethielleux, 1901), pp. 17–8. My whole theory of the saint's play takes its point of departure from Sepet's work.

20. Gastoué, *La Cantique populaire en France* (Lyon: Janin Frères, 1924), p. 17.

21. *La Chanson de sainte Foy*, ed. Ernest Hoepffner and Prosper Alfaric (London and New York: Oxford University Press, 1926), II, 70.

22. Zumthor, *Histoire littéraire de la France médiévale* (Paris: Presses universitaires de France, 1954), p. 84. François J. Fétis observed in the nineteenth century that "il est hors de doute qu'à certaines fêtes de saints . . . des épîtres farcies étaient chantées sur d'anciens airs populaires." He was referring to the tenth and eleventh centuries. (*Histoire générale de la musique*, V, 100–1.)

23. Faral, *Les Jongleurs en France au moyen âge* (Paris: Honoré Champion, 1910), pp. 48–51. Faral cites in support Gaston Paris' edition of the St. Alexis legend: *La Vie d'Alexis*, ed. Pannier and Paris, Bibliothèque de l'École des Hautes Études, VII, 265.

24. Gastoué, p. 17; Dominica Legge, *Anglo-Norman Literature and its Background* (Oxford: Clarendon Press, 1963), p. 243.

25. Faral, pp. 46–8.

26. E. K. Chambers, *The Mediaeval Stage* (Oxford, 1903), I, 59. The pertinent extract from de Cabham's *Penitential* is given in Chambers' second volume, Appendix G.

27. Zumthor, p. 141; Karl Uitti, *Story, Myth and Celebration in Old French Narrative Poetry, 1050–1200* (Princeton, 1973), pp. 8–26.

28. Rychner states quite positively that the recitation of the *chanson de geste* was a dramatic art, and that the reciter *played* his song, as an actor does his role. His book is not a study of dramatic techniques but of themes and motifs, with their relationship to unity of epic construction. (*La Chanson de geste. Essai sur l'art épique des jongleurs* [Geneva: E. Droz, 1955], p. 17.)

29. Bruno Roy, "Arnulf of Orleans and the Latin 'Comedy,'" *Speculum*, 49 (April, 1974), 261–2.

30. Young develops his definition of drama in the opening chapters of his Vol. 1.

31. Faral surveys European scholarship on the mimic tradition rather harshly in his opening chapter. Since he was writing within the decade that had produced E. K. Chambers' *The Mediaeval Stage*, with its chapters on medieval minstrelsy as the fusion of mimic and bardic traditions, much of Faral's commentary here reads like a challenge to the British writer.

32. Hippolyte Delehaye discusses in his preface the *poetic* here involved. (*The Legends of the Saints*, 4th ed., 1955. tr. Donald Attwater [New York: Fordham University Press, 1962], p. xviii.) In more recent terminology, Professor Karl Uitti places the literary problem in the context of the popular imagination as a shaping force in legend. See above, n. 27.

33. Charles Muscatine's discussion of nonrepresentational style in the French romance provides a basis for understanding the style of the saint's legend. (*Chaucer and the French Tradition*, Berkeley, 1957.)

34. Gastoué, p. 22. With questionable accuracy, he calls this piece a farced epistle.

35. Fétis, V, 100–1.

36. *Ibid.*, V, 106.

37. R. Pascal speculates on this matter in his essay "On the Origins of the Liturgical Drama of the Middle Ages," *MLR*, 36 (1941), 369–87. He cites on p. 377 Robert Stumpfl's survey of historians who support the notion of Germanic folk song as related to trope melodies (*Kultspiele der Germanen als Ursprung des mittelalterlichen Dramas* [Berlin, 1936], pp. 76ff.).

38. P. Wagner, *Introduction to Gregorian Melodies*, cited by Pascal, p. 377, n. 3.

39. Dominica Legge, p. 243.

40. Gastoué, p. 20.

41. Pierre Aubry, *La Musique et les musiciens d'église en Normandie au XIIIᵉsiècle* (Paris: H. Champion, 1906), pp. 34 and 40.

42. Richard B. Donovan, *The Liturgical Drama in Medieval Spain* (Toronto: Pontifical Institute of Mediaeval Studies, 1958), p. 38.

43. The discussion of folk drama and dance is handled speculatively by Chambers in I, 188ff.

44. Chambers, I, 188, n. 2. The reference to Du Méril is made without title but is apparently to *Origines latines du théâtre moderne* (1849), p. 65.

45. Curt Sachs, *World History of the Dance*, tr. B. Schönberg (New York: W. W. Norton, 1963), p. 246.

46. L. Gougaud, "La Danse dans les églises," *Revue d'histoire écclesiastique*, 15 (1914), 10–14; Jules de Douhet, "Danses consacrées," in *Dictionnaire des mystères, moralités, rites figurés et cérémonies singulières* (Paris: J. P. Migne, 1854), col. 285; Chambers, I, 161, esp. n. 2.

47. J. D. Ogilvy, "Entertainers of the Early Middle Ages," *Speculum*, 38 (1963), 616; Alfaric, *La Chanson de Sainte Foy*, II, 74–77.

48. Gougaud, p. 7 and pp. 19–20.

49. Sachs, p. 246.

50. Chambers, I, 164.

51. Beleth's remarks are to be found in his *Rationale Divinorum Officiorum*, in Migne's *Patrologia Latina*, Vol. 202, Chapters 70, 72 and 120. Durandus

of Mende has a treatise by the same title as that of Beleth, and considers religious dance in Book VI, 86, 9. I have used the edition of 1560 (Lugduni: Apud Haeredes Iacobi Iuntae, 1560), p. 369.

52. Chailley, "Un Document nouveau sur la danse ecclésiastique," *Acta Musicologica*, 21 (1949), 18–24.

53. Axton presents dance as one of three secular elements of pagan origin impinging on medieval religious drama. His chapter on the dance begins with twelfth century dance-games and gives no consideration to saints' plays. See my review of this book (*European Drama in the Early Middle Ages* [London: Hutchison, 1947]) in a forthcoming issue of *Comparative Drama*.

An Analysis of the
Narrative Motifs in the
Legend of St. Eustace

THOMAS J. HEFFERNAN

The legends of the saints have often fallen foul of scholarly judgment and have been found unsatisfactory because of their lack of "organic development" or because, when compared with romance they were found thin in descriptive detail. The "passivity" and lack of "roundness" in the characterization might be cited as evidence of the lack of literary artifice in the legends. In this paper I hope to be able to point out that the qualities desired by modern readers are not prominent in the Lives for three reasons: first, because hagiography depends less on "organic" structure to move the narrative line than on what I shall call a unitary or episodic narrative sequence; second, the apparent lack of descriptive detail results from the narrative's primary interest in action and response; and third, "character" is differently conceived as the three very different Middle English variants of the Eustace Life demonstrate. I shall then try to account for the markedly increased and continued interest in the Eustace legend from the late eighth century on by arguing that it is a popular tale adapted by the clergy as a homiletic aid. Finally, I shall show how, by examining an incident in the Middle English variants of the Eustace legend, we can come to some appreciation of the great variety possible within this neglected and "conservative" literary genre.

I

The telling and retelling of the Life of St. Eustace was very popular throughout the Middle Ages at least from the eighth century,[1] and it persisted into the eighteenth century.[2] The ability of any fictional narrative to maintain itself through the vicissitudes of ten centuries bespeaks a potent and continually gratifying coalescence of theme and event, admirably able to engraft itself on the popular imagination of the day. A. B. Lord, in assessing this phenomenon of longevity with special reference to oral verse, derives a conclusion that is equally applicable in our consideration of a hagiographic narrative, "For it is of the 'necessary' nature of tradition that it seek and maintain stability, that it preserve itself. And this tenacity springs neither from perverseness nor from abstract principles of absolute art, but from a desperately compelling conviction that what the tradition is preserving is the very means of attaining life and happiness."[3] The hagiographer is a custodian of such tradition, a religious one, and as such writes not merely to amuse (though this is clearly an aspect of his intention), nor merely to interest, but to conserve, to construct, and to edify.

The legend of St. Eustace employs a narrative imbued with some historical detail and setting focused around a fictional personage. This type of hagiography may draw and select incidents from written, oral, and indeed pictorial sources as, for example, the work of Agnellus of Ravenna[4] and Prudentius' *Peristephanon* testify.[5] In a similar vein, Bishop Brunton, the fourteenth-century bishop of Rochester, repeating a classic remark of Gregory the Great, calls the visual representations of the saints the books of the laity, "ymagines et picturae sanctorum, et precipue crucis christi, sunt libri laicorum."[6] What may then be perceived as a lack of wholeness or thematic unity is a deliberate result of this magpie compositional style. Rather like a palimpsest, the narrative blocks of the legend reveal their earlier, often crudely disguised, progenitors and, as a result of this marked heterogeneity, these units take on a quasi-independence within the narrative structure. However, although they appear autonomous, these blocks are held together by a thematic attraction.

The legend of St. Eustace divides into three major narrative units: the conversion, the sufferings, and finally the martyrdom. The functions which the *dramatis personae* carry out in each of these units have been drawn from the international popular tale, eastern legend, Greek Romance and biblical narrative (see section VI). Before we examine the considerable debt the Eustace Legend owes to certain of these diverse traditions, I will give a brief summary of the legend as it appears in the tenth-century Latin Life printed by the Bollandists.[7]

II

Placidas, a virtuous heathen, was a favorite of the Roman Emperor Trajan and a great military man and hunter. One day, while out hunting he pursued a great stag into a wilderness. There he saw a brilliant vision of the crucified Christ between the stag's horns, "et huic demonstravit inter cornua cervi formam sacrae Crucis supra claritatem solis splendentem, et in medio cornum imaginem Domini nostri Salvatoris Jesus Christi." The stag directed him to take his wife, Theopistis, and two sons, Agapetus and Theopistus to the "pontificen Christianorum" for baptism and then return for further instruction. This accomplished, Eustace (formerly Placidas) returned the following day and was told that because he had deserted the service of Satan by becoming Christian, he would now be severely tested. Eustace returned home and the trials were initiated. First a pestilence struck which killed all his servants and livestock; then thieves stripped him of all his wealth. The family, ashamed at their poverty, fled into Egypt. On route Eustace's wife was seized by a sea captain, "Et videns dominus uxorem Eustathius quod esset decora facie valde concupivit eam." Shortly after both his sons were stolen by wild beasts. Eustace, dejected, settled in a small village, and lived there fifteen years.

Meanwhile, Trajan who was again in need of military leadership, sent troops out to search for the former commander, Placidas. He was discovered by two former military companions, "Et confestim exilientes osculabantur eum." The three comrades returned to Rome, where Eustace resumed his military career. One day, following a great battle, his sons, who unknown to Eustace were soldiers in his army, discovered in conversation that they were brothers. Their mother, dwelling in the same house and having overheard their conversation, considered whether they might be her long lost sons. The following day, having petitioned the military governor, she recognized him as her husband Eustace "vidit signa, quae erant in marito suo." She informed him of the conversation between the two youths. He at once summoned the two young men and the joyous recognition was complete. The entire family returned to Rome. There the Emperor Hadrian, a most severe persecutor of Christians, "gentilem ipsum pejorem impietatibus," now reigned. Hadrian asked Eustace to sacrifice to the God Apollo. Eustace refused, professing his Christianity, "Ego supplico Christum Dominum meum et offero incessanter ei preces." The emperor, enraged, ordered the family into the arena. After miraculously surviving death by a lion, they were finally martyred in a furnace into the form of a brazen bull. Christians came in the stealth of night and secretly removed their bodies. Their feast day is celebrated on the Kalends of November.

III

The first mention in the West of St. Eustace is generally considered to be by John of Damascus in his "De Imaginibus" written in 726.[8] John wrote his account in Greek, but it was translated almost immediately into respectable Latin prose. In his brief prose account, "Ex martyrio sancti Eustathii, qui et Placidas," of fifty lines the translator renders the legend only up to the beginning of the first vision, "In cervi cornibus sanctae crucis ipso sole longe fulgentiorem figuram, atque inter cornua divini sui corporis, quod pro nostra salute sumere dignatus est, effigem ostendit." However, he must have had access to a more complete variant of the legend because he quite definitely refers to the martyrdom of the saint "ex martyrio sancti Eustathii." This gives more support to Meyer's argument for an earlier text (see section V).

John's account begins with the hunt scene ". . . per densissima silvae praeruptaque loca in nemus prosiliit," and ends with Christ explaining the reason for his coming to the still-heathen Placidas, "Idcirco quippe ad terras, ea quam cernis specie veni, ut generi hominum salutem afferrem." John stresses the providence and mercy of God, "At sapientissimus clementissimusque Deus," as the essential theme of his narration. This aspect of the legend receives less emphasis in the later *vitae* and is neglected in the vernacular lives which amplify (as we would expect) the central section, the sufferings.

Every century from the ninth to the fourteenth produced a Latin recension of the legend. The earliest complete Latin text extant is a tenth century (or perhaps late ninth century) metrical rendering in trochaic five-line strophes.[9] The prose *vita* printed by the Bollandists has been dated from the tenth century. There is an eleventh century version in hexameters[10] which displays a marked self-conscious Virgillian flourish and yet another in leonine hexameters attributed to Peter of Rheims.[11] There is an elaborately rhetorical example in distichs from the fourteenth century.[12] The standard collections of exemplary and moralized tales of the thirteenth and fourteenth centuries are also well represented: Johannes Junior's "Scali Coeli,"[13] Jacobus de Voragine's "Legenda Aurea,"[14] Vincent of Beauvais' "Speculum Historiale,"[15] and the anonymous "Gesta Romanorum."[16] The tale was also popular in virtually all European vernaculars and occurs as early as the tenth century in Anglo Saxon.[17]

The derivation of the vernaculars from the earlier Latin texts is exceedingly difficult to work out. None of the Latin Lives that I have studied seems to have been a direct source for any of the vernacular authors. However, the standard account of the relationship drawn between the "Legenda Aurea" and the "South English Legendary" seems to be wrong (see section VII). Before discussing the possible reasons for the wide popularity of the legend in the West in the late eighth and early ninth centuries, it is well to note that the legend was also popular in the East; there is a very complete tenth century Coptic text which clearly does not derive from any of the extant Latin texts.[18]

I V

The popularity of the Eustace legend is most marked and coincides with the Ottonian Age, an era which has been called the age of hagiography.[19] It is from this period that we begin to have mention of the saint both in *vitae* and in liturgical and martyrological books. How is this relatively sudden popularity to be explained?

It is my hypothesis that this signal popularity is a result of the ecclesiastical hierarchy sanctioning the clergy's use of an existing narrative with a proven popular appeal as a homiletic exemplum. Undoubtedly the Eustace legend had a local unofficial popularity for some time prior to the ninth century. John of Damascus' version (726 A.D.) is surely based on an even earlier text (see section III).

The narrative's theme of reward for patient suffering, its identification with the plight of the poor, and its ennobling of deprivation and hardship were certain to arouse the sympathy of its audience. Poverty was endemic in the seventh and eighth centuries,[20] and the tale of Eustace and his family, with its celebration of their heroic triumph over both material and spiritual poverty, contained the narrative ingredients which accounted for its popularity. Thus the legend of Saint Eustace possessed certain important features which a vernacular homily movement initially depends on, that is, it already had a proven popularity, which as it were, guaranteed audience approval and understanding. Furthermore, it has as its theme patience and reward – two obvious homiletic themes.

The earliest mention of St. Eustace is contemporary with the iconoclastic controversy, and moreover is by John of Damascus, the leading opponent of the iconoclasts. Damascus was an ardent supporter of the belief that it was in images that God made the invisible readily visible, and considered visual representation a valuable pedagogic tool.[21] It seems likely that the Eustace legend with its use of miraculous images, especially that of the stag, would be favored by this anti-iconoclastic faction of the clerical hierarchy fresh from their triumph at the Second Council of Nicea (787).[22] Indeed, it was most plausible that they would have supported its use as a text suitable for use in vernacular preaching.

St. Eustace first appears in the pseudo-Jerome martyrology and then consistently in the ninth century martyrologies, for example Usuardus' martyrology, but he does not appear in Bede's martyrology nor in the tenth century Anglo-Saxon martyrology. A church was erected in his honor in Rome during the Pontificate of Gregory II (715–731). However, if we were to believe the theory that Eustace was an oriental saint whose cult was imported into the West, we would expect his church to have been built around the Colosseum, the traditional site for shrines to oriental martyrs. However, Delehaye's researches have located it in the Champs du Mars. The anniversary date also varies: Roman missals and breviaries cite September 20 (the date given by Usuardus), while most other western European service books cite November 2nd, 3rd, 4th, 5th, 9th and, rarely, May 20th. The pseudo-Aelfric variant reflects, perhaps, some of this uncertainty concerning celebration date: it gives the date of the martyrdom in the translation as the Kalends of November, but the text appears in Aelfric's collection of saints' Lives under the date 20 September. Yet all the extant Benedictine calendars of the eleventh and twelfth centuries of English houses agree on the 2nd of November as the anniversary date. These inconsistencies reflect wide popularity and local manifestations of piety.

Notwithstanding the relative scarcity of vernacular hagiographic or homiletic texts from this period, it is still demonstrable that preaching in the vernacular, though in its infancy, was slowly beginning to emerge from under the dominance of Latin. In 813 both the Second Council of Rheims[23] (convened by Charlemagne) and the Third Council of Tours called for preaching in the "lingua romana."[24] Shortly after, the First Council of Mayence 847[25] repeated verbatim (see canon 2) the injunction of preaching in the vernacular stipulated by the Third Council of Tours; indeed these conciliar injunctions are a commonplace through the eleventh century. The preachers preparing to meet this renewed episcopal demand for vernacular preaching were thus in need of suitable sermon materials. Certain of these early sermons are little more than ready-made homilies borrowed literally from the Fathers; unadorned expositions of the Sunday Gospel or versions of the earlier Latin legends of the saints. The tradition of reading brief accounts of a martyrdom during the Mass was already quite ancient – St. Cyprian thought it efficacious and it received official sanction by the church at the Third Council of Carthage in 397.[26] The Eustace legend, which was popular at this time (the late eighth century) and which probably had enjoyed some popularity for over a century – is now incorporated into the teaching canon of the church where it serves as a homiletic exemplum.

Though strictly speaking the Life of St. Eustace is not a sermon, the dividing line between hagiography and sermon literature can be and often was indistinguishable. They are both narrative didactic forms which have as their ends the edification of their listeners. For example, a thirteenth century Anglo-Norman verse Life of St. Eustace (despite the zealous protests of Alain de Lille reproving verse homilies) refers to itself in the opening lines as "qui weult öir sarmon novel." [27] Further, besides their use as surrogate sermons, some saints' Lives were probably chanted in church services, as suggested by the Clermont manuscript of St. Leger and the eleventh century Anglo-Saxon St. Goderic which both retain musical notation; and a fourteenth century English "Speculum Sacerdotale" containing sermons for saints' days refers to saints' Lives "that have been read and sung on their feasts." [28]

V

The historical milieu helps to account for the increased use of and interest in the legend that are observed from the mid-eighth century. The church, we suggested, adopted a narrative that had an historically proven intrinsic popular appeal. However, historical forces alone are insufficient to account for the narrative's wide appeal. A legend's popularity also depends on its ability to incorporate and embellish popular narrative themes and motifs. The hagiographer was especially concerned to use deliberate verbal reminiscence of earlier texts (principally biblical) in constructing his narrative, and relied on his listeners' familiarity and recognition "anagnorisis" of these passages to delight his audience.

A motif central to the first narrative unit of the saint's Life, "the conversion," is the religious rebirth of Placidas through the medium of the miraculous stag. Indeed, without this motif the moral of the sufferings would remain purely secular and completely within the conventions of the international popular tale.[29] Gaster traced the ancestry of the motif of the stag as the manifestation of divinity, and concluded that it ultimately derived from a Buddhist Jataka of the third century B.C.[30] The similarity of the incident described by Gaster, while showing certain strong parallels with the Eustace legend (the king as a mighty hunter, the deer with the radiantly brilliant horns, the Bodisatta assuming the appearance of a stag, and the conversion of the king by the stag), appears somewhat exaggerated, especially in light of the currency of stag symbolism in Christian authors.

The stag is an ancient and widely diffuse motif in the Christian West and East. The stag symbolism in the Eustace legend (a narrative composed almost a millennium after the Buddhist text) is more likely to derive from Christian sources than Indian. For example, St. Ambrose proposes that the qualities of innocence, simplicity, and trust embodied in Christ may also be observed in the stag;[31] Gregory of Tours discusses the stag as a divinely appointed guide;[32] printed in the *Patrologia* among Bede's *dubia et spuria* is a gloss on Psalm 28 which draws an analogy between the stag and Christ;[33] Origen in a commentary on the Song of Songs, a text which was extremely popular in the West and especially in monastic communities (most of the Latin Lives were written by monks), discusses the frequency with which the stag appears in the pages of Scripture;[34] the *Physiologus* depicts the stag as the mortal enemy of the serpent/ Satan;[35] and Alanus de Insulis compares Christ's Resurrection and triumph over Satan with the stag's awakening from sleep;[36] all of these diverse Christian authors represent a very deep and abiding interest in this rich symbolism.

Hagiography is also well represented as Eustace is only one of many saints who are involved in some fashion with stags. Indeed, the incidents in the lives of Saints Meinulf and Hubert appear to be consciously modeled on the Eustace incident. The striking image of the glowing cross between the stag's horns had wide appeal, and in the legend of St. Fantino, the image is multiplied thus: "huic multae inter cornua cruces exstabant"; the single brightness of the cross becomes a brilliant "red and azure" in the legend of St. Felice of Valois. Thus, while appreciating the significance of the narrative aspect (the speaking stag) of Gaster's eastern analogue, I think it more probable that the stag image in the Eustace legend developed from the frequent comment and discussion from the Patristic Age onwards.

A. D'Ancona proposes the interesting thesis that the conversion scene may have been the nucleus of the Eustace legend, onto which the "man tried by fate" motif was later grafted.[37] W. W. Meyer, in a very learned discussion,[38] is of the opinion that neither of these motifs can be derived quite so clearly or directly from these oriental sources, and that the probable transmission of the "man tried by fate" motif was from the West to the East. Meyer argues that the Eustace legend almost certainly derives solely from an early Latin variant, found in manuscript Caessensis 145. After a paleographic examination he dates this variant to the fifth or sixth centuries. He demonstrates how this manuscript, Caessensis 145, was the probable source for a Greek version of the seventh century which was in turn retranslated (rather literally) into Latin about the year 800, and it is this second text that remains the influential variant for the later Middle Ages. Though exceedingly interesting and of considerable importance, Meyer's thesis is highly idiosyncratic and has a great number of opponents.[39]

VI

The biblical influence in the Eustace legend has been neglected in comparison with the amount of scholarly investigation that has gone into the influence of the popular tale and eastern legend, yet the Vulgate was throughout the Middle Ages a dominant influence. For example, the story of Balaam (Numbers 22:2), Cornelius (Acts 10:1), Paul's conversion on the road to Damascus (Acts 9:1–9), and the books of Job and Daniel are all potent allusions in the Eustace narrative. It is notable that the Latin Lives seem always to maintain the above biblical allusions; the English Lives usually retain only the allusions to Job, with the single exception of the Northern Homily Cycle version, which makes brief mention of the Old Testament figures Abraham and Tobit. But these biblical narratives, allusions to which in the Latin versions occur rather like prefaces to each of the three distinct units of the legend (the conversion, the sufferings, and martyrdom), are the very models underlying and shaping the specific functions, incident by incident, developed by the narrative. Further, as will be seen, the actual dialogue used in the narrative is in part often drawn from the language of the Vulgate.

In the Latin Lives the Old Testament story of Balaam is mentioned immediately before the stag's address to Placidas, "Antea quique asinae Balaam dedit ora loquelae." [40] The allusion here serves as a *figura* with which the hagiographer is attempting to underline the miraculous nature of the speaking stag (as a manifestation of God's infinite power) and also to point to the simultaneity of the events within Christian history; all events are, as it were, viewed by God "sub specie aeternitatis" and thus exist at the same time. The existence of the one, far from detracting from the importance of the other, only increases the richness of the parallel. As Balaam achieved wisdom through the "dumb" beast, so too is Eustace to be enlightened through the intermediary of the stag.

This motif, Balaam's ass, achieved some considerable degree of popularity in the Middle Ages. This can probably be accounted for, especially in the Germanic North, by their rigorous rejection of the pagan muses, which led them to substitute the biblical narrative of Balaam's ass as proof that God can bestow eloquence. This is certainly true of the Anglo-Saxon Aldhelm; the example was also used by Caelius Sedulius in his *Carmen Paschale,*

> Angelicis tremefacta minis adfatur asella
> Sessorem per verba suum, linguaque rudenti
> Edidit humanas animal pecuale loquellas.[41]

Bede, in his *Vita Cuthberti Metrice,* makes use of the same example and appears to be echoing Sedulius in this line, "Qui facit humanas asinam reborare loquelas."[42] The Balaam incident is also alluded to by Orientius in his *Commonitorium,*

> Mandato cum iussa tuo superaverit omnem
> Naturam, nostra voce fruens asina
> Et stimulis propria subigentem terga Balaam
> Terruerit miro quadrupes alloquio.[43]

It appears in Odo of Cluny's *Occupatio* "Qui dedit os asinale loqui."[44] Hence the hagiographer was using an image that would have been recognizable and understood by a large number of his audience.

The character of Placidas/Eustace itself is rather complex and appears to be a composite modeled chiefly after Cornelius the virtuous heathen, (Acts 10), Paul, the zealous persecutor of Christians (Acts 9), and Job, the model of patient endurance. The parallel between Cornelius and Placidas is made quite deliberately in the *vita:* "Justum Cornelium exemplis fuit ille imitatus." Both persons are god-fearing, alms-giving pagans and officers in the Roman Army; their families are said to resemble them in their virtuous behavior. Similarly both are saved because of their good work, and both, finally, are baptized by popes. Each is told in a vision that the Lord has offered him salvation because of his charitable life: the angel says to Cornelius (Acts 10:4), "orationes tuae et elemosynae tuae ascenderunt in memoriam in conspectu Dei," and the stag (in rather similar language) to Placidas, "eloemosynae quas facis indigentibus coram me steterunt."

In the *vita,* the allusion to Paul's conversion on the road to Damascus shows the borrowing in an even more striking and direct fashion, "sed sicut Paulum insequentem per suam ostensionem." Here the hagiographer has at least in part drawn closely from the biblical narrative as it is presented in Acts 9:1 – 30, 22:3 – 16, and 26:13. Notice also the similarity of the language of the two narratives. In the Vulgate, God asks Paul, "Saule, Saule, quid me persequeris"; and the stag (echoing this verbatim) asks Placidas, "Placidas, Placidas, quid me persequeris." Both men are astounded and fall to the ground: Paul "et cadens in terram" and Placidas, "et cecidit de equo in terram." The vision is described in both accounts as being brighter than the sun: in the Vulgate "supra splendorem solis circumfulsisse me lumen" and in the *vita*, "Quae splendore suo solis radios superabat." These examples show the legend's close dependence on the Bible for the action of the *dramatis personae*, the layered quality of "characterization," and in certain instances (as we have seen above) actual dialogue.

The central section of the legend, the sufferings or adventures, is rather more complicated in terms of identifying probable sources of the narrative. For example, it has been suggested that the motif of long separation and subsequent reunion, a popular theme in Greek romance, was an influence in the Eustace legend.[45] Achilles Tatius' "The Love of Leucippe and Clitophon" (c. second century A.D.) and Heliodorus of Emesa's "Aethiopica" (c. third century A.D.) may have been at least an indirect inspiration in the hagiographer's composition. H. Dorrie, however, proposes that the martyrology of Leucippe and Clitophon in the "Acta Sanctorum" for November 5 accounts for the survival and wide propagation of the pagan romance.[46] It was a widespread belief amongst the Christian community at this time (though apparently without foundation) that both Tatius and Heliodorus were bishops of the Church. This seems a simple case of converting a potentially scandalous pagan author of romance to the "truth," thereby somehow sanctioning his work. That some of the early Christians were troubled by their love for the classics is notoriously illustrated in St. Jerome's dream when Christ rebukes him for being a Ciceronian rather than a Christian.

However, notwithstanding the very general and diffuse influence stemming from Greek Romance, and the even more direct influence of the popular motif of the "man tried by fate" discussed by Gerould, the Book of Job is the single most important biblical antecedent in this central section of the legend. For example, the speaking stag in the second vision directs Eustace to look to Job as a model for his behavior in the difficult period ahead, "oportet enim et in his temporibus alterum Job demonstravi per temptationes et victorem diaboli te ostendi per tolerantiam." The sufferings of both Job and Eustace are remarkably similar and more significantly follow the same chronological sequence in the narratives. Immediately following the loss of his two sons, Eustace ardently appeals to the Lord to recognize that his sufferings have now surpassed those of Job's, his historical paradigm. It is a scene which is quite effective even in the straightforward prose of the *vita*:

Heu mihi, qui in abundantia nimia fueram, mode captivatis more desolatus sum. Heu mihi, qui magister militum, multitudine exercitum circumdatus fueram, modo solus relictus sum, nec filios concessus sum habere! Sed tu, Domine, ne in finem derelquas me, nec despicias lacrimas meas. Memini, Domine, dicentem te, quoniam oportet te temptari, sicut Job. Sed ecce plus aliquid in me fieri video. Ille enim, esti possessionibus caruit, tamen stercus habuit, supra quod sedere concessum est illi: ego vero peregre eadem patior tormenta. Ille amicos habuit compatientes ei, ego vero in deserta immites feras habeo in consolationem, quae filios meos rapuerunt. Ille etsi ramis caruis caruit, sed radicem uxoris respiciens secum consolabatur; ego vero infelix undique sine radice factus sum, sed sum similis ramis in deserto, qui undique procellis conquassantur." [47]

Besides this most explicit statement of the parallel between Eustace and Job, the very language of the Book of Job seems to have exercised some influence on the hagiographer in the composition of this unit of the legend. For example, Job, on hearing of the loss of his children, is moved to great sorrow, "tunc surrexit Iob et scidit tunicam suam et tonso capite corruens in terram . . ."; Eustace, immediately following the seizure of his sons by the wild beasts, expresses a similar sorrow, "coepit evellere capillos capitis sui . . . voluit se projicere in aquam. . . ." Now it may be argued that both these utterances are standard formulae used to express extreme grief, but the correspondence of such similar language in equally parallel events, sequence following sequence, is sufficient evidence to demonstrate the influence of the one text on the other. Further, both these despairing cries are next followed by strikingly similar utterances: Job laments his plight as "nudus egressus sum de utero matris meae et nudus revertar illuc . . ."; Eustace uses this same metaphor of nakedness in describing his condition, "ut arbores, modo vero nudatus sum." The simile of the tree occurs in Job (14:7 – 10) in a passage which considers the finality of death and which concludes with a reflection that echoes Eustace's above re-marks, "homo vero cum mortuus fuerit et nudatus." Admittedly, the connection in this comparison of the simile of the tree and the idea of nakedness in birth and death is not as straightforward as the other instances. However, it is my feeling that the author of the St. Eustace Life was so immersed in the biblical narrative of Job that it was virtually part of his living tissue.[48] Let us look at one last example from Job in complet-ing our argument of filiation between the two texts. Job, near the end of his apology to the Lord, prays for the strength to control his tongue, "manum meam ponam super os meum . . ." (39:4) and shortly before, ". . . non loquentur labia mea iniquitatem nec lingua mea meditabitur mendacium" (27:4). Similarly, Eustace prays in parallel language at the end of his plaint to the Lord for a like strength, "Pone, Domine, custodiane ori meo (et ostium munitionis circa labia mea), ut non declinet cor meum in verba malifiae, et ejiciar a facie tua." As I suggested above, the English versions of the Eustace Life as a rule severely restrict the biblical allu-sions; but even when the allusion is retained, as is the one to Job, the incidents stressed in the vernacular Lives are kept to a minimum.

Before going on to discuss the influence of the Vulgate in the third and final episode of the Eustace Life, the martyrdom, I should like briefly to account for the deliberately symbolic use of the number fifteen in Eustace. The *vita* tells us that Eustace is a penitential exile in the desert for fifteen years and that his return journey out of Egypt to Rome took fifteen days. The use and repetition of this number fifteen, especially as it occurs in the return from exile, is probably an allusion to the fifteen "Psalms of Ascent," sung by the Israelites in their exodus out of Egypt. As the Exodus signified the beginning of a new covenant for the children of Israel, so Eustace's return from exile signifies a covenant, the covenant of martyrdom. An ancient tradition had it that Solomon's temple in Jerusalem had fifteen steps leading up into the sanctuary; this rather obscure numerology continued to influence the Middle Ages, and indeed there are Renaissance paintings of the fifteen steps leading to the sanctuary (i.e., G. di Milano's Mary enters the Temple School, c. 1470). This passage from exile sets the stage for our analysis of the third and final major narrative unit in the legend, the martyrdom.

The martyrdom as it occurs in the Life of St. Eustace is founded on the two very popular incidents in the Book of Daniel: the unsuccessful martyrdom of Shadrach, Meschach, and Abednego, and Daniel in the lion's den. The brazen bull motif (the agent of their martyrdom) is not biblical. The use of a brazen bull for torture is first attributed to the Sicilian tyrant Phalaris (fifth century B.C.). The Eustace Life reverses the order of the episodes as they occur in the Book of Daniel, placing the confrontation with the lion before the immolation in the brazen bull. The biblical narrative says that Daniel is saved from the lions by an angel who miraculously caused their mouths to be closed. Likewise in the Eustace narrative the lion is made docile and gentle through the power of the Lord. This miracle is meant to underline the immanence of divine power and is a commonplace of hagiography.

However, the parallel with the three young Jewish martyrs is much more explicit than the incident concerning Daniel, the *vita* drawing a deliberate comparison, "sicut tres pueri (Babylone) per ignem probati sunt. . . ." The sequence of events in the narratives of both immolations is identical; in both instances, the refusal to obey the sovereign's command to worship an idol is the direct cause of the martyrs' being cast into the furnace. This refusal combined with a declaration of religious principle is an ancient *topos* in the hagiographic narrative. In the early historical Christian passions, for example, "The Martyrdom of Perpetuae and Felicitas," "The Letters of the Churches of Lyons and Vienne," and "The Acts of St. Cyprian," to cite some of the better known, it is in this section that we can expect to find some instances of the actual consular interrogations. In the later legendary *acta* this section allows the hagiographer a great opportunity to illustrate the efficacy of Christian apologetics and heroism in the at times interminable debates between heathen king and Christian saint.

Returning to the narrative, we notice some similarity in the actual immolation: the three young biblical martyrs praise the lord in prayer and song; so do Eustace and family. Further, in both narratives their bodies are spared from the ravages of the flames; this becomes a commonplace of the legendary Lives. The description given of the bodies in both accounts and the attention given to similar detail is noteworthy: in the biblical narrative, "et cappilus quoniam nihil potestatis habuisset ignis in corporibus eorum, et capillus capitis eoreum non esset adustus, et sarabara eorum non fuissent inmutata et odor ignis non transisset per os," and in the *vita*, "et non tetigit eos ignis, neque capillus capitis sensit odorem ignis." The Anglo-Saxon variant of the Eustace Life erroneously ascribed to Aelfric and included in his collection of Saints' Lives follows a Latin variant even more faithful to the Book of Daniel than the *vita* in this instance. For example, the Daniel narrative (3:50) describes the heat of the brazen furnace as being cooled by a wet dew, "et fecit medium fornacis quasi ventum roris flantem," and in Aelfric's version "þaet þyes fyres hæto sy gecyrred on wætne deaw."

VII

The conversion scene, the first of the three singular episodes (conversion, suffering and martyrdom) which constitute the legend, is treated rather differently in the three Middle English variants of the legend. This is an especially interesting scene to examine because it initiates the ensuing action of the narrative: Placidas is converted by the stag, which in turn leads to his sufferings and ultimately martyrdom.

The Life of St. Eustace accompanies the gospel for Quadragesima Sunday in the "Northern Homily Cycle" as an illustrative tale and is referred to both in the text itself and the manuscript margins as "narracio," "tale," "play," and "spell." This version, which focuses on the exemplary character of Eustace almost exclusively, was probably not preached following the gospel during the morning mass but rather at the informal Sunday afternoon service, and thus is a good example of the presumably many church-sanctioned alternatives to secular romance.[49]

Saints' Lives may have been narrated by the laity outside the church as Thomas de Chabham's (c. 1230) "Penitential" suggests, "joculatores qui cantant gesta prinicipum et vitas sanctorum."[50] And Ordericus Vitalis in his "Historia Ecclesiastica" reports Gerald of Avranches, chaplain to Earl Hugh of Chester, and his efforts to draw the courtiers to a more godly life by describing the heroism of the saints: "Luculenter enim enarrabat conflictus Demetrii et Georgii, Theodori et Sebastiani, Mauricii ducis et Thebaeae legionis, et Eustachii praecelsi magistri militum cum sociis suis, qui per martyrium coronari meruerunt in coelis."[51] Further, Robert Mannyng tells us that saints' Lives were very popular with the people;[52] William of Nassington, who approves the telling of saints' Lives (and specifically the Eustace Life), condemns in his *Speculum Vitae* even those romances closely modeled on the earlier saint's Life as "vayn carpyng" of "mynstralles and jeestours" that "makys carpying in many a place/ Of Octovyane and of Isambrase."[53]

The Northern Homily version uses formula, repetition, contrast, and parallelism more effectively than any of the other Middle English Lives to elucidate the patterns of paradox intrinsic to the theme. It contrasts the conventional theme of ideal life/Christian life with real life/earthly life; and the contrast of the two, seen as opposites, gives rise to the paradox: that to live totally in the world is to die to life, that is, to die to the eternal life of the spirit.

The conversion episode in the Northern Homily variant of the St. Eustace Life[54] occupies approximately 25 percent of the entire text (241 out of a total 1060 octosyllabic lines). The event as it occurs here is a composite of two distinct visions and their fulfilment. The four distinct movements which comprise this first unit are approximately the same number of lines in length: first and second visions 71 and 96 lines respectively and the first and second fulfilment 36 and 37 lines. The homilist is no doubt deliberately balancing these parallel events which form a composite of four different but thematically related actions. The divisions in this first unit, the conversion, exist not only to continue the action of the narrative but also to record the progressive change in the character of Placidas from virtuous pagan to Christian pilgrim. Placidas is shown as a different individual following each encounter with the stag. This change is realized through contrast, which compares his present state of mind with those things, now inadequate, which formerly brought pleasure.

The initial vision is fast drawing to a close, and the now-convinced believer Placidas addresses the vision of Christ between the stag's horns, asking how he may best serve the Lord:

> And seide: lord, þou me say
> hou I schal serue þe to pay!
> (ll. 121–2)

Christ's response is given rather baldly:

> Crist onswerde and seide hym þan
> how he schulde bi come cristene man,
> "And aftur come to me here,
> Mo of my priuetes to lere!"
> (ll. 123–6)

The transition from the place of the vision to the fulfilment (in this instance the baptism of Placidas and family) follows immediately:

> Whon þis was seid hom he ede,
> þenkyng on crist and on his rede.
> he fond al his men in o place
> But hedde he no talent to chase.
> (ll.127–30)

The sudden juxtaposition of the vision and the hunt freezes the character of these two incidents into sharp contrast. It isolates the tranquility of the wood, in which the vision occurs, from the associations of violence and death connected with hunting. Placidas' departure from the miraculous stag bridges the transition from the stasis of the vision to the kinesis of the hunt; it is the "via media" between the divine and earthly realms. The departure is also the time for reflection and decision making: it begins the gradual humbling process necessary for his salvation.

This is no longer that same man,

> Sire Placidas over alle thyng
> Touede veneyre that is hontyng,

but a man now moving from an old established set of values toward a new and difficult ideal, who now "has no talent to chase." The metamorphosis accomplished by that "gret ferly," has changed Placidas from the great "hethene" hunter, who stood foremost among men, into a member of the Christian community. It might be construed as his first lesson in Christian humility, for as in the hunt, so in the Christian community: there is but one leader and as Christ tells Placidas,

> ffor þe hert spak to hym wiþ mouþ
> And seide: whi hast þou chased me?
> I am come to take þe:
> To me leof and dere þou is . . .
> (ll.94–7)

Ironically the roles have completely reversed; the hunter has become the hunted. This is no longer an ordinary hunt, but a unique one in which ultimately the prey, although loved by the hunter (Christ in the guise of a stag), must first demonstrate his worth before the hunter accepts the victim.

This change of place, with the corresponding change in attitude it brings about, occurs in this first scene four times, first vision and baptism, second vision and sufferings. Marking each division is a couplet exemplifying Placidas' change from a pagan hunter to a Christian. On his departure after the first vision,

> he fond al his men in o place
> But hedde he no talent to chase.
> (ll.129–30)

On his return for the second vision,

> And eode to wode as he wolde chas
> And wente from his men In hast.
>
> (ll.164–5)

On his departure following the second vision,

> And hamward glad eode sire Eustas –
> But he hedde no wille deor to chaas!
>
> (ll.257–8)

The effect of these steps is to indicate to the listener the cumulative change in the character of Placidas following each point of separation.

> And ouer come his wikkednes
> wiþ pacience and Mekenes;
> Let Mekenes beo þi scheld and
> spere . . .
>
> (ll.193–6)

Placidas must be changed, changed not only from a heathen to a Christian, but from a Christian man to a Christian saint. The *vita* makes clear that this process of enlightenment will entail self-sacrifice: "Oportet ergo, te humiliari de alta tua vanitate, & rursus exaltari in spiritualibus divitiis." Placidas through his actions must become the visible means for other men to achieve this transformation. The changes to be wrought in this instance result from the forthcoming life and death struggle between Eustace and Satan:

> ffor þou hast geten nou my graas
> And þou hast cast sathanas
> And fald hym as traitour in plas –
> And wiþ þe is he wroþ forþi
> But of o þyng þe warne I:
> Þat he wol fonde ful bisily
> T(o) Cuiþe to þe his feleny;
>
> (ll.180–6)

The divisions occurring in the narrative, separating these four incidents, unequivocally mark the progressive change in Eustace born out of the divine revelations with Christ, and following from this those that will result from the forthcoming struggle with Satan. They also serve a more practical and pastoral purpose, in that they assist the preacher to record cumulatively those edifying incidents which constitute a saint's life. Indeed at times the preacher becomes so concerned lest we misunderstand, that he feels it necessary to underline the moral of Christ's second revelation to Eustace, for example:

> ffor, euere þe betere and þe holyere
> Þat cristene Men in þis world here,
> Þe fastore fondeþ sathanas
> To fonden hem as his dedly fos.
>
> (ll.219–22)

and then wryly self-conscious, he moves on,

> But heer my prechynge leue wol I
> And tellen ow forþ of Eustas stori.
> (ll.231–2)

The late thirteenth century version found in manuscript Digby 86, "Ci Comence La Vie Seint Eustace qui out noun Placidas,"[55] is one of the earliest examples of the tail-rhyme stanza in English[56] which were thought very highly of by K. Horstmann, one of its early editors, "sie sind echt volksthumlich, Eustas zugleich echt epish in dem staten Forttrieb der Handlung u. in der Fulle der Stimmung."[57] Gerould's judgment is more accurate, however, when he speaks of its tendency to confuse and omit events and its inadequate handling of emotions as, "poor imitations of the meaner romances."[58] It not only fails to record such critical events in the legend as the loss of Eustace's wife, but even more seriously it neglects to exploit the reason for the sufferings and reunions, namely the fulfillment of the divine promise.

On a less exalted level its matter-of-fact treatment of the recognition scenes reduces the plausibility of these moments; and yet this apparent neglect, which is so striking, may be an attempt to utilize a poetic idiom more concerned with action and statement than motive.[59] The eldest brother has just completed his rather lengthy description of his past life:

> Wel softeliche ich was ared
> And brout in a softe bed,
> I-herd be god almiʒtte!
> A riche man of þat ilke londe
> Al þat me ned was, he me founde
> And dobede me to knʒtte.
>
> (ll.343–8)

The younger brother listening quietly receives this revelation and utters one single word of recognition:

> A, broþer, let me tellen þe
> A wolf þere com and kipte me
> And ber me in his mouþe.
> (ll.349–51)

Then he proceeds immediately to tell the story of his youth, ending with an account of his recent knighthood which parallels his brother's:

> And seþþen a levedi me fedde
> And dobbede me to kniʒtte;
> (ll.356–7)

The recognition passes so swiftly that one is, for a moment, not certain it has occurred. The single utterance "A, brother," complete in a breath, is the sum total of emotional response. It is terse to a fault. But it is more than an omission or "chopped" development. It is a clear and direct state-

ment, that this text is not much concerned with interpreting the inter-
actions of its fictional characters. Perhaps this statement by O. Pächt, in a
discussion of the gestures in the Bayeux tapestry will help clarify my
meaning, "they [the gestures] are never the organic result of the action
in which the figures are involved. . . . It is the beholder who is addressed
by these gestures; the actors of the drama speak to us, the spectators, not
to the protagonist in whose company they appear on the stage."[60]

The recognition between the brothers succinctly closed, the narrative
moves on to fit the next piece of this roughly hewn mosaic. Each stanza
is a complete unit, a "picture," the effect of the piece depending on the
cumulative arrangement of these stanzas. The recognition between husband and wife is dispatched with equal brevity. Theopistis addresses her
husband Eustace:

> Mi louerd, ich I-cnowe þe
> Bi one wonde, that ich I-se
> Oupon þi neb I-sene.
> (ll.379–81)

She then characteristically, without even as much as a sign or word of
recognition, begins to describe the events of her separation:

> Lemman, ich haue harde I-fare,
> I-lad mi lif in mikel kare,
> Ich wot, and nouht ne wene.
> (ll.382–4)

The conversion episode, which comprises eighty lines out of the total
four hundred and twenty-six (approximately 20 percent of the text) in
this Digby version, suffers primarily from the absence of the second
vision. Less serious but also omitted is the parallel vision of Theopistis, all
mention of any proper names with the one exception of "Troian" in
line 2, the choice to accept the sufferings now or later in life, all biblical
allusions to Baalam, Cornelius, Paul, Job, and the Book of Daniel. There
is little dialogue in the Digby conversion episode, whereas fully one-third
of the same narrative section in the Northern Homily Cycle is dialogue.

Further, and of more significance in hagiography than in romance, there
is no indication in the Digby text of the change the conversion is supposed to have wrought on Eustace. For example, an angel (the motif
supplied in place of the second vision of Christ) appears to Eustace
shortly after his baptism and reveals the future woe which is to befall him
and his family:

> þey þou lete lond and lede,
> Halle and bour and heye stede,
> Ne be þou nout sori!
> þou art I-turned to cristindome:

> Þe fend þe wille sechen I-lome
> And ofte þe fondi.
>
> (ll.85–90)

Eustace's reaction to this appallingly bad news is mechanical, and without so much as a murmur,

> To his hous he wente anon,
> So swiþe so he miȝtte gon,
> Mid wif and children two.
>
> (ll.97–9)

There is no indication of the difficulty this command must have presented for Eustace until his actual departure from home, "Al þat he louede, him wente fram." Could this inattention to so plausible an emotional response have afforded the narrator "joculator" an opportunity for personal expression, "amplificatio"?

In order to illustrate more vividly the baldness of emotional response in the Digby text, let us review briefly this incident as it appears in the Northern Homily version. Here the incident is treated with greater attention to the individual personal response to his plight, albeit divinely planned. Christ in the second vision tells Eustace of his coming misery:

> Crist onswerde and seide þan
> To seint Eustas þis holy man . . .
> And wiþ þe is he wroþ forþi
> But of o þyng þe warne I:
> Þat he wol fonde ful bisily
> T(o) Cuithe to þe his feleny.
>
> (*North. Hom.* ll.177–8; 183–6)

Indeed, he even gives Eustace the reason for this trial:

> he wol þe fonde on mony wyse,
> ffor þou leuest his seruyse –
> Þeih he do so nis no ferly:
> ffor me he fondet bysily.
>
> (*North. Hom.* ll.187–90)

And finally Christ reveals to Eustace how he should overcome this trial:

> And ouer come his wikkednes
> wiþ pacience and Mekenes;
> Let Mekenes beo þi scheld and
> spere . . .
>
> (*North. Hom.* ll. 193–5)

Eustace's response to this prophecy of his coming hardships indicates once again the homilist's concern that the character of Eustace should emerge as a realized exemplum. The Northern Homily version portrays Eustace less in the convention of the heroic saint and more in the guise of "everyman." This is in sharp contrast to the essentially heroic, romantic character exemplified in the Digby text. There is no question that the homilist's Eustace will triumph over Satan's trials, but his triumph is won with God's help and difficult physical struggle. His spiritual heroism is continually balanced against his physical frailty,

> But, leoue lord, ȝif me miht
> To stonde a ȝeyn þe fend in fiht,
> Þat I ne leose wiþ grucchyng
> Þe Muchel Mede of my fondyng!
> A ȝeyn þe fend I falle in place,
> But þou help me wiþ þi grace.
> *(North. Hom.* ll.243–8)

whereas in the Digby version the contest is purely one of a great and heroic struggle, a struggle divorced from the frailty of human beings, a struggle between forces rather than personalities.

The version preserved in the "South English Legendary"[61] is approximately contemporary with the Digby text (last quarter of the thirteenth century), but shows less influence from the romance tradition and remains closer to the traditions of hagiography. It is 331 lines of unremarkable end-rhyme couplets. T. Wolpers summarizes the main critical judgements on the "South English Legendary" since the publication of Horstmann's text. Horstmann considered the work a lesser work, "Als reine Dichtung, als Schöpfung wirklicher Dichter, tritt die Legende zuruck," and Brandl's remarks are no more favorable, "Künstlerische Feinheit sei bei einem solchen Massenprodukt nicht zu erwarten. . . ." Gerould considered the "South English Legendary" an uninspired translation of an earlier Latin variant and W. F. Manning concurs, specifying the Latin source as the "Legenda Aurea": "the translations are [Manning is speaking of the entire "South English Legendary" and its dependence on the "Legenda Aurea"], for the most part close and the author's dependence on his Latin source is evident from the preservation of the order of episodes and the retention of dialogue and descriptive detail."[62]

I disagree both with the judgment of Gerould and with Manning's identification of the "Legenda Aurea" as the parent text of the "South English Legendary." For example, if we compare some instances of the conversion episode in both the Latin and English texts, we notice that the Christian names received at baptism are given in the "Legenda Aurea," but are missing in this and the Digby text, the only English analogues to omit them. The topographical description of the first vision is markedly different: in the "Legenda," the stag appears (as usual) on top of a rocky precipice, "ceruus tandem super quandam rupis altitudinem conscendit et Placidus approprians"; and in the South English analogue, "tho huy comen opon a fair hul: this best with-stod at the last." In the actual vision itself, the omission of biblical allusion and change of emphasis is pronounced. The "Legenda" preserves the allusion to Balaam and describes in careful detail the vision of the glowing cross, "Qui cum cervum diligenter consideraret, vidit inter cornua ejus formam sacrae crucis supra solis claritatem et imaginem Jesu Christi, qui peros cervi, sicut olim per asinam Balaam, sic ei locutus est dicens: Placide, quid me persequeris?" The "South English Legendary" takes little pains in preserving either allusion or in qualifying the nature of the miracle:

> Bi-twene is hornes he i-saiȝh: ane creiz schine briȝhte
> with gret leome ase it were of sonne: þat vnneth bi-holde he it miȝhte.
> "Placidas, seide the heort: ȝwy woltthou weorri with me?"
>   (*South English Leg.* ll.19–21)

Further, the "Legenda Aurea" retains the "choice" motif, "Si modo tentationes vis accipere aut in fine vitae," which is not present in the Legendary. There is a marked difference of emphasis in the way both variants treat Placidas' response to his sufferings: in the "Legenda," he is advised to resist the torments of Satan with a patient humility, "Dyabolus enim eo, quod ipsum dereliqueris, contra te saeve armatur; oportet igitur te multa sustinere, ut accipias coronam victoriae; oportet te multa pati, ut de alta saeculi vanitate humilieris et rursus in spirtualibus divitiis exalteris. Tu ergo ne deficias nec ad gloriam pristinam respicias, quia per tentationes oportet te alterum Job demonstrari"; whereas in the English text the incident has a pronounced martial air, and Placidas is advised to war against Satan,

> For þou hast þene deuel ouer-come: he armeth him aȝen þe:
> Þolie þou schalt wo and sor: ase Men schule in bataylle;
> Ȝif þou wolt þolie and a-ȝein him fiȝhte: of is wille he schal faille.
> He shal þe, ase he dude Iob: mid alle wo þe fonde;
> Seie me ȝif þou it þolie wolt; and faste a-ȝein him stonde!
>   (*South English Leg.* ll.44–8)

There are other important differences between both texts. For example, Christ's revelation of the Christian faith, "Ego, sum Christus, qui coelum et terram creavi . . ." which runs to seven lines in the "Legenda Aurea" is completely absent in the "South English Legendary." These differences are sufficient to show that the "South English Legendary" variant of the Eustace legend is clearly something rather more than a close translation (as Manning suggested) of the "Legenda Aurea."

The "South English Legendary" version omits all biblical allusions with the single exception of the reference to Job. It omits all proper names with the exception of Eustace and the two Roman Emperors, Trajan and Adrian, and contains the entire conversion episode within fifty-four lines out of the total of 331 ((approximately 16 percent of the complete text). There are twenty-four lines of dialogue in the conversion: Eustace has five, his wife two and the remaining seventeen lines are spoken by Christ. This reduces the dramatic effect, which is strengthened through dialogue, and exploits the didactic nature of the piece, which succeeds best when there is a single point of view.

Rather, like the "Northern Homily Cycle" version, the conversion episode is built on the two separate visions and their fulfilments. However, the actions of Placidas after each vision are autonomous events, and not made to serve as visible indications exemplifying progressive interior change as they do in the "Northern Homily Cycle." For example, the first vision is just drawing to a close:

> Þo nuste ȝware þe heort bi-cam: þis kniȝt in grete þouȝte
> wende hom and þonkede god: þat swuch tiþingue him brouȝhte.
> his wiue he tolde it priueliche: "sire, merci," heo seide.
> (*South English Leg.* ll.31–3)

This is not without some charm, but there is little effort here to convey an indication of Placidas' emotional state following this extraordinary event other than through the use of straightforward statement. There is virtually no use made of contrast or parallelism which are used in the Northern Homily incident, to underline the change:

> Whon þis was seid, hom he ede,
> Þenkyng on crist and on his rede.
> he fond al his men in o place,
> But hedde he no talent to chase.
> whon he com hom, his wyf he told
> how crist to his knowynge him cald.
> (*Northern Homily Cycle*, 11.127–32)

And yet the three above lines from the "South English Legendary" ("tho must he ȝware," etc.) do adequately bridge the transition from the causally related vision and baptism incidents, which the Digby analogue treats in a more independent and isolated fashion. In stanza 10 of the Digby text, Christ tells Placidas to take himself and his family to baptism:

> Þou nim þine children and þi wif,
> And wendeþ al wiþ-oute strif
> And cristineþ ou bitime!
> (*Digby*, ll.55–7)

And in stanza 11 the command is obeyed:

> He nom is children and is wif,
> And wenten al wiþ-outen strif
> To þat follovstone
> Þere hy weren I-cristened bein,
> (*Digby*, 11.64–4)

The "South English Legendary" treatment of the stag is interesting and singular in all the English analogues. It appears less a messenger of God's divine will and more a wondrous beast in its own right, "this holie best he saiȝh tho eft-sone: aftur he wende al-so." This version adds none of the conventionally qualifying explanations, made in virtually all other variants both English and Latin, that this miracle is solely the result of God's power manifesting itself through the beast. For example, in the *vita*, printed by the Bollandists, "imaginem Domini nostri Salvatoris Jesu Christi. Qui etiam humanam vocem imponens cervo;" and in John of Damascus, "inditaque cervo voce humana."

Indeed all of the Latin versions, with the one important exception of a ninth-century metrical variant, follows the *vita*. The late ninth-century Latin text gives a curiously similar rendering to that in the "South English Legendary,"

Stanza 3:   Vidit in cornibus eius   crucis imaginem
            Et inter cornua pulcram Christi effigiem

Stanza 4:   Placidas dum stupendo   istud aspiceret,
            Vocem sibi dicentem   audivit taliter:
            'Placidas, (o) Placidas, quid me persequeris?[63]

And in the "South English Legendary,"

Bi-twene is hornes he i-saiȝh: ane creiz schine briȝhte
with gret leom ase it were of sonne: that vnneth bi-holde he it miȝhte.
"Placidas," seide the heort: "ȝwy woltthow weorri with me?"
(ll.19–21)

That this is a detail of considered import is obvious from the number of different variants of the legend and the singleness of their renderings. The St. Eustace Life in the Scottish Collection of Legends, reflecting the strength of the tradition, makes a point in the narrative which appears to reflect the changed emphasis and novel handling found in the "South English Legendary,"

Bot he saw betwene his tyndis brycht
A verray croice schenand lycht,
& one þat croice þe liknes
Of Jhesu Crist saw, mare na les.
Þane spak þe hart to Placydas,
As to Balame quhil dyd his as –
Bot sume mene sais It is to lak
Þat þe hart to þe knycht spak,
Bot erar þat mene suld treu
Þat in hyme spak swet Jhesu –
& sad til hyme: þu Placydas,
Quhat mowis þe me to chas?
& I for cause of þe apere
In to þis best þat þu seis here;[64]
(*Scottish Legendary*, ll.105–18)

Briefly to sum up the main themes of this paper, we have examined the presence of other literary (and certain nonliterary "folk") traditions, but especially the extraordinary (and hitherto neglected) influence of the

Vulgate in the narrative structure of the Eustace legend. I have tried to show how the hagiographer has made deliberate and very often skillful use of the verbal reminiscences of certain of these earlier texts in constructing his narrative; that he has relied on his audiences' familiarity with these passages (read orally) to produce a corporate delight derived from their recognition, "anagnorisis." We have seen how the church was able to adopt and use most effectively a preexisting popular tale in its efforts to develop preaching in the vernacular, "lingua romana," and thus contribute considerably to the wide popularity of the legend in the later Middle Ages.

I have argued that while hagiography does follow an aesthetic built on adherence to the convention, nevertheless there was much scope for individual authorial interpretation, as the three very different approaches to the Life of St. Eustace the Middle English variants so aptly demonstrate. For example, while the "Northern Homily Cycle" life emphasizes the exemplary characteristics of the saint, the Digby text, which reflects a substantial amount of influence from romance (specifically Anglo-Norman texts), is less concerned with exemplary qualities and more with a secular heroic ideal, indeed less concerned with patient forbearance than with dramatic portrayal of action and statement. Finally, I have shown how the "South English Legendary," lack of dialogue, singularity of point of view, and thoroughgoing didacticism all point to its probable use as a pious reading at a conventual refectory.

NOTES

1. John of Damascus, *De Imaginibus Oratio* III (*PG* XCIV, 1382).
2. Angelo Monteverdi, "I Testi Della Leggenda Di S. Eustachio," *Studi Medievali*, 3 (1908–1911), 489–98.
3. A. B. Lord, *The Singer of Tales* (London, 1960), p. 220.
4. Agnellius, "Liber Pontificalis Ecclesiae Ravennatis," ed. O. Holder-Egger, *MGH, Scriptores Rerum Langobardicarum*, xviii, 32.
5. Prudentius, *Liber Peristephanon* (*PL* LX, 275–594).
6. G. R. Owst, *Literature and Pulpit in Medieval England* (Oxford, 1966), p. 137.
7. *Acta Sanctorum*, "De Sanctis Eustachio, Uxore ejus et Filiis," September, 6 (Antwerp, 1757), 123–37; H. Knust, *Dos obras didácticas y dos leyendas sacadas de mss. de la. Bibl. del Escorial* (Madrid, 1879), pp. 107–21.
8. John of Damascus, *PG* XCIV, 1382; *Bibliotheca hagiographica græca seu Elenchus Vitarum sanctorum*, 3rd. ed. (Brussels, 1954), p. 201; *Bibliotheca hagiographica latina antiquæ et mediae ætatis* Brussels, 1898–1901), I, 2760–71.
9. K. Strecker, "Rhythmi Aevi Merovingici Et Carolini," *MGH, Poetae Latini*, 4 (1923), 593–9; see also, E. Dummler, "Rythmen Aus der Carolingischen Zeit," *Zeitschrift für Deutsches Alterthum*, 23 (1879), 273–80. Dummler prints an identical text with the one exception of an additional stanza between lines 252 and 253; A. Ebert, "Zu den Carolingischen

Rythmen," *Zeitschrift für Deutsches Alterthum*, 24 (1880), 148–50; F. Seiler, "Zu den Carolingischen Rythmen," *Zeitschrift für Deutsches Alterthum*, 25 (1881), 27–8; F. Seiler, "Noch Einmal Der Rhythmus von Placidas-Eustathius," *Zeitschrift für Deutsches Alterthum*, 26 (1882), 197–9; F. Zarncke, "Zu der Rhythmischen Version der Legende von Placidas-Eustathius," *Zeitschrift für Deutsches Alterthum*, 26 (1882), 96.

10. H. Varnhagen, "Zwei Lateinische Metrische Versionem Der Legende Von Placidus-Eustachius: Eine version in hexametern," *Zeitschrift für Deutsches Alterthum*, 24 (1880), 1–25.

11. M. Charles Fierville, "Notice et Extraits des Manuscrits de la Bibliothèque de Saint-Omer," *Notices et extraits des Manuscrits de la Bibliothèque Nationale*, 31 (1884), 49–88.

12. H. Varnhagen, "Zwei Lateinische Metrische Versionem Der Legende Von Placidus-Eustachius: Die version distichen," *Zeitschrift für Deutsches Alterthum*, 24 (1884), 241–54.

13. Johannes Junior, *Scala Coeli* (Louvain, 1485), sig. 08ᵛ. Johannes Junior also seems to have been known as Johannes Gobius; L. Hain, *Repertorium Bibliographicum* (Paris, 1831), II, 159–60.

14. Jacobus de Voragine, *Legenda Aurea*, ed., Th. Graesse (Leipzig, 1850), pp. 712–8.

15. Vincent of Beauvais, *Speculum historiale*, 3 vols. (Augsburg, 1474), I, folio 296v.

16. H. Oesterley, *Gesta Romanorum* (Berlin, 1871), pp. 44–51.

17. W. W. Skeat, *Aelfric's Lives of the Saints* (London, 1881–1900), pp. 190–219.

18. E. A. W. Budge, trans., *Coptic Martydoms in the Dialect of Upper Egypt* (London, 1914), pp. 356–80.

19. There seems to be a consensus of opinion amongst scholars that the Benedictine revival originating in Cluny in the ninth century was a major contributing factor responsible for the renewed interest in hagiography; see Rosemary Woolf, "Saints Lives," *Continuations and Beginnings in Old English Literature*, ed. E. G. Stanley (London, 1966), p. 39; S. C. Aston, "The Saint in Medieval Literature," *Modern Language Review*, 65 (1970), 30; Carl Selmer, *Navigatio Sancti Brendani Abbatis* (Notre Dame, 1959), p. xxix, discusses the communications between Benedictine houses on the continent and the British Isles; Gisbert Kranz, *Europas Christliche Literatur von 500–1500* (Munich, 1968), p. 182, describes a growing tendency on the part of monastic communities to write Lives that would have appeal for the prominent laity as well as the clergy. He cites the work of Odo of Cluny as an early example of this trend.

20. C. W. Jones, *Saints' Lives and Chronicles* (Ithaca, 1947), p. 2.

21. John of Damascus, *De Imaginibus Oratio* (PG, XCIV, 1266); see also, Theodore of Studium, *Antirrheticus* (PG, XCIX, 327–51).

22. J. Mansi, *Sacrorum Conciliorum Nova, Et Amplissima Collectio* (Florence, 1759–1798), XII, col. 977.

23. Mansi, XIV, col. 78.

24. Mansi, XIV, col. 85.

25. Mansi, XIV, col. 899.

26. Mansi, III, col. 891.

27. Holger Petersen, "La Vie de Saint Eustache," *Societé des Anciens Textes Francais* (Paris, 1928), p. 1. Although medieval names of genres are often unstable, it does seem that the Latin word "sermo" was widely understood

to mean sermon in England from at least the middle of the twelfth century, see R. E. Latham, *Revised Medieval Latin Word-List: from British and Irish Sources* (London, 1963), p. 435.

28. G. R. Owst, *Literature and Pulpit in Medieval England*, p. 123.
29. K. H. Jackson, *International Popular Tale and Early Welsh Tradition* (Cardiff, 1961), p. 5. Jackson's discussion of the narrative characteristics of the popular tale suggests certain parallels in hagiography.
30. M. Gaster, "The Nigrodah-jataka and the Life of St. Eustathius-Placidus," *Journal of the Royal Asiatic Society of Great Britain and Ireland*, N.S., 26 (1894), 335–40; for the relationship between the legend of Eustace and its oriental analogues see: G. H. Gerould, "Forerunners, Congeners & Derivatives of the Eustace Legend," *PMLA*, 19 (1904), 338. Gerould suggested that the central motif of the Eustace legend was the man tried by fate; he then concluded that the legend ultimately derives through Arabic and Pahlair from Sanskrit; S. Thompson, *Motif-Index of Folk Literature* (Copenhagen, 1958), 5, N251. Leo Jordan, "Die Eustachius-legende, Christians Wilhelmsleben, Boeve de Hanstone und ihre orientalischen Verwandten," *Archiv für das Studium der Neueren Sprachen und Literaturen*, 21 (1908), 361.
31. Ambrose, *De Interpellatione Job et David* (PL, XIV, 849–50).
32. Gregory of Tours, *Historia Francorum* (PL, LXXI, 234).
33. Bede, *De Psalmorum Libro Exegesis* (PL, XCIII, 624).
34. Origen, *Homiliae in Canticum Canticorum* (PG, XIII, 56, 198–9).
35. F. J. Carmody, ed., "Physiologus Latinus Versio Y," *University of California Publications in Classical Philology*, 12 (1941), 131.
36. Alanus De Insulis, *Liber in Distinctionibus Dictionum Theologicalium* (PL, CCX, 737). See Psalm 42, vs. 2: "Quemadmodum desiderat cervus ad fontes aquarum, ita desiderat anima mea ad te, Deus."
37. A. D'Ancona, *Poemetti Popolari Italiani* (Rome, 1881), p. 400.
38. W. W. Meyer, "Die alteste lateinische Fassung der Placidas-Eustasius Legende," *Nachrichten von der Koniglichen Gesellschaft der Wissenschaften zu Gottingen* (1916), 767.
39. Hippolyte Delehaye, "La legende de saint Eustache," *Bulletins de la Academy Royale de Belgique, Classe Des Lettres* (1919), 210; W. Bousset, "Die Geschichte eines Wiederkennungsmärchens," *Nachrichten von der Koniglichen Gesellschaft der Wissenschaften zu Göttingen* (1916), 542–3; and J. Murray, "The Eustace Legend in Medieval England," *Bulletin of the Modern Humanities Research Association*, 1, No. 2 (1927), 36–8.
40. H. Varnhagen, "Eine version in hexametern," p. 5.
41. Sedulius, *Carmen Paschale* (PL, XIX, 569).
42. Bede, *Vita Metrica Sancti Cuthberti* (PL, XCIV, 577).
43. Orientius, *Commonitorium* (PL, LXI, 977–8).
44. Odo of Cluny, *Occupatio*, ed., A. Swoboda (Leipzig, 1900), p. 68.
45. A. Monteverdi, "I Testi Della Leggenda . . . ," p. 188; a very similar series of events can be observed in the *Pseudo Clementine Recognitions*, which were immensely popular in the Middle Ages, and survive in over one hundred manuscripts.
46. H. Dörrie, "Die griechischen Romane und das Christentum," *Philologus* 93 (1938), 274; B. E. Perry, *The Ancient Romances* (Berkeley, 1967), pp. 346–7.
47. *Acta Sanctorum*, "De Sanctis Eustachio . . . ," p. 128.
48. The daily cursus of public prayer "Opus Dei" and spiritual reading

"lectio divina" certainly contributed to a thoroughgoing familiarity with biblical texts. John, Abbot of St. Albans (1195–1214), is credited with the remarkable feat of repeating the entire psalter backwards, verse by verse: H. Riley, ed., *Gesta Abbatum Monasterii Sancti Albani* (London, 1867) I, 231.

49. For examples of the clergy's scorn for these secular romances see: P. Meyer, "La Vie de St. Grégoire Le Grand," *Romania*, XII (1883), 147; M. D. Legge, *Anglo-Norman Literature* (Oxford, 1963), p. 213.

50. C. Haréau, "Notice Sur Un Penitentiel Attribué A Jean De Salisbury," *Notices Et Extraits Des Manuscrits De La Bibliothèque Nationale*, 24, 2 (1876), 285.

51. Ordericus Vitalis, *Historica Ecclesiastica* (PL, CLXXXVIII, 451–2).

52. Robert Mannyng, *Handlyng Synne*, ed. F. J. Furnivall (London, 1901–1903), p. 3.

53. William Nassington, "Speculum Vitae" (unpublished) cited in G. R. Owst, *Literature and Pulpit in Medieval England*, p. 13.

54. C. Horstmann, "Die Evangelien Geschichten des Ms. Vernon," *Archiv für das Studium der Neueren Sprachen und Literaturen*, 57 (1877), 262–72. All lines cited are from this edition. I am currently engaged in editing a critical text of the earliest redaction of the Northern Homily Cycle.

55. C. Horstmann, *Altenglische Legenden, neue folge mit Einleitung und Anmer Kungen* (Heilbronn, 1881), pp. 211–9.

56. C. Strong, "Tail Rhyme Strophe in Latin, French & English," *PMLA*, 22 (1907), 372–414; L. Braswell, "Sir Isumbras and the Legend of Saint Eustace," *Medieval Studies*, 28 (1965), 129; D. Klausner, "The Nature and Origins of Didacticism in some Middle English Romances," Diss. University of Cambridge, 1967, p. 134.

57. C. Horstmann, *Altenglische Legenden*, p. 213.

58. G. H. Gerould, *Saints' Legends* (New York, 1916), p. 212; T. Wolpers, *Die Englische Heiligenlegende des Mittelalters* (Tubingen, 1964), p. 196, shares Gerould's view.

59. E. Vinaver, *The Rise of Romance* (Oxford, 1971), p. 11.

60. Otto Pächt, *The Rise of Pictorial Narrative in Twelfth-Century England* (Oxford, 1962), p. 10.

61. C. Horstmann, *The Early South-English Legendary* (London, 1887), pp. 393–402.

62. T. Wolpers, *Die Englische Heiligenlegende*, p. 212.

63. K. Strecker, "Rhythmi Aevi Merovingici Et Carolini," *MGH, Poetae Latini*, 4 (1923), 593.

64. C. Horstmann, *Barbour's des Schottischen Nationaldichters Legendsammlung* (Heilbronn, 1881–82), p. 12.

The Joseph of Arimathie

English Hagiography in Transition

VALERIE M. LAGORIO

The close alliance of hagiography and romance is nowhere more clearly illustrated than in the accretive legend of Joseph of Arimathea, which had its inception in the early era of Christianity and its fullest flowering in medieval France and England. It will be my purpose to examine the durability, credibility, and adaptability of the legendary Joseph of Arimathea, based particularly on his featured appearances in the French Grail romances, a derivative English romance, the *Joseph of Arimathie*,[1] and the hagiographic encomium written by John of Glastonbury toward the end of the fourteenth century. Throughout this study I will follow W. W. Skeat's delineation between the legendary which, resting on longstanding ecclesiastical tradition, remains within the bounds of probability, and the fabulous, which has purely fictional origins.[2]

The *fons* of Joseph's legendary status resides in his rather slight biblical mention as a secret disciple of Christ and wealthy Arimathean, who buried the Savior in his own tomb.[3] Subsequently, his legendary roles of favored disciple of Christ, guardian of the Blessed Virgin Mary and thus a surrogate Joseph of Nazareth, and intrepid apostolic missioner were extolled in such popular apocryphal gospels and *acta* as the *Evangelium Nicodemi, Narratio Josephi, Transitus Mariae, Vindicta Salvatoris* and *Cura Sanitatis Tiberii*, both of which incorporated Joseph into the Veronica legend,[4] the *Syndonia Legend*,[5] and the Georgian *Legend of Lydda*.[6] These apocryphal narratives expanded their minimal Scriptural base with a mixture of doctrinal content, thaumaturgy, and liberal borrowings from secular fiction to produce a distinctive literary form,[7] closely allied to the historical romance. Accordingly, the biblical Joseph of Arimathea was transformed into an idealized hero of ecclesiastical romance at an early date.

In addition to his above-cited legendary roles, Joseph was widely acknowledged as the collector and guardian of the Precious Blood. This was effected through a coalescence of symbolic interpretations of the Mass, such as the *Gemma animae* of Honorius of Autun,[8] with medieval accounts of the origin of Precious Blood relics at Bruges, Fécamp, and other monastic institutions.[9]

It is no wonder then, that when Robert de Boron initiated the Christianized Grail romances in the late twelfth century,[10] he elected Joseph of Arimathea as the Grail guardian and missioner par excellence, thereby introducing the legendary Joseph of hagiographic fame into the realm of Arthurian romance. He also added a significant new dimension to Joseph by making him a stalwart pro-Christian knight of Pontius Pilate, who, in payment for his military service, requested and received Pilate's permission to bury the crucified Christ. This knightly vocation, based on St. Mark's appellation *nobilis decurio,* was assigned to Joseph in all of the Grail romances, as well as in much of the non-Grail literature of the Middle Ages. Robert's work, which drew heavily on the apocryphal accounts of Joseph, served as the seminal story for early thirteenth-century French romances, such as the *Perlesvaus,*[11] the Continuations of Chrétien's *Conte du Graal,*[12] and the Vulgate *Estoire del Saint Graal.*[13] The indebtedness of these works to hagiography is especially marked in the *Estoire,* which was an amalgam of several well-known hagiographic corpora: The apocryphal gospels, *Vitae Patrum,* and the *Clementina* were major informing influences on the events in the Holy Land and Near East, just as the Lives of Pan-Brittonic saints inspired many of the later adventures in Britain.[14] Moreover, all three works amplified Boron's account to include the conversion of Britain by Joseph and his followers, a romance innovation which was to have an important bearing on the English hagiography of Joseph.

Shortly after the appearance of the *Estoire,* Glastonbury Abbey, which in 1191 had acclaimed itself as the Avalon burial place of King Arthur, quietly appropriated Arthur's romance compeer, Joseph of Arimathea. Heretofore, the abbey's origins had been ascribed to twelve disciples of St. Philip and St. James. However, through a series of interpolations in William of Malmesbury's prestigious *De antiquitate Glastoniensis ecclesiae,*[15] the monks credited Joseph with the foundation of the abbey and an evangelizing career which ended with his death and interment at Glastonbury. Owing to this fortuitous conflation of Glastonbury and Grail romance accounts concerning Britain's conversion, Joseph reentered the hagiographic domain, with the enhancing dimension of Apostle of Britain added to his legendary status.[16]

The subsequent English interest in Joseph, coincident with the increasing propagation of his Glastonbury cult,[17] was manifested by the *Joseph of Arimathie.* It has been called an homiletic romance because the author combined story motifs and stylistic devices taken from both romance and hagiography, but imposed a distinctive moral and religious interpretation on the content.[18] As the *Joseph* was derived solely from the *Estoire del Saint Graal,* a comparative source study was conducted to determine the extent and nature of substantive change, if any, in the English work. For, as Robert Ackerman points out in his discussion of the dependence of English romance authors on French literature, in their adaptations and often in their translations as well, the English writers, who were addressing a later audience, tended to create a type of romance quite distinct from the French. . . . Certainly, it is not irrelevant to inquire whether the author was merely attempting a translation of a French work, or whether he was striking out with a free and independent adaptation of a traditional story.[19]

It is equally important, according to Dieter Mehl, to note, what the English romance authors have actually taken from their sources, as to record what they have omitted.[20]

The *Estoire del Saint Graal* relates how Joseph, Pilate's knight, buried the crucified Christ and, in the process, collected the Precious Blood in the vessel (*escuele*) used by Christ at the Last Supper. Condemned by the angry Jews for these actions, Joseph is imprisoned for forty-two years, and sustained solely by the miraculous powers of the Holy Grail until his liberation by Vespasian during the destruction of Jerusalem. After being baptized by St. Philip, he is commanded by a heavenly voice to lead a band of converts, including his wife and son Josephe, on a westward mission, with the Grail to provide their needs. As Joseph and his followers approach the mythical city of Sarras, he is enjoined by God to convert the royalty and people of that area, and promptly begins to preach the gospel to King Evelake of Sarras. Up until this point, the *Estoire* account of Joseph is largely legendary, and consonant with his long-established roles as guardian of the Precious Blood and zealous evangelizer. At this juncture, however, the fabulous elements begin to predominate, with Josephe replacing his father as protagonist, and with the narrative concentrating on the conversion of Sarras and the protracted wanderings of the Sarras royalty until their reunion with Joseph and Josephe in Britain. The *Estoire* ends with the conversion of Britain by Josephe, aided to a minor extent by his father, and the establishment of the Grail castle Corbenic, where the Arimathean line will continue to guard the Grail for 400 years, until the time of Arthur.

From this brief summary, it is evident that, in content, the *Estoire* has much in common with hagiographic romance. However, because it was written as a retrospective sequel to the Vulgate *Queste*, its tripartite purpose was to present a wonder-filled account that would integrate the Holy Grail into the Arthurian romance cycle; to substantiate and amplify references to the Grail's early history already present in the Vulgate romances; and to justify the recurring honorific, "kin of Joseph of Arimathea," which was attached to the notables both of the Grail line and Arthur's Round Table. Since its primary intention was not to provide an exemplar of Christian zeal and fortitude, in the person of Joseph or his son, it is more a secular romance than a strictly hagiographic work.

The converse is true of its English derivative, the *Joseph of Arimathea*, which is a fragment of 709 lines, the first 100 lines having been lost. In his adaptation, the English author was clearly not aiming for an exact translation, a task which would be slavishly accomplished by Herry Lovelich in 1450.[21] Rather, he selected, modified, and drastically abridged the early portion up through the conversion of Sarras. His choice of material was undoubtedly dictated by the predominance of the legendary Joseph in this part of his source, and by the markedly fabulous nature of the post-Sarras events, in which Joseph played an insignificant part. Possibly, too, he was influenced by the biblical overtones of this earlier portion, where Joseph is depicted as a New Testament Moses, guarding the Ark of the Grail, leading the chosen band of Christians to the Promised Land of Britain, and constantly relying on and responding to divine guidance. While there is no overt reference to the Glastonbury claim, the author's characterization of Joseph accords with the abbey's account of his pre-Britain missionary endeavors. Finally, the authorial concern for the rapid movement of the story, a characteristic shared by other Middle English romances, might account in some measure for the extensive curtailment of the source material. Yet, far from a haphazard attempt at verbal economy, the work represents a determined attempt to impart an English *sen* to the French *matière* on Joseph.

The first evident difference between the two works is the English de-emphasis of the Holy Grail. Prior to the exodus from Jerusalem, the *Estoire* records God's command that Joseph take nothing with him but the vessel, with the implication that it will sustain the Christians on their westward journey (19.17–9). This reference is omitted in the English work, in which Joseph reassures his followers, "He þat ledes vs · þis wei · vre herborwe schal wisse." (l.32) God's subsequent command to enshrine the vessel in a wooden ark is included in both works, but in the *Joseph* is ascribed to Christ:

> & anchois que tu ten partes de cest bois feras
> tu a mescuele vne huche en quoi vous le porteres
> & cascun iour feres vous asflixions devant cele
> huche que on apelera arche en quoi vos le porteres
> por avoir lamor de uo createur . & quant tu voldras
> a moi parler si ouuerras larche si que tu tos sels
> voies lescuele apertement . Mais iou ne voeil mie
> que nus touche a lescuele fors tu & tes fils .
>
> (20.34–36, 21.1–3)
>
> 'Iosep[h], marke on þe treo . and make a luytel whucche,
> Forte do in þat ilke blod . þou berest a-boute;
> whon þe lust speke with me . lift þe lide sone,
> þou schalt fynde me redi . riȝt bi þi syde,
> And, bote þou and þi sone . me no mon touche.'
>
> (ll.39–43)

It will be noted that the English author omits the request for daily prayer before the ark, since at no time does he treat the vessel either as an object of supplication or source of provisions. He also specifies and thus emphasizes the contents of the container, "ilke blod," not the container itself, as he will continue to do in the other three references to the relic in the poem (ll.52, 297, 708). Christ's assurance of His abiding presence within the ark is retained to underscore the mystery of Transubstantiation which is manifest in the sacred relic. Similarly, the English version preserves the divine appointment of the two Josephs as ark guardians in recognition of their sanctity and fitness for this task, as well as for their forthcoming guardianship of Christ's earthly flock. While the *Estoire* assigns the Grail a prominent place in the subsequent climactic vision within the ark (33.4 – 7, 32 – 3; 34.18 – 9; 41.7 – 8), the *Joseph* gives only a passing reference to the "disch wiþ þe blod" (l.297). It is clear, therefore, that for the English writer, the vessel is simply a reliquary of the Precious Blood, worthy of veneration, but not the miracle-working and mysterious talisman of the French version. This interpretation may be due to the lack of ecclesiastical sanction for the Holy Grail, a matter about which the English were evidently more scrupulous than the French. At the same time, however, this treatment is consonant with Joseph's legendary affiliation with the Precious Blood.

The second noticeable departure from the French source is the consistent omission of links with the Grail's future Arthurian destiny. Both works cite God's command to Joseph to beget a second son, Galahad. In the *Estoire*, this event occurs just before the Grail party embarks for England, and it is predicted that Galahad will be a most valiant and renowned knight (209.7 – 11). A variant version, contained in the Royal 19C. XII manuscript, places the incident shortly after Joseph's first confrontation with Evelake of Sarras, with the following accolade for Galahad:

de cestui Galat descendi la haute lignie qui essaucerent la loi ihesu crist . & honorerent la terre de la grant bretaigne . (30 fn 5)

The author of the *Joseph* evidently followed the Royal manuscript, both in the earlier placement of the incident and in its praise of Galahad:

> "þat goodnesse schal reise
> þe Aventurus of Bruytayne . to haunsen and to holden"
> (ll.231–2)

The phrase "Aventurus of Bruytayne," with its Arthurian overtones, may, on the one hand, indicate the author's confused or disinterested conflation of Joseph's second son with the future Grail knight. Yet, as this is the only reference to Britain in the entire work, it more likely refers to the forthcoming conversion of Britain and continuing Christian endeavors of the Arimathean line. According to the French romance, the holy chrism used for Josephe's consecration will anoint all of the future Christian kings of Britain, down to Uther Pendragon, father of King Arthur (36.26 – 36), a reference that is absent from the *Joseph*. Finally, the poem concludes rather abruptly with "þe blod" entrusted to two men, and Josephe and Seraphe, now christened Nascien, leaving Sarras on an unspecified evangelical mission:

> But þere an vnsely kyng . in prison hem caste,
> wiþ muche serwe to him-self . siker atte laste;
> For þe kyng Mordreyns . com with such strengþe,
> forte liuere hem out . on lyue he lafte none.
>
> (ll.704–707)

This incident is excerpted from the end of the *Estoire*, when the evil king of North Wales imprisons the Grail band, and Mordrains (Evelake's baptismal name) is summoned by Christ to their rescue. The suppression of this link again points to the English author's interest in those events which pertain to the lengendary Joseph and his corresponding lack of concern with romantic Arthuriana.

Perhaps the paramount difference between the *Estoire* and the *Joseph* is in the latter's emphasis on Joseph's career as an apostolic missioner. Adhering closely to its source, the English romance recounts God's command to Joseph to convert his family and friends, lead them out of Jerusalem, and preach the gospel in foreign lands (Fr. 19.10–23 = ll.21–25). On the approach to Sarras, there is a second injunction from God (21.19–26), which, in the English poem, is spoken by Jesus Christ Himself:

> 'And Iosep[h], walk in þe world . & preche myne wordes
> to þe proudest men . A parti schul þei here.
> pauȝ þei þe of manas . melen, and þe þreten,
> beo þou no þing a-dred . for non schal þe serue.'
> 'lord, I was neuer clerk . what and I ne cunne?'
> 'Louse þi lippes a-twynne . & let þe gost worche;
> Speche, grace, & vois . schul springe of þi tonge,
> & alle turne to þi mouþ . holliche atenes.'
>
> (ll.44–51)

Undoubtedly the English author translated this entire speech not only as it adumbrates the biblical *topos* of the reluctant prophet and his New Testament counterpart, the apostolic missioners, but also because it recalls Christ's actual words to His disciples, enjoining them to go and teach all nations, and assuring them that the Advocate, the Holy Spirit, will teach them all things.[22] Its inclusion, therefore, reinforces Joseph's status as one of Christ's leading disciples. Joseph immediately undertakes Evelake's conversion, expounding the Christian mysteries of the Trinity and Incarnation. While the *Estoire* is far more prolix (Fr. 22–26 = ll.75–150), the English version incorporates all of the salient points of the discourse, as well as an abbreviated rendition of the two heavenly visions given to Evelake to prove the truth of Joseph's teaching (Fr. 27–29 = ll.175–211). As a further testament of Joseph's apostolic fervor, the English poem also includes Joseph's prayer for God's help in converting Evelake, and God's assurance of success in this endeavor. This colloquy is followed in both works by the ark Christophany and Josephe's episcopal consecration. Since the expansive French account of these events stresses the rising importance of Joseph's son, the English work drastically condenses both episodes (Fr. 31–41 = ll.258–304), and omits the French tribute to Josephe as the first bishop of Christendom, both in the order of his consecration and of primacy. In so doing, the English author accords greater significance to Christ's commission to the two Josephs for the continuing care of His faithful, which had already been anticipated by their joint guardianship of the ark:

> I seiȝe, Ioseph þi fader . schal bodiliche hem ȝeme,
> And þou gostliche . nou ȝemes hem boþe.
> (ll.309–10)

Both romances then turn swiftly to the dramatic confrontation between Joseph and his son and Evelake and his wisest clerk, a confrontation which concludes with one of the prime biblical and apocryphal *topoi*, the iconoclastic miracle. At this point in the *Estoire*, Joseph of Arimathea is superseded by his son Josephe, a role reversal that does not occur in the *Joseph*. One can reasonably argue that the English poet was confused by the nominal similarity between the French Joseph and Josephe. Yet, the *Estoire*'s glorification of Joseph *fils* is as unmistakable as the English poet's determination to extol Joseph *père* as an exemplar Christian rather than his purely fictional offspring.

Owing to these changes, the *Joseph of Arimathea* is closely linked to the hagiographic romance, as its incorporation in the predominantly religious Vernon manuscript attests. Its homiletic bent is also evident in the large number of lines assigned to the catechizing of Evelake (ll.65–299, 324–402) and to the mystical ark vision and ensuing ceremony (ll.240–311), all of which also point to Joseph's apostolic prowess and Christ's special favors to Joseph and his son. Even the conflict between the forces of Sarras and Tholomer of Egypt, which occurs shortly after Joseph's arrival at Sarras, is depicted not as a stirring romance episode, but rather as additional proof of Christian right over might, much in the vein of the battles in the Charlemagne cycle. With its consistent praise of Joseph of Arimathea, in his legendary roles of apostle and preserver of the Precious Blood, the work establishes a pattern for subsequent English encomia to Joseph, and thus qualifies as English hagiography in transition.[23]

This pattern is especially evident in John of Glastonbury's *Chronica*,[24] a purported history of Glastonbury Abbey which, however, lacks the veracity of William of Malmsbury's earlier chronicles. An ingenious composite of apocryphal and abbey legends, conjoined with the Arthurian Grail romances, the work testifies to John's eclectic and creative imagination, the Glastonbury monks' audacious lack of discrimination in matters hagiographical, and, above all, the alacrity with which Joseph of Arimathea transits the fluid boundaries between hagiography and romance.

John's proem identifies his source as a book which Emperor Theodosius found in Jerusalem during Pilate's reign. This is a modified borrowing from the *Evangelium Nicodemi*, which was purportedly translated by Ananias in the reign of Theodosius. John then adds a *caveat lector* to dispel all doubts regarding his veridical proof of the antiquity of Glastonbury Abbey. The history proper opens with the *Evangelium Nicodemi*'s account of Joseph's first imprisonment by the Jews and his liberation by Christ, which also corresponds to the opening episode in the *Estoire*. Significantly, the *Vindicta Salvatoris* account of Joseph's second imprisonment and deliverance by Vespasian is omitted, for this event ostensibly occurred in A.D. 70, whereas the revised abbey claim cited Joseph's arrival at Glastonbury in A.D. 63. Possibly, too, John did not want to duplicate the extant legend of the Holy Blood of Hayles, based on the Grail romances which alleged that the relic was taken from a pious old Jew who had been imprisoned for forty-two years until his liberation by Roman leaders.[25]

Because of St. Philip's prominence in earlier Glastonbury legends, John next includes the *Estoire* report of the baptism of the two Josephs by St. Philip, in order to establish Joseph's close relationship with that apostle. The apocryphal *Transitus Mariae* supplies the following episode, in which Joseph attends the Blessed Virgin in Jerusalem, at St. John's request. He subsequently witnesses her Assumption into heaven, along with Philip and the other disciples, and preaches the gospel in diverse lands for fifteen years, finally arriving in France. This latter claim is supported by legendary accounts of Julianus[26] and Flavius Lucius Dexter,[27] which placed Joseph in Gaul. Moreover, Freculfus, another of John's putative sources, recorded Philip's evangelical activities in Gaul.[28] With Joseph and Philip successfully united, John inserts the *Estoire* information that Joseph is accompanied by his son, whom Christ had consecrated as bishop at Sarras, but whom John consistently treats as a minor helpmate of his saintly father.

Practicing adroit hagiographic *entrelacement*, John returns to the Glastonbury legend, testifying how St. Philip sent his dear friend Joseph of Arimathea, his son, and ten disciples to convert Britain. Next, John interjects an abridged version of the *Estoire*'s fabulous recounting of the Christian band's miraculous voyage to Britain on Josephe's shirt and Solomon's Ship, their imprisonment by King Crudel of North Wales, and their subsequent rescue by Mordrains and Nascien of Sarras. In John's hands, this *Estoire* interpolation becomes a signal manifestation of God's favor to his disciple Joseph and, at the same time, provides a smooth and logical transition back to the Glastonbury version of Britain's apostolic conversion in A.D. 63, as interpolated in William of Malmsbury. Impressed with the sanctity of Joseph and his followers, Auviragus, King of Britain, endows them with the island of Yneswitren, which John carefully identifies as Avalon/Glastonbury, an oblique reference to the abbey's Arthurian claim:

> Intrat aualloniam duodena caterua virorum,
> Flos armathie ioseph est primus eorum:
> Iosephes ex ioseph genitus patrem comitatur;
> Hijs alijsque decem ius glastonie propriatur.

At the command of no less a heavenly personage than Archangel Gabriel, the missionaries construct an oratory to the Blessed Virgin, which is consecrated by Christ. In this way, John skillfully accounts for the genesis of the *vetusta ecclesia,* by which Glastonbury merited its accolade "*Fons et origo totius religionis.*" Owing to their unceasing vigils and prayers, the Blessed Virgin aids the apostolic twelve in their times of need. In addition, two pagan kings give them twelve hides of land surrounding Glastonbury, where they continue to lead holy lives until their death and burial near the *vetusta ecclesia.* John's pseudohistory ends at this point but, it should be noted, neatly synchronizes with the then prevalent belief that Christianity was brought to Britain in A.D. 167 by two missionaries, Phagan and Deruvian, sent by Pope Eleutherius at the request of King Lucius of Britain. According to a Glastonbury addendum, these two latecomers found the *vetusta ecclesia* in ruins on their arrival at Glastonbury, and restored it to the greater glory of the Virgin Mary.[29]

As his principal *auctoritas* for this extraordinary opus, John cites a book relating the deeds of King Arthur, Lancelot du Lac and the Round Table knights, and the quest of the Holy Grail. Undoubtedly, his acknowledgment of this wholly secular source was sanctioned, at least in part, by the abbey's well-established Arthurian claim. As yet another borrowing from the Arthurian Grail romances, or as a possible concession to Glastonbury's Celticists, he appends a vatic writing of the Welsh seer Melkin, who antedated Arthur's sage Merlin. This prophecy not only discloses Joseph's approximate burial site, but also the fact that within his sarcophagus are two cruets filled with the blood and sweat of the Prophet Jesus; and when his tomb is found and opened, there will be no drought on the ancient isle of Britain. Evidently it was one thing to claim the Arthurian Grail book as a source, but quite another to associate Joseph with the ecclesiastically suspect Grail. Accordingly, John, wishing to capitalize on Joseph's established connection with the Precious Blood, substituted the two cruets, and thus harmonized his account with other English, Church-sanctioned accounts of the origin and transmission of this priceless relic.[30]

As a fitting coda to his composition, John appends a genealogy, proving Arthur's descent from Joseph through the *Estoire's* line of Grail guardians. He thereby confers on Arthur the honorific "kin of Joseph of Arimathea" which was denied to him in the Arthurian Grail works. Thus an hagiographic seal of approval is stamped on Glastonbury's dual claim to Arthur, Britain's hero king, and to his saintly ancestor, Joseph of Arimathea, Britain's own apostle, a claim which ironically has its true *auctoritas* in Arthurian romance.[31]

This survey upholds the truism that the line of demarcation between hagiography and romance, in terms of content, is faint indeed, if not nonexistent. It would seem that in Joseph's case, any work which, despite its heterogeneous content, could be construed primarily as a *laus* of his *gesta, signa,* and *virtutes*[32] deserved an *imprimatur.* In the fifteenth century, more scrupulous hagiographers would follow the pattern established in the *Joseph of Arimathea,* and gradually excise the fabulous content drawn from the Arthurian Grail romances.[33] At the same time, they retained the legendary core of Joseph's *vita,* and particularly the Glastonbury accretion regarding his British apostolate. As a result, Joseph of Arimathea, whom Roger Loomis aptly dubbed "an evangelist by error,"[34] merited Britain's ultimate hagiographic tribute by his inclusion in the *Nova Legenda Angliae,*[35] the calendar exclusively devoted to England's greatest saints.

NOTES

1. Walter W. Skeat, ed., *Joseph of Arimathie, EETS OS* 44 (London, 1871). All quotations in this study are taken from this edition. An abbreviated version of this paper was read at the Medieval Section of the Eighty-Ninth Annual Convention of the MLA, New York, 28 December 1974.
2. *Ibid.,* pp. xxviii–xxxv.
3. Matthew 27:57–61; Mark 15:42–6; Luke 23:50–5; John 19:38–42.
4. These five works are contained in M. R. James, *The Apocryphal New Testament* (Oxford, 1926), pp. 94–115; 158–61; 216–18. For a full exploration of the Veronica legend, see Ernst von Dobschütz, *Christusbilder: Untersuchungen zur christlichen Legend* (Leipzig, 1899), pp. 177–262.
5. W. H. Hulme, ed., *The Middle-English Harrowing of Hell and Gospel of Nicodemus, EETS ES* 100 (London, 1907), p. lix.
6. Ernst von Dobschütz, "Joseph von Arimathie," *Zeitschrift für Kirchengeschichte,* XXIII (1902), pp. 4–17.
7. E. Hennecke and W. Schneemelcher, *New Testament Apocrypha,* tr. R. M. Wilson, 2 vols. (Philadelphia, 1962), I, pp. 444–77. Concerning secular romance content in hagiographic genre, see H. Delehaye, *Les Passions des Martyrs et les Genre Littéraires* (Bruxelles, 1921), pp. 316–364; and René Aigran, *L'Hagiographie* (Paris, 1953), pp. 128–55.
8. *Patrologia Latina* CLXXII, cols. 543–738. Also see Richard O'Gorman, "Ecclesiastical Tradition and the Holy Grail," *Australian Journal of French Studies,* VI (1969), p. 3–8.
9. A. Waite, *The Hidden Church of the Holy Grail* (London, 1909), pp. 33–35.
10. Robert de Boron, *Le Roman de l'Estoire dou Graal ou Joseph d'Arimathie,* ed. W. A. Nitze (Paris, 1927).
11. W. A. Nitze and T. A. Jenkins, eds., *Le Haut Livre du Graal: Perlesvaus,* 2 vols. (Chicago, 1932 and 1937).

12. William Roach, ed., *The Continuations of the Old French Perceval of Chrétien de Troyes*, 4 vols. (Philadelphia, 1949, 1950, 1952, 1971).

13. H. O. Sommers, ed., *The Vulgate Version of Arthurian Romances*, I. *Estoire del Saint Graal* (Washington, D.C., 1909). All citations are based on this edition.

14. See the writer's "Pan-Brittonic Hagiography and the Arthurian Grail Cycle," *Traditio*, XXVI (1970), pp. 29–61.

15. *Patrologia Latina* CLXXIX, cols. 1683–1686. Owing to William's reputation as a scrupulous medieval historian, Skeat, *op. cit.*, pp. xxix, FN 1 and xxxv, placed great credence on this entry in the *De antiquitate*. J. A. Robinson, *Two Glastonbury Legends: King Arthur and Joseph of Arimathea* (Cambridge University Press, 1926), pp. 28–50, has clearly shown the entry to be a later and thus spurious interpolation.

16. A balanced discussion and assessment of Glastonbury's legendmaking proclivities are contained in Robinson, *ibid.*

17. For the complex historical, political, and ecclesiastical considerations promoting the cult of Joseph in England, see the writer's "The Evolving Legend of St. Joseph of Glastonbury," *Speculum*, XLVI (1971), pp. 209–231.

18. Dieter Mehl, *The Middle English Romances of the Thirteenth and Fourteenth Centuries* (London, 1968), pp. 17–26, 120–8.

19. R. S. Loomis, ed., *Arthurian Literature in the Middle Ages* (Oxford, 1959), p. 481.

20. Mehl, *op. cit.*, p. 14.

21. Herry Lovelich, *The History of the Holy Grail*, ed. F. J. Furnivall, *EETS OS* 20 (1874); (1875); 28, 30, 95 (1877).

22. Matthew 28:18–20; John 14:26.

23. This same interest in and characterization of Joseph is reflected in the *Titus and Vespasian*, another homiletic romance of the later fourteenth century (J. A. Herbert, ed., *Titus and Vespasian or The Destruction of Jerusalem* (London, 1905), which expands its French source, *La Venjance Nostre Seigneur*, with amplified versions of the *Evangelium Nicodemi* and *Vindicta Salvatoris*.

24. *Johannes Glastoniensis Chronica*, ed. Thomas Hearne (Oxford, 1728), I, pp. 48ff.

25. Carl Horstmann, *Altenglische Legenden* (Heilbronn, 1881), pp. 275–81.

26. *Acta Sanctorum* VIII, col. 509.

27. *Ibid.*, IV, col. 455.

28. *Patrologia Latina* CVI, col. 1147.

29. Robinson, *op. cit.*, p. 36.

30. See Grosseteste's account in Matthew Paris, *Chronica Majora*, ed. H. R. Luard, Rolls Series No. 57 (London, 1882), VI, 138–44.

31. For an even more fabulous amalgam of Grail romances and Glastonbury legends, see John Hardyng's *Chronicle*, ed. Henry Ellis (London, 1812), p. 83ff.

32. C. W. Jones, *Saints' Lives and Chronicles in Early England* (Ithaca, N.Y., 1947), p. 59.

33. These encomia are found in Skeat, *op. cit.*, pp. 27–52.

34. R. S. Loomis, *The Grail From Celtic Myth to Christian Symbol* (New York, 1963), pp. 223–48.

35. Carl Horstmann, ed., *Nova Legenda Angliae*, 2 vols. (Oxford, 1901), II, pp. 78–82.

Didacticism and Drama
in Guy of Warwick

DAVID N. KLAUSNER

The tenuousness of the border between romance and legend is emphasized by the alacrity with which writers in each genre borrow from one another. The extent to which this borrowing may be conscious is difficult to determine, for in all the romances any explicit connections with a hagiographic predecessor appear to have been carefully avoided.[1] In some cases this may be due to a radical change in the didactic purpose of the story, and of this *Guy of Warwick* is an excellent example. None of the three surviving English versions nor the Anglo-Norman romance on which they are based gives any hint that part of the story is a secular pastiche of elements from the legend of St. Alexis.[2] In the romantic reworking, furthermore, the original purpose of the legend has been almost entirely lost, and a completely new didactic structure has arisen around the figure of Guy. This article will be concerned with these changes and with the presentation of the moral teaching in *Guy*. It does not purport to be a full discussion of the romance, which has in recent years suffered a heavy critical trouncing.[3] In general this is deserved, but I wish to show that the romance has some merit based largely on its didactic presentation.

From the thirteenth through the sixteenth centuries, the tale of Guy held its popularity among English audiences, and it seems clear that this attraction was due largely to the didactic bases of the story. Lydgate makes the story's nature clear in his poem on Guy's pilgrimage and death when he portrays himself in a brief apologia more as the dutiful hagiographer than the romance storyteller:[4]

> The parfight lyf, the vertuous gouernaunce,
> His wylful povert, hard goyng, and penaunce
> Brought on-to me a chapitle to translate:
> Yif ought be wrong in metre or in substaunce,
> Putteth the wyte for dulnesse on Lydgate.

The tale is bipartite.[5] Guy passes through a series of battles in order to win the love of his high-born lady, Felice. His ultimate success is crowned by their wedding, but shortly afterwards Guy is stricken with remorse that he has given no thought to God in his many battles. He leaves home as a pilgrim and undertakes a further series of battles for God, aiding the poor and distressed. These battles culminate in the rescue of England through the defeat of a Danish champion. Guy dies as he is reunited with Felice. Clearly only the second part of the romance is didactic in any specific sense, and it is with this part of the tale that I will be concerned. I will limit discussion to the version contained in the Auchinleck manuscript, much the best of the English texts from a literary point of view.[6]

The basic outline of Guy's "wylful povert, hard goyng, and penaunce" is drawn from the legend of St. Alexis. In its most familiar form the legend tells of a wealthy and generous Roman couple, Eufamian and Agloes, whose prayers for the relief of Agloes' barrenness are at length heard. The son born to them is called Alexis; he is well educated and grows daily in piety. When the appropriate age is reached his father arranges a marriage. Alexis submits dutifully, but left alone with his bride he elicts from her a promise of chastity, gives her a gold ring, and sets out on a pilgrimage. In Edessa he distributes his goods among the poor and lives as a beggar for seventeen years. An image of Our Lady reveals his presence, and he is forced to flee to preserve his anonymity. He embarks for Sicily, but the boat is driven by a storm to Rome. Alexis meets his father coming from church and begs charity. He is taken into his parents' house where he lives as a beggar, enduring the taunts of the servants. After a further seventeen years he is warned of his impending death by an angel; in preparation he acquires pen and paper and writes his story. An angelic announcement is made of the presence of a holy man in the city, and the Pope is directed by the angel to Eufamian's house. Alexis is dead when he arrives, the manuscript clutched in his hand. It is read aloud to the assembled multitude and the family laments his death.

In addition to a host of Latin and Greek texts, six English versions of widely varying quality follow these details.[7] None is particularly distinguished, but they give an idea for the sort of vernacular materials with which the romance writers may have dealt. At least one fifteenth-century life may have undergone back-contamination from the Guy of Warwick story, for it opens very much in the manner of a romance, citing valor and strength rather than piety:

> Alle þat willen here in ryme
> Hou gode Men in olde tyme
> Loueden god almiȝth,
> Þat weren riche of grete valoure,
> Kynges sones and Emperoure,
> Of bodies strong & liȝth. . .
> *(Laud* 1–6)

Added to the tale of Alexis' shipwreck on the Roman coast is a *digressio* on the subject of Jonah and the whale, explained as an exemplum of God's

redirection onto the right path. This episode (unique to *Laud*) corresponds in position to the story of Guy's rescue of Earl Jonas; indeed, the
legend calls the recalcitrant sailor "Ionas." There is a further connection
in Alexis' explanation on leaving his bride that his penance will be for
her as well:[8]

> "And half þe godenesse þat I do
> Graunte þee god almiȝth."
>
> (*Laud* 233–4)

which parallels Guy's words to Felice:

> "Of alle þe dedes y may do wel
> God graunt þe, lef, þat haluendel . . ."
>
> (st. 26, 10–11)

The author notes the popular accomplishments which Alexis forsook –
they are, of course, the accomplishments of Guy:

> . . . to be Man of valoure
> And lernen chiualrie,
> Of chesse pleieyng & of tablere;
> Of huntyng & of Ryuere,
> Al nas worþ a flye . . .
>
> (*Laud* 986–90)

In order to examine the changes which were made in the tale in its
transition from saint's life to romance, a comparison of the texts of a
scene of both dramatic and didactic importance will be useful. In discussing Guy's departure scene, reference will be primarily to the English
romance and the English and Latin saint's Lives, but comparisons will
also be drawn from the Anglo-Norman *Gui de Warewic*.[9]

Some of the changes made in the adaptation of the Alexis tale can be
related to the exigencies of the first part of Guy's story. Guy's marriage
decision is obviously his own rather than his father's, and the lavish
character of the wedding feast and the conception of a child on the
wedding night are alien to most versions of the legend. These changes
have been strictly calculated, for the poet's intention is to provide the
greatest possible contrast between the free-living warrior's sumptuous
marriage and the ascetic life to which he turns. This is the greatest departure from the legend: the moral force of Alexis' life is embodied in the
perseverence of his search for humility; in Guy's story it derives from his
sudden but voluntary change of life, his "wylful povert," in contrast to
the worldly glory of his earlier life.

Alexis' search for humility becomes in the romance a further series of
adventures, albeit in the guise of a pilgrim and in the service of God.
Through this the didactic orientation of the story is further altered.[10]
Guy takes his pilgrimage half as a penance and half to do to God the
honor he has done Felice in the first half of his life. He leaves in a spirit

of piety and asceticism, visits the Holy Land, and dies a hermit, but between these points he retains much of his old character. "Frohen muts schikt sich denn auch Guy – er est der alte wieder – zum heissen waffengange."[11] Yet this is not altogether fair, for there is now a great difference in Guy's exploits: they are undertaken for God alone. Guy takes on Alexis' insistence on anonymity, if for a rather different reason than the saint. Guy honors God the only way he knows – by deeds of arms, and so his change is, as Schelp points out, from worldly warrior to *miles Christi.*[12] Tanner assumes that Guy's penance aught to be ascetic in character, and while the ascetic note is strong in Guy's departure:

> "To bote min sinnes ichil wende
> Barfot to mil liues ende,
>   To bid mi mete wiþ care."
>   (st. 22, 10–12)

it is overshadowed by the thought that God should be honored on the same terms, if in greater degree, as Felice:

> "Ac ȝif ich hadde don half þe dede
> For him þat on rode gan blede
>   Wiþ grimly woundes sare,
> In heuene he wald haue quit mi mede,
> In joie to won wiþ angels wede
>   Euer-more wiþ-outen care
> Ac for þi loue ich haue al wrouȝt:
> For his loue dede y neuer nouȝt.
>   Iesu amende mi fare!"
>   (st. 25, 1–9)

The proximity of the romance to the legend is evident in some minor details; the relationship is often the more striking in that these details are inessential to the narrative. In most versions of the legend, the saint gives his bride a gold ring as a remembrance token. The motif is taken up in the romance with the greater significance of a recognition token.[13] The characters are reversed; Felice gives the ring to her departing husband who returns it to her in order to reveal his presence at the hermitage. Both the Earl of Warwick and Eufamian send messengers in search of the two pilgrims, and both searches are unsuccessful. Guy recognizes Herhaud in his search just as Alexis recognizes his father's envoys. The pilgrim Guy approaches the German emperor as he comes from church just as Alexis accosts his father after a service. Their requests for charity are granted in similar terms; Alexis is taken into his father's house, Guy into the emperor's court. The celestial announcement of death is narrated in very similar fashion in both romance and legend, while the angel's announcement to King Athelstan of the presence of the pilgrim parallels the revelation of Alexis' presence by the icon of Edessa. Athelstan is told to find the pilgrim at the north gate of the city; the sacristan will find the beggar Alexis at the church door. The miraculous sweet odor of the corpse is an almost invariable detail of both legend and romance, and the refusal of Alexis' body to yield up the manuscript is perhaps related to the refusal of Guy's body to be moved from the hermitage.

Guy's soliloquy and his subsequent argument with Felice are largely original to the romance and constitute the most significant addition to the story. Alexis' state of mind leading to his decision is shown to us in glimpses if at all, while both the French and English romances take great pains to make Guy's thoughts clear. Alexis' wife is generally a passive figure who, if she says anything, merely assures her husband of her continued chastity. Felice is a different person entirely. Her attempts to answer her husband's arguments become the basis not only of the dramatic tension of the scene, but also of its didactic presentation.

The munificence of Guy's wedding feast, in which he is shown at the height of earthly glory and happiness, would be out of place in the saint's life. Alexis' wedding is a time of rejoicing primarily for the parents whose desires have at last come to fulfilment. Similarly inappropriate would be the delay of fifteen days between the wedding and Guy's departure, for the essence of the legend is the flight from the marriage bed, the desertion of the bride before the consummation of the marriage.[14] Guy, in contrast, fathers a child before his departure. His initial decision to leave comes as a greater surprise to the audience than in the legend, for all the events preceding this change of heart point to the imminent fulfilment of all Guy's desires. Alexis is not shown to be pleased with his situation in any clear way. His education and piety are emphasized, and from what we learn of him before his departure it is certain that he is capable of turning to God at any moment. Furthermore, he has no cause to be especially pleased with his marriage; it is a family affair in which he plays but a minor role until his father sends him off to bed.

Alexis' decision is usually narrated very swiftly, for it is the result of a sudden recognition of the impossibility of his position. Only in a few versions do we find Alexis retiring to the marriage bed already considering how to avoid it; more often, as in the Old French *Vie de S. Alexis*, it is a moment of shock as he sees the bridal bed and is struck by the full horror of fleshly desires. The Latin text, in the "pale and intangible style of the late antique legend,"[15] gives even less information. Alexis goes to his bride and preaches to her; there is no hint of his thoughts: "Ut autem intravit, coepit nobilissimus juvenis, & in Christe sapientissimus instruere sponsam suam."[16]

The English legends vary widely in their treatment of the scene. Although Alexis' state of mind is less essential to the narrative than Guy's, most of the better texts include some hint of his thoughts. In *Laud*, Alexis' chaste intentions seem to have been developing over the course of his education. His father's direction to the marriage bed comes as no surprise; he has been dreading the moment:

> And whan Alexius herd þat word,
> It priokèd his hert as speres oord,
> So sore it gan him rewe . . .
>
> (*Laud* 199–201)

The following scene, though it revolves about the two characters of Alexis and his bride, does not seem much concerned with them dramatically. There is no discourse; Alexis' preaching is reported blandly. The bride does not speak. Of the effect of Alexis' words upon her it is simply said that "þi holy gost hir lauȝtte" (219). She accepts his sermon unquestioningly; there is no hint of any conflict. The high point of the scene is not, as in the Old French *Vie*, the moment of confrontation, but Alexis' departure and the glimpse of the woman grieving for her husband who is, for her, already dead:

> Alexius þus his leue tooke;
> Rewely his wijf gan on hym loke
> Þat was so fair & briȝth . . .
>
> (*Laud* 235–7)

No effort is made to reinforce the precepts of chastity and humility; Alexis' reasons for leaving are not clearly defined, and his wife accepts his decision because she is directed by the Holy Ghost.

If the *Laud* text is rather average, the *Titus* version is a monstrous mistake. More consideration is given to Alexis' feelings prior to his marriage. He understands the transitoriness of the world and the necessity of placing God above all things:

> he loued god in all his thought
> And of thys worllde gaffe he nought:
> he sawe thys worllde was butt gylle,
> for hit showld laste but a whyle.
>
> (*Titus* 49–52)

Much of this opening is good in its concern for the saint's thoughts and motivations. It is when we come to the confrontation with his bride that the problems begin:

> Into a chaumbur he com ful ryght,
> and redy there he founde hys bright,
> And toke here in his armys twoo,
> and downe they layde bothe twoo.
> "dame," he sayde, "nou it ys soo
> O fflessche are wee all so,
> Nowe may we be gladde of þis lyffe,
> ffor thowe art bothe moder and wyffe . . ."
>
> (*Titus* 87–94)

Not only does the marriage appear to be consummated, but the birth of a child is even suggested. All this is disastrous to the theme of the legend, and Alexis' ascetic character is quite demolished. This peculiar change may well have come about through a back-contamination from the *Guy* tale, to which both consummation and child are essential. However, they are very much out of place in the saint's life.

The *Vernon* life is very much better. The whole scene is organized about the theme of chastity, reaching a climax in Alexis' sermon to his bride. It is an effective piece of preaching; the virgin bride is advised to turn to Jesus, "Maidenes spouse" (60), and to emulate the purity of "þat Maiden clene" (64).

The *Laud-Trinity* version is better yet. It is the only English text to use the "moment of revelation" of the Old French *Vie,* and the drama of the scene is caught more vividly than in the other texts. The flatness and occasional banality of the other lives becomes here a touching simplicity, as in the bride's attempts to cheer her startled husband:

> Ne myht glade him his fere
> with wordes ne wiþ fair chere
> þat stod shred in palle.
> (*Laud-Trinity* 124–6)

In contrast to the other versions, Alexis' bride speaks, and her tone follows that of Felice in the similar situation. She is at first angry, and then laments wildly with tears and tearing of hair. She calms down to give her vow of chastity and her assurance that she will grieve for him:

> "Al myrthe I wile forsake
> & euere more sorwe take
> & shone al plawe."
> (*Laud-Trinity* 166–8)

The departure scene is a climax, rather than a transition as in the other texts.

The *Scottish Legend Collection* text is far more consciously literary than the others. The hand of the author is more evident in the guiding of events, and his didactic purpose is more clearly shaped (despite some very indifferent verse). The tale is dominated by the tone of the preacher, set at the opening with a lengthy sermon on chastity and matrimony. We are presented with a wealth of examples of chastity and wedded continence from Anna to the Scottish Queen Margaret:

> sume aftyre weding, sume aftir syne
> þai wex chast, & hewine cane wine.
> (*SLC* 61–2)

Far better, continues the preacher, are those happy souls who "fra þe byrth lifit þame chast" (64). The tale is told much in this vein and, like many a sermon, it is all on rather the same level – the argument is not varied with tensions and relaxations, but *seriatim* examples reiterate a single point. As in most of the English Lives, Alexis' decision is not a revelation, though it becomes more meaningful in its relation to the opening sermon. We see Alexis planning beforehand, and the course of his thoughts is laid before us:

> Of fleschly lust he had na thocht,
> bot beyisit hyme how he mocht
> gere hyre consent to chastyte.
> (*SLC* 123–5)

He presents this ideal of chastity to his bride in language of some passion, to which references to Judgement Day and the transitoriness of earthly life lend a strong sense of urgency:

> "fore al mone de, man & wyf,
> & sic as we are fundyne here
> before þe Iuge we sal apere,
> & gyf reknyne þat Iuge til
> of al dedis, gud & Il,
> & fore oure dedis, nocht to layne,
> resawe oþire Ioy or payne."
> (*SLC* 130–6)

The opening sermon looms large throughout the story, so that the point of each episode is evident without explanation. The story is an *exemplum* to the sermon.

The *Northern Homily Collection* life is a case of unfulfilled potentials, for although the poet achieves several striking moments, they are far above the general level of the narrative. The austerity of Alexis' thought is contrasted with the lavish preparation of the bridal bed:

> Bot þo bokis lufid he inwardlie
> Þat spak oght of God all-mightie.
> (*NHC* 55–6)
> When þis bridegome suld go to bed,
> Þat richeli wiþ pall was sprede –
> Gayli was his chaumbir graithid
> Wiþ riche clothis, in flore laide . . .
> (*NHC* 81–4)

The motif is effective enough on its own, but there is little attempt to weave the comparison into the fabric of the tale. A similar problem arises in the scene with Alexis' bride. As in the Scottish life, Alexis presents his decision in terms of chastity, emphasizing her chastity over his own, but here the author takes the occasion to point out that such chastity must also be selfless:

> He prechid here of maidenhede
> & sithen of þat mikil mede
> Þat þai sall haue þat ʒemes here

> Þaire maidenhed on gode manere –
> Wiþouten ani priue pride,
> Þat fele wymen er wont to hide
> In þaire hert for þaire maidenhede:
> Þat geres þaim laytheli tyne þaire mede:
> For who so duse gode dede in rose,
> He tynes all þat euere he duse.
>
> (*NHC* 91–100)

Caught up in an expansion of the phrase "in gode manere," the poet only succeeds in obscuring the primary lesson of the passage, the overwhelming importance of chastity itself. The tension of the moment is broken with irrelevance.

The success of the presentation of the moral precepts in these legends is largely governed by two factors: the consistency and organization of the explication and exemplification of the moral itself, and the integration of this with the dramatic flow of the narrative. That is, the first requirement is the coherent presentation of the moral theme, in such manner that there are both tension and release in the didactic argument as well as in the drama. The second requirement is the coincidence of this didactic argument with the dramatic argument; the one must reinforce and complement the other. The success of the Old French *Vie* stems directly from this, as does the failure in some way or another of most of the other versions, including the Latin *vita* in which there is no drama at all.

With the romances these same principles hold although the situation is somewhat altered, for the essence of *Guy*'s moral seriousness is contained largely in those elements foreign to the Alexis story, namely Guy's lament for the evils of his past life, and his consequent longing for the bliss of heaven. Guy's decision, since it is so much less expected, is much more fully explained, and is expanded into a scene of considerable tenderness and beauty. There are important differences between the versions. The English Guy returns from a hunting party of a fine summer's day. At night he climbs alone onto one of the castle towers and, looking at the stars, is moved to think of Jesus:

> To a turet sir Gij is went,
> & biheld þat firmament,
> Þat thicke wiþ steres stode.
> On Iesu omnipotent,
> Þat alle his honour hadde him lent,
> He þouȝt wiþ dreri mode . . .
>
> (st. 21, 1–6)

He laments his past life, in that throughout his fighting he has never done anything for the love of Christ:

> "For neuer in al mi liif biforn
> For him þat bar þe crown of þorn

Gode dede dede y nare . . ."
(st. 22, 4–6)

Guy's recognition of the necessity of penance and his acceptance of this
follow immediately. He will "wende barfot" to the end of his life and
beg his bread.

The Anglo-Norman romance, while giving almost precisely the same
details as the English, contributes a greater sense of calm by giving a
more lengthy description of the evening scene.[17] Through the beauty of
the evening, Gui's decision (though not his subsequent argument with
Felice) is at once more moving and more convincing. Gui returns from
the hunt delighted with his marriage, "Mult joius e lé se feseit" (7567),
and this feeling of pleasure is continued in the description of the beautiful
night in which Gui stands upon the tower:

> A une vespree, que bele esteit,
> Gui en une tur munta,
> En halt as estres se pua;
> Le pais envirun ad esgardé
> E le ciel, qui tant ert esteillé,
> E le tens, qui ert serré e cler.
> (7568–73)

As in the English romance, Gui ponders his earthly honor, given by God,
and the number of men he has killed to obtain it:

> Gui comence dunc a penser
> Cum Deus li out fait grant honur,
> Unc a chevaler ne fist greignur:
> Que unc ne fu en liu n'en estur
> Qu'il ne fu tenu al meillur,
> E cum il ert home de grant afaire
> E preisé en estrange terre,
> E que tanz homes aveit oscis,
> Turs e citez par force pris . . .
> (7574–81)

Gui's thoughts concentrate on the evil he has done, and there is less
emphasis on his lack of good deeds for God's sake than in the English
romance. He speaks only briefly of the "servise" (7594) he owes God,
and returns to the thought of his victims:

> "Pur vus ai fait maint grant desrei,
> Homes ocis, destruites citez,
> Arses abbeies de plusur regnez . . ."
> (7608–10)

The thoughts of the English Guy in contrast are organized around the
distinction between the earthly love of woman which he bears towards
Felice, and which has heretofore been his primary motivation, and the
love of Christ which he has neglected. The argument which follows is

somewhat more extended than in the French.[18] Felice begins by asking Guy the cause of his sorrow, and he replies that since he first saw her, he has been so bound by her love that he has done no good deed, but has slain men instead. Had he done half of this for Christ, he would be saved, but he has done all for the love of a woman, not for God:

> "Ac for þi loue ich haue al wrouȝt:
> For his loue dede y neuer nouȝt."
>   (st. 25, 7–8)

The whole of the passage in the Auchinleck text is dominated by this dichotomy: Guy has lived for the love of woman, now he must live for the love of God.

Guy determines immediately upon his pilgrimage, and in his words the ascetic impulse is stronger than in the French, where Gui merely decides to devote himself to God:

> En sun corage se purpensa
> Que tote sa vie changera
> E en Deu servise se mettra.
>   (7592–4)

The English Guy goes beyond the idea of "servise"; he will go "barfot to mi liues ende, Mine sinnes for to bete" (st. 26, 5–6). A further part of his penance will be a search for humility in the tradition of St. Alexis:

> "Þat whore so y lye aniȝt
> Y schal neuer be seyn wiþ siȝt
>   Bi way no bi strete."
>   (st. 26, 7–9)

This suggestion of the legend is unique to the Auchinleck text. Throughout the passage Guy speaks of the love of God to which he must turn, while the French Gui reminds Felice of the men whom he has killed for her sake. It is only the French hero who adds to these wrongs his own sufferings out of love for Felice:

> "Puis que primes vus amai,
> Tanz malz pur vus sufferz ai,
> Ne qui que home fust unc né
> Qui tantes dolurs ait enduré
> Pur une femme cum jo ai pur tei."
>   (7603–7)

In the light of the situation this seems a bit tasteless. The husband who reminds his wife of the torments he has suffered for her love while on the point of leaving her is not the sympathetic character whom Guy at this stage should be. After its fine opening, the scene in the Anglo-Norman romance is disappointing in its lack of tenderness, in its emphasis on bloodshed rather than love.

Felice, so different from the wife of Alexis, replies in all the texts that Guy must have a second wife in foreign parts whom he wishes to join. Her anger is quickly calmed, and she pleads with Guy to remain at home and take his penance in the form of good works – almsdeeds, the building of monasteries, and constant shrift. She cannot see the mutual exclusiveness of the two loves of which Guy speaks, nor does she see the necessity of a penance commensurate with the sin itself – Guy must point this out to her bluntly:

> "Þat ich haue with mi bodi wrouȝt
> Wiþ mi bodi it schal be bouȝt . . ."
> (st. 29, 10–11)

Guy requests that she not sorrow after him, but place their son in the care of Herhaud and explain his departure to her parents. The Anglo-Norman version, although similar, lacks the organizing theme of the contrasting loves of God and woman.[19] The references to Gui's bloodshed stand out strongly in the French and the episode takes on a more desperate tone. The English Guy, in contrast, is almost exultant about his decision.

The two loves of which Guy speaks are also employed briefly in the version of the story contained in the *Gesta Romanorum*. Christ appears to Guido exhorting him to change his life, and speaks of the two loves in a manner which would serve to justify the romance Guy's continued knight-errantry: "Guido, Guido, sicut bella sepius commisisti pro amore unius puelle, tempus est ut pro meo amore studens viriliter contra inimicos pugnare." His later battles are cited as examples of this love of Christ: "plurima bella pro Christi amore commiserunt."[20] As the Anglo-Latin *Gesta* can be dated most probably from the end of the thirteenth or beginning of the fourteenth century, it is possible that it was known to the redactor of the Auchinleck *Guy*.

It is clear that the scene of Guy's departure is based in outline on the legend of St. Alexis. Yet the differences are many. There is little of moral significance to be drawn from Alexis' departure; it is simply the beginning of the road to sanctity, the preparation for which began with his early education. For Guy the pilgrimage is a great change, and because of the moral tone of this change the scene is easily expanded into a dramatic episode which is the vehicle for a considerable amount of didactic material. Principally there is the doctrine, reiterated in innumerable texts throughout the Middle Ages, of the necessity of penance. Guy's penance follows the formula repeated by the preachers and the penitential manuals. He first confesses his sin (*confessio*), expresses his sorrow for it (*contritio*), and takes penance in expiation (*penitentia*). Guy is here an exceptionally successful figure – the common man who has through his own merit worked his way to the height of earthly glory, to the position he has long desired. In his battles he has never been on the side of what the audience would recognize as the wrong, yet it is pointed out through his repentance that these deeds of bloodshed cannot truly be accounted good works. Guy must recognize the insufficiency of his past life:

> "For neuer in al mi liif biforn
> For him þat bar þe croun of þorn
> Gode dede dede y nare . . ."
> (st. 22, 4–6)

The audience too must realize that there are good deeds and good deeds; that those which Guy has done in the winning of Felice are not those which will win him the bliss of heaven. "For him þat bar þe croun of þorn" is not merely a formula (although it is that as well), it is the essence of the argument. Contrasted with this rejection of the past is a great longing for the future, for the heavenly joys to which Guy has hitherto given no thought:

> "In heuene he wald haue quit mi mede
> In joie to won wiþ angels wede . . ."
> (st. 25, 4–5)

The strength of his passion is indicated by his words to Felice; his rejection of the past life almost extends to regretting his attachment to her:

> "Seþþen y þe seȝye first wiþ ayn
> ('Allas þe while,' y may sayn) . . ."
> (st. 24, 4–5)

Out of this juxtaposition of the past and the future – the rejection of the one and the embracing of the other – grows the theme of the two loves, secular and sacred, which quickly comes to symbolize his former life and his future hope. The contrast is strengthened by the alternation of passages of despair,

> "Now may me rewe al mi liue,
> That euer was y born o wiue,
> Wayle-way þat stounde!"
> (st. 24, 10–12)

and passages of hope:

> "Bot god is curteys & hende,
> & so dere he haþ bouȝt mankende,
> For noþing wil hem lete."
> (st. 26, 1–3)

Such emotions, as well as the dichotomy which fosters them, are alien to the legend, for St. Alexis has not lived the life of a sinner even in Guy's limited sense.

Unlike the Alexis legend, the essence of Guy's story is his confrontation with his wife and his defense of his position. She phrases her objections to his decision in much the same language in which he has propounded it to her. "God is curteys & hende," he had said of his salvation through penance; "So curteys he is & hende," Felice replies, that he will forgive simply on the basis of shrift and almsdeeds. Her arguments are strong, so strong that the audience is tempted to identify with her. She puts her case as an established fact, not as a proposition:

> "Schriue þe wele in word & þouȝt,
> & þan þe þarf dout riȝt nouȝt
> Oȝaines þe foule fend."
> (st. 28, 4–6)

The depth of Guy's sin is not apparent to her, and his task is to impress upon her its seriousness. He is forced to put it as bluntly as possible: "ich haue destryued mankin" (st. 29, 7). He has not merely killed the Saracens or exterminated wrong-doers, he has murdered his fellow man. Felice can offer no counter to this argument and is silent for the rest of the scene. It is not merely for drama that she stands between Guy and his journey, that the family ties must be broken more forcibly than those of Alexis. Felice constitutes a necessary part of Guy's penance, as the living symbol of the world from which he must break away.

Auerbach suggested that "the first elevated style of the European Middle Ages arose at the moment when the single event is filled with life," and that this development coincided with the dramatic confrontation of lively characters.[21] Guy's departure is such a scene, the conflict of two persons in whose concerns the poet has aroused his audience's interest. Even the Old French *Vie* is less a confrontation of two people than of Alexis with the specter of the flesh, for there is little life in the character of his bride. The tension of Guy extends beyond the abstract tension of ideals, as well as beyond the internal tension of characters. In this scene both Guy and Felice take on an added dimension through their argument and its familiar subject, and the scene is played against an emotional background common to the audience. The spectators are drawn into the argument and forced to take sides. The result of this emotional involvement is, of course, a moral involvement, and it is in this that the didactic success of the Guy story lies. By making the characters alive, the moral precepts involved are presented on a ground which is essentially real and related directly to the life of the audience.

Still, the aims of the legend are not those of *Guy*. The saint's life is a study in humility and piety, viewed through the ascetic tradition of *imitatio Christi*. Unlike many of the popular legends it is not based on miracles, and does not rely upon fantastic events to excite wonder. This is effected merely by the story of Alexis' perseverance in his search for humility. Everything in the legend is aimed toward the support of this feeling and toward the excitement of admiration. Alexis' desertion of his bride is not the sacrifice it is for Guy; it is the only conceivable action consistent with his character. Miracles, such as there are, are subordinate to this ideal of selflessness; the icon of Edessa reveals his presence as a test of humility, and when Alexis flees the adoration of the public he is directed back onto the testing ground by a storm. What in later years is remembered of Alexis is not the revelation in Edessa or even the wonders surrounding his death, but his assumption of pilgrim's cloth or his return as a beggar. It is a simple, quiet, and devout story, perhaps most effective in contrast to the violence of many of the popular legends.

While most of the Alexis legends can boast little more than cardboard figures, and while even the Old French *Vie de S. Alexis*, for all its poetic beauty, presents us with characters who rarely show any fullness, the romance of *Guy* gives us two characters confronting with very human reactions the familiar questions of penance and salvation. The audience of *Guy* may have contained no one of the moral fiber of its hero; nonetheless, the emotional background of his confrontation with Felice would have been immediately and deeply felt. The husband deserting his wife and her attempts to stop him; this is the cloth into which the thesis of the two loves and the doctrine of penance are worked.

It has been a critical commonplace for many years that a didactic bent is sufficient grounds for dismissing a romance. This opinion must be revised in the light of the acceptance of the didactic or exemplary romance as a genre with its own esthetics and requirements. As Schelp has shown, the didactic romance is different from the purely narrative poem and must be seen through its exemplary purpose.[22] This is not to excuse the bad writing which we frequently find in the romances, but to indicate that the critical ground must be shifted sufficiently to consider the poet's teaching as well as his dramatic and poetic success.

Like Chrétien's characters, Guy moves predominately in a world whose political ambience does not extend beyond the crusading spirit. In the final scenes of the romance, however, all is changed by the assumption of a pseudohistorical reality. Guy is no longer fighting nameless Saracens, defending imaginary kings and earls; he is defending England and King Athelstan against the Danes, and though Guy's battle with Colbrond may be fanciful, the Danish invasion was hardly a figment of the author's imagination. The political reality informs the scene with life and gives it a final dramatic impetus which does not end with the defeat of the Danes. The sense of reality lingers, and it is in Athelstan's England, not in some vague kingdom of romance, that Guy's story is concluded. The familiarity of the setting adds to the didactic force of the story. Guy's piety and humility are less distant than Alexis' self-abnegation, in part because of the audience's emotional contact with the character himself, in part because of their awareness of the real setting for his last actions.

Through this appeal Guy held for generations the affection of the English popular audience.

NOTES

1. An exception is the mention of St. Eustace in the Spanish romance *El Cauallero Zifar*, ed. C. P. Wagner, Michigan University Publications, Language and Literature 5 (Ann Arbor, 1929), i, pp. 90–1.
2. L. H. Loomis, *Medieval Romance in England* (Oxford, 1924), pp. 137–8; C. W. Dunn in *A Manual of the Writings in Middle English 1050–1500*, ed. J. B. Severs (New Haven, Conn., 1967), i, pp. 27–31.
3. For example, M. D. Legge, *Anglo-Norman Literature and its Background* (Oxford, 1963), pp. 162–71.
4. John Lydgate, *Minor Poems*, ed. H. N. MacCracken, EETS OS 192 (1933), pt. ii, ll. 580–4.
5. Tripartite, if the tale of Guy's son Reinbrun is included.
6. *Guy of Warwick*, ed. J. Zupitza, EETS ES 42 (1883), 49 (1887), 59 (1891).
7. *Laud:* C. Horstmann, "Alexiuslieder," *Archiv*, lix (1878), 79–90. *Titus:* Horstmann, "Alexiuslieder," 90–101. *Vernon:* C. Horstmann, "Zwei Alexiuslieder," *Archiv*, lvi (1876), 391–401. *Laud-Trinity:* Horstmann, "Zwei Alexiuslieder," 401–16; citations are from the *Laud* text and Horstmann's abbreviations have been expanded. *SLC: Legends of the Saints*, ed. W. Metcalfe, Scottish Text Society (Edinburgh, 1896), i. pp. 441–57. *NHC:* C. Horstmann, *Altenglische Legenden* (Neue Folge, Heilbronn, 1881), pp. 174–88; citations are from the Ashmole text.
8. Here *Laud* follows the Auchinleck *Guy*; the Caius version of *Guy* and the Anglo-Norman source agree in saying, "I grant you half the benefit . . ."
9. *Gui de Warewic*, ed. A. Ewert, Classiques français du moyen âge 74–5 (Paris, 1932–1933). All citations will be from this edition.
10. An early fifteenth-century Irish version shifts the didactic ground even more. Either its author or the author of its unknown English source also had access to a late thirteenth-century homiletic poem, the *Speculum Gy de Warewyke*, a verse rendering of Alcuin's *Liber de Virtutibus et Vitiis* which was attached to Guy of Warwick probably through confusion with the patron of Alcuin's work, Guido of Tours. The Irish tale describes Guy's call to Alcuin for spiritual guidance after his decision to abandon his worldly life.
11. A. Tanner, *Die Sage von Guy von Warwick* (Heilbronn, 1877), p. 14.
12. H. Schelp, *Exemplarische Romanzen in Mittelenglischen*, Palæstra 246 (Göttingen, 1967), p. 138.
13. This is, of course, a common romance motif and need not necessarily have come from the legend.
14. It is also found in several other legends; B. de Gaiffier, "Intactam sponsam relinquens; àpropos de la Vie de S. Alexis," *Analecta Bollandiana* lxv (1947), pp. 157–95.
15. E. Auerbach, *Mimesis*, tr. W. Trask (Princeton, N.J., 1953), p. 118.
16. *Acta Sanctorum*, quæ . . . collegit . . . J. Bollandus, etc., Jul. iv, p. 252.
17. Mehl notes that "the English versions follow their Anglo-Norman source for the most part rather closely and do not change the character of the poem to any significant degree." D. Mehl, *The Middle English Romances*

of the Thirteenth and Fourteenth Centuries (London, 1968), p. 220. The first part of this is quite true, but the second as I shall show is not altogether so.

18. In Auchinleck only; in Caius it is reduced to about one-third the length.
19. The theme also appears in Malory's Grail story. *The Works of Sir Thomas Malory*, ed. E. Vinaver (Oxford, 1947), ii, p. 897.
20. *Gesta Romanorum*, ed. H. Oesterley (Berlin, 1872), p. 564.
21. Auerbach, *Mimesis*, p. 120.
22. Schelp, *Exemplarische Romanzen*, p. 252.

John Capgrave's Life of St. Katharine *and* Popular Romance Style

DEREK PEARSALL

Hagiography and romance have, in general, a good deal of common ground, and the close relationships between the Middle English metrical saints' Lives and the Middle English metrical romances have often been noted.[1] Both forms employ narrative, usually with a single protagonist as hero; both exemplify and celebrate certain kinds of ideal behavior; and, in their typical popular form in the fourteenth century, both are designed to appeal to the same comparatively unsophisticated audience. Further complexities of relationship are introduced by the adaptation as romance of fundamentally hagiographical materials,[2] and by the imitation in popular hagiography of the style and mode of address of the romances. Didactic purposes, of course, are dominant, and the blurring of form which so perplexes the modern scholar, preoccupied with matters of generic definition, is the precise goal of these writers, whether they be entertainers with a touch of piety or hagiographers with an eye for their audience.

The adaptation of romance style in saints' Lives is perhaps one of the simpler ways in which this theme of interconnection can be explored. Indeed, it is a technique which the writers of saints' Lives are very conscious of and which they cultivate deliberately as a means of enhancing the appeal of their work and absorbing the naturally profane instincts of their audience. The opening lines of saints' Lives often echo the mode of address of popular romances,[3] and the author of the prologue which appears in some manuscripts of the *South English Legendary* is quite explicit in his recognition of the need to compete with the romances in both subject matter and style:

> Men wilneþ muche to hure telle . of bataille of kynge
> And of kniʒtes þat hardy were . þat muchedel is lesynge
> Wo so witneþ muche to hure . tales of suche þinge
> Hardi batailles he may hure . her þat nis no lesinge
> Of apostles & martirs . þat hardy kniʒtes were
> þat studeuast were in bataille . & ne fleide noʒt for fere.[4]

However, the more sophisticated type of saint's Life – introduced into English by Chaucer – with its elevated style and rhetorical interpolations,[5] makes no such appeal, and in the elaboration of the type by Lydgate there is a studied avoidance of the popular style and tone of address.[6] It is therefore all the more interesting that there should be traces of the influence of popular romance style in the *Life of St. Katharine of Alexandria* by John Capgrave,[7] who on the whole, as might be expected of such an eminent scholar and theologian, can be counted as a follower of Chaucer and Lydgate in his writing of English verse.

John Capgrave (1393–1464) was born and brought up in Norfolk, probably at Lynn,[8] and entered the order of Friars Hermits of St. Augustine, commonly known as the Austin friars, at an early age. This order had been created by papal decree in 1256 as an amalgamation of separate communities following the rule of St. Augustine. By the end of the reign of Edward II the order had about thirty houses in England,[9] mostly in the prosperous towns of the midlands and eastern part of the country, including Huntingdon, Oxford, Lincoln, York, Norwich, Cambridge, Grimsby, Lynn, Orford, Yarmouth, Boston, and Hull. The order had a reputation for learning,[10] and was active in the mendicant and Wycliffite controversies of the fourteenth century. In the fifteenth century, a number of Austin friars obtained fame as scholars and bookcollectors. None, however, could dispute the preeminence of Capgrave. He was educated at the Austin house in London (1417–1422), and at Cambridge (1422–1425), and probably spent most of the rest of his life at the Austin friary in Lynn, where he was prior at the time of Henry VI's visit in 1446. By this time he had written Latin commentaries on books of the Bible, some of them dedicated to Humphrey, duke of Gloucester,[11] and probably other theological works as well. He had also written a major historical work in Latin, the *Liber de Illustribus Henricis* (completed 1446),[12] and his two works in English verse, the *Life of St. Norbert*[13] dedicated to John Wygenhale, abbot of the Premonstratensian house at West Dereham, near Lynn (Norbert was the founder of the Premonstratensian order), in 1440, and the *Life of St. Katharine*,[14] probably about 1445.[15] In 1450, Capgrave visited Rome for Holy Year, his expenses being paid by Sir Thomas Tudenham of Oxburgh, near Lynn, and on his return wrote *Ye Solace of Pilgrimes*,[16] a guidebook to the antiquities and churches of Rome which has been called "the most impressive English medieval description of Rome,"[17] remarkable alike for its "powers of observation and astonishing accuracy."[18] In 1451 Capgrave composed his English prose *Life of St. Gilbert* for Nicholas Reysby, master of the order of Sempringham, who had admired his earlier *Life of St. Augustine,* also in English prose, and wished for the life of his order's founder to be "translat in þe same forme."[19] These works, along with the *Sermon* on the orders of St. Augustine published at the same time,[20] are part of Capgrave's self-imposed task of creating concord among the different orders that followed the rule of St. Augustine.[21]

In 1453 Capgrave reached the summit of his career when he was elected Prior Provincial of his order in England, a position he held until 1457. He then resumed his work of writing and scholarship, composing a commentary on Acts[22] and a treatise, *De Fidei Symbolis*,[23] both dedicated to William Gray, bishop of Ely. The *Chronicle of England*,[24] in English prose, perhaps his major work, was dedicated to Edward IV some time after 1461. It is clear that during these years Capgrave was operating something close to a publishing house from his headquarters at Lynn, with himself as the main scribe and with other scribes and a binder working under his direction, producing copies of Capgrave's own works, in a standard "house style" of spelling and punctuation, for dedicatees and perhaps for other patrons.[25]

Capgrave's *Life of St. Katharine* was derived, he tells us in his Prologue, from an incomplete and little-known English version, marred by obscurity, "Ryth for straungenesse of hys derk langage" (Prologue, 62),[26] made by a fourteenth-century parson of St. Pancras from an early Latin Life by "Arrek," in turn translated from the Greek Life of the saint by Athanasius. This parson died at Lynn "many ȝere a-goo" (Prologue, 219) and Capgrave took it upon himself to "translate" his work into English and "set it more pleyn" (233).[27] The story is told in five books (8624 lines, with the Prologue): Katharine is brought up, a studious girl, in the household of her father, King Costus, after whose death she is crowned queen (Book I); a parliament is summoned to persuade her to marry, but in vain, since she will have none but a peerless immortal (II); she visits the cell of the hermit Adrian where, in a vision of the Heavenly City, she is united with Christ in mystical marriage (III); she returns, incognito, to Alexandria, where Maxentius, having become emperor, decides to silence her attacks on his pagan idolatry by setting her to dispute with fifty wise men, all of whom she converts (IV); after converting more members of the court, she is finally martyred (V).

In many ways the work can be seen as a continuation of the Chaucer-Lydgate tradition of embellished rhetorical hagiography.[28] The choice of verse form (rhyme royal), the division into books, the apparatus of prologues and envoys, all emulate the elevated style of those writers, and particular passages, such as the exclamation on Fortune,

> O very onsekyrnesse, o chaungand & variable!
> Þou werdly lyffe, for euyr art þou vn-stable!
>
> (i. 874–5)

and the interpolations on the hidden ways of God with his chosen servants,[29] are reminiscent of their methods of amplification. In addition, there are some particular echoes of Chaucer in individual lines and phrases, of which the following may serve as specimens:

> What schuld I lenger in his preysyng tary?
> Cf.   What shold I lenger in this tale tarien?[30]

> It nedyth not herfore to legge auctrorite (ii. 434)
> Cf.   Ther nedeth noght noon auctoritee t'allege
> > (*Knight's Tale*, I.3000)
>
> His wordes wer acordyng to his visage (ii. 574)
> Cf.   Accordant to his wordes was his cheere
> > (*Squire's Tale*, V.103)[31]

Some other apparent echoes are probably drawn from a common stock of proverbial and similar expressions:

> For as wyth me, dunne is in þe myre
> Cf.   And seyde, 'Sires, what! Dun is in the myre!'
>
> This leude doctryne is noʒt wurth a flye
> Cf.   and swich folye
> > As in oure dayes is nat worth a flye.[32]

There are features of Lydgate's style too, in the tendencies toward a pompous and inflated diction which are difficult to avoid for writers working with Latin sources in an exacting verse-form. However, Capgrave is held only fitfully within the orbit of the Chaucer-Lydgate stylistic tradition, and there are other influences at work.

The handling of the rhyme royal stanza, for instance, shows an almost total neglect of its inherent structure. Capgrave uses a form of stanzaic enjambement[33] so licentious that it makes of the stanzaic rhyme scheme a mere episode in the verse paragraph. In individual lines, where there is attention to stress-patterns, which is often not the case,[34] a characteristic tendency is for the pentameter to break down into a loose four-stress line, under the influence of older structural patterns:

> A goode man was he, þis is þe grounde:
> Meke as a mayde, manful at nede,
> Stable & stedfast euyr-more I-fownde,
> strong man of hand, douty man of dede,
> helper of hem þat to hym hade nede.
> > (i. 36–40)

The traditions of alliterative verse are no doubt at work here, as elsewhere in fifteenth-century pentameter verse,[35] but the alliterative phrases are common currency,[36] and on the whole it is the shorter four-stress line of the romances and early Chaucer that asserts itself more in Capgrave's versification:

> If ʒe wyll wete qwat þat I am
> > (*Prol.* 239)
>
> A full longe tyme er he was bore
> > (i. 62)
>
> To kepe his lawes þei shuld not fayle
> > (i. 83)

What distinguishes Capgrave from Chaucer and associates him with
the romances is his technique of rhyming, in particular his resort, under
pressure, to the characteristically arbitrary and inane formulae and phrases
with which the professional romancers fill out their lines. It is these
pressures that produce some of the memorably inconsequential couplets
of *Havelok*, where new "matter" is created out of technical constraint:

> Þe tale of Hauelok is i-maked;
> Hwil he was litel, he yede ful naked.[37]

Capgrave is as frank as any in his recourse to such devices, particularly in
the fifth and seventh lines of the stanza:

> Ther was a preste, of flesch he was ful wan
> > (*Prol.* 47)
> hyr modyr fel down as rownd as any balle
> > (ii. 1461)
> þan fell þat qween down plat to þe grounde,
> hyr corown sche toke of þat was ful rownde
> > (iii. 1175–6)
> After my blood be spilt heere on the grownde.
> Farweel thys world that is shape soo rounde!
> > (v. 1777–8)

The effect of these usages is different from the effect created by the
employment of those conventionally meaningless tags (*ywis, out of dout,
withouten faile,* etc.) which are habitual in all Middle English poetry.
Such usages as the former affect the *sense,* affect it in random ways, and
are not readily acceptable as matters of stylistic texture. In Chaucer they
are subjects for parody only, as with Thopas's "semely nose" (*CT,*
VII. 729).

Sometimes these rhyming line-fillers are systematized according to set
patterns, such as the "numerical" pattern, for which *Havelok* may again
provide a model:

> And fel it so, þat yunge men,
> Wel abouten nine or ten . . .
> > (1009–10)

So with Capgrave:

> And tell forthe of babel & of oþer men
> Whech long to þe kynred, mo þan .ix. or ten.[38]

Chaucer uses such phrases too, but in this case he and Capgrave are borrowing independently from a common source. What we see in Capgrave
is the reversion of these tags – to which Chaucer had given a fresh effec-
tiveness in dramatically appropriate contexts, or which at least he made
part of the *sense,*[39] – to their original cruder functions as line-fillers in
the popular romances.

A favorite type of phrase in *Havelok* is the "inclusive" formula, which provides a rhyming variant for "all men" (or "at all times," "everywhere," etc.) by coupling words of opposite meaning. Simple types of the formula are very common in all Middle English poetry (*more and less, rich and poor, young and old, early and late, east and west,* etc.) but *Havelok* seems to make particularly prominent and varied use of the formula[40] (variation, of course, tends to emphasize the arbitrariness of the usage). One type of formula, *kniht and sweyn,*[41] is characteristically expanded to give a comprehensive list of social ranks, as in the eulogy of King Athelwold:

> Him louede yung, him loueden olde,
> Erl and barun, dreng and thayn,
> Kniht, [and] bondeman, and swain,
> Wydues, maydnes, prestes and clerkes.[42]

Katharine is very similar, in a similar context:

> he was so wel I-know boþe styll & lowde,[43]
> All dede hym homage bothe fer & nere;
> kyng, duke, erle, baron, & bachilere.[44]

Another variant in *Havelok,*

> Alle greten swiþe sore,
> Riche and poure þat þere wore;
> And mikel sorwe haueden alle,
> Leuedyes in boure, knihtes in halle
> (236–9)

seems to provide the model for Capgrave:

> 'þis thyng is not lykly,' þus seyd þei alle,
> ladyes in þe chaumbyre & lordys in þe halle.
> (i. 209–10)

Elsewhere there are variations on the "everywhere" formula:

> God yeue him mikel god to welde,
> Boþe in tun, and ek in felde.[45]

> Cf. he schall haue fortune down for to bete
> All þe bate & stryffe in toun or in strete.
> (iii. 1292–3)

and what looks like an amplification of the "over hill and dale" formula:

> he is now goo forth in hys vyage,
> Be hyllys & pleyn, felde & wyldyrnesse.[46]

Only one character in Chaucer journeys "over hill and dale," and that is Sir Thopas (*CT* VII. 2027).

It would be possible to multiply examples of Capgrave's use of other types of formula, such as the characteristic similes of romance,

Ech lord which had þere any lady & make,
Was ʒoue to courseres, of whech þe on
Was blak as cole, þe othere wythe as bon,
Wyth sadyll & brydyll of gold & of sylke . . .
Sume were ʒoue mantellis wyght as þe mylk,
On whech were many a broche & many a beye[47]

and of his use also of homely proverbs and sayings.[48] Enough has been said, however, to communicate in some measure the impression that a reading of Capgrave's poem invariably gives – namely, that he had access to and used, to a limited extent, the stylistic idiom of the metrical romances.

It will not have passed unobserved that one romance, *Havelok*, has been used extensively for comparative quotation in the above analysis. *Havelok* would in any case serve as an apt representative of the form, but there are particular reasons for thinking that Capgrave knew this very poem. The impression that he had some acquaintance with romance idiom is first created and never again so fully evoked as in the description of the wise, just rule of King Costus, Katharine's father, with which book I begins (l.1–56). It is a description that has no particular function in Capgrave's narrative, or in that of his source.[49] However, it is strongly reminiscent of an impressive passage at the beginning of *Havelok* (27–105), the description of the wise, just rule of King Athelwold, which has a very significant function in the poem's structure.[50] Writers of saints' Lives, as we have seen, were particularly conscious of the need to create an impact at the beginning of a poem, to tap the sources of poetic energy that lay to hand in the romances, and convince their audiences that they could rival the romances in narrative vigor and appeal. Capgrave may have recognized and attempted to profit by the success of a particular romance: the description of Athelwold's reign is a *locus classicus* of its type, and may well have had a special fame. It is a passage from this description that is definitely echoed in the Auchinleck text of the *Anonymous Short English Metrical Chronicle*,[51] and there are interpolated allusions to Havelok in several texts of the *Chronicle*[52] which suggest that the story, and probably the English poem, were widely known. Robert Mannyng, of course, also knew the poem well.[53] The evidence would suggest, in fact, that the poem of *Havelok*, having a recognized claim as history, would have been well known to professional chroniclers, both monastic and secular, and perhaps not unreasonably therefore to a writer like Capgrave.

Capgrave's description of the reign of King Costus is also a gathering-place for other echoes of *Havelok*:

Were it clerc, or were it kniht (77)
Wore he yung, [or] wore he old (1035)

Cf.   Were þei marchauntis, were þei marineris,
      Alle were þei þan to hym as omageris (i. 20–21)

Wis man of red, wis man of dede (180)
Cf.   strong man of hand, douty man of dede (i. 39)

When we find his borrowings from romance idiom falling into a pattern which can readily be deduced from a knowledge of *Havelok*, and when we further find Katharine's coronation celebrated

As well in wrestyllyng as puttyng at þe ston
(i. 763)

as if in reminiscence of Havelok's coronation in Denmark,

Wrastling with laddes, putting of ston
(2324)[54]

we may think it not implausible that Capgrave knew the poem.[55]

Havelok is a poem with strong Lincolnshire associations,[56] and one which, it may be thought, could have been well known in an area so close to the Lincolnshire border as Lynn. Only two manuscripts of the poem survive, one in Bodley MS Laud Misc. 108, the other a series of fragments discovered in the Cambridge University Library early this century and now catalogued as C.U.L. MS Add. 4407 (19).[57] There is evidence to suggest that both manuscripts, the former from the early fourteenth century, the latter from the late fourteenth century, are the work of scribes in West Norfolk.[58] The manuscripts are textually unrelated, which indicates that at least two more manuscripts were in circulation, and almost certainly more. One can do no more in such a situation than create possibilities, but certainly there was nothing to deny Capgrave access to the poem. It is further interesting that *Havelok*, together with *Horn*, forms one part of a tripartite manuscript,[59] the other sections of which are a text (with some additions) of the *South English Legendary*,[60] also of the early fourteenth century, and three saints' Lives from the fifteenth century,[61] together with the poem *Somer Soneday*.[62] The association of *Havelok* and *Horn* with collections of saints' Lives is suggestive, even though it is only the work of a fifteenth century collector or binder, of unexpected ways in which poems like these may have circulated. It would be tempting also to make use of Sir Frederick Madden's early speculation[63] that Havelok's founding of a priory of "monekes blake" (2521) at Grimsby, in memory of Grim, refers to the house of Austin friars there, founded in 1293.[64] The date is right for the poem, which would thus find a historical occasion for its pervasive piety and a direct connection with another Austin friary not far away; but Austin friars are not normally called "monekes blake."[65]

The *Life of St. Norbert*, Capgrave's only other English poem, written somewhat earlier than *Katharine*, makes little use of the features of romance style described above. The treatment of the stanza is similar,[66] and from time to time the movement of the verse has the colloquial four-stress patterning,

> Thei went in reyn thei went in þe snow
> On to þe kne sumtyme. sumtyme to þe thy
> Were þe weye hy or elles were it low
> (f. 6v)

but on the whole the style is sober, dignified and restrained.[67] This is in keeping with the purpose and occasion of the poem – the life of the founder of the order – written at the request of the abbot of the nearby Premonstratensian house at West Dereham, presumably to be read aloud to the assembled canons of the house.[68]

The tone of *St. Katharine* is rather different. Here there is coarse and boisterous detail for the burning of the wise men,

> Weel is hym that may a fagot bere
> To brenne the clerkis! . . .
> There is not ellis but fette, renne and lepe,[69]
> Blowe now faste, the foweris shal not slepe
> (v. 286–92)

and for the making of Katharine's wheel,

> Thei arn called foorth, bothe robyn and Iohn,
> Carpenters and smyghtes, as faste as þei may goon;
> Thei hewe and thei blewe ful soore, leueth me!
> The wheeles musten be redy with-inne dayes thre.
> (v. 1299–302)

There is a touch of rough humor for the death of the sinful Galerius:

> he stank on erthe as ever dede carayn –
> lete hym goo walke on sarysbury ployn.
> (iv. 118–9)

One might admit that the life of a famous and sensationally martyred virgin-saint lends itself in any case more readily to such treatment than the comparatively sober life of the historical Norbert, but there is a further difference. There is much discussion and exposition of Christian dogma in *Katharine*, where Katharine is being questioned by the wise men, and Capgrave consistently abbreviates the arguments put forward by the pagan philosophers against such matters of belief as the Trinity and the dual nature of Christ:

> I suffer tho leuys to ly[e]n stille ful softe,
> lete other men here hem that loue nugacyon.
> (iv. 2114–15)

We may accept his own explanation that his purpose is to avoid prolixity,

> Supposynge that þis same prolyxite
> Wulde make men wery of reedynge to be
> (iv. 2155–6, cf. 2279)

or that the arguments introduced are repetitious (e.g. iv. 2112, 2145),[70] or
that it is difficult to put into English such un-Christian notions:

> It is ful hard swiche þingis for to ryme,
> To vtter pleynly in langage of oure nacyon
> Swhiche straunge doutes þat longe to the
> incarnacion.
> (iv. 2194–6)

But the impatience with such hair-splitting, which we find also elsewhere
(e.g. v. 908 – 12), is no characteristic of the scholar and theologian: it
is characteristic rather of presentation to the uninstructed. It cannot be
good to let layfolk hear any more than the most fatuous arguments against
the faith, and on one occasion Capgrave explicitly refrains from a detailed
description of pagan burial customs for this reason:

> & mych othere thyng
> Was seyd & do, whech nedyth not to rehers,
> For happyly sume folk myght than be þe wers
> To here swech maummentrye & swych-maner rytes.
> (i. 474–7)

It would not be wise to overemphasize this element in the presentation
of the poem, to suggest, for instance, on the basis of such remarks as
that which follows, that the work has been deliberately prepared for oral
presentation to a lay audience:

> Be whom & be whos dayes, ȝe shal sone here,
> If ye wyl be stylle & no man now speke
> But I my-selue.
> (i. 528–30)

Such formulae of delivery[71] are not to be interpreted at face-value, since
they can easily be seen as relics, whereas a reference to 'ȝe reders of þis
lyffe' (iii. 22) is more impressive as evidence of an expectation of private
reading. Perhaps the safest inference is that both kinds of "publication"
are anticipated by the writer, as an envoy in MS Arundel 20 suggests:

> He þat thys lyue wryȝtis, redis or els cvthe here.[72]

Nor would it be wise to underemphasise the sober seriousness of Capgrave's
purpose, the care, for instance, with which he handles the debate in book
II, and the frequent learned interpolations, some of them his own.[73] We
are not in any sense dealing with a "popular" work.[74] But there do seem
to be some concessions to a kind of audience somewhat different from
that to which Capgrave is accustomed, that is, men of religion and learning like himself. It is perhaps for this reason that he has availed himself to
some extent of the traditional style of romance.

It is worth remarking in conclusion that *Katharine* is exceptional among Capgrave's literary production not only in its style of address but also in its bibliographical status. It is the only work of Capgrave's that appears nowhere in an autograph or holograph manuscript,[75] the only work that appears in conjunction with other texts, the only work that has no declared occasion or patron, and the only work that appears in more than two manuscripts. In one of these manuscripts, Rawlinson poet. 118, *Katharine* occurs in conjunction with two short pious tales in the popular style, "The Adulterous Falmouth Squire" and "The Tale of an Incestuous Father and Daughter."[76] It would not do to argue from this that the work is not Capgrave's, nor that, if he wrote it, he was unconcerned about its fate. Nevertheless, it is clear that the *Life of St. Katharine* has a unique place in the Capgrave canon, and that it was, in both senses of the word, the most "popular" of his works.[77]

NOTES

1. E.g. T. Wolpers, *Die englische Heiligenlegende des Mittelalters* (Tübingen, 1964), pp. 188, 190, 195–7, 234, 253–8, etc.; D. Mehl, *The Middle English Romances of the Thirteenth and Fourteenth Centuries* (London, 1968; first published in German, 1967), pp. 17–20, 26, 32, *et passim.*
2. Two valuable recent articles deal with this kind of adaptation: Laurel Braswell, " 'Sir Isumbras' and the Legend of Saint Eustace," *Mediaeval Studies*, 27 (1965), 128–51, and Kathryn Hume, "Structure and Perspective: Romance and Hagiographic Features in the Amicus and Amelius story," *Journal of English and Germanic Philology*, 69 (1970), 89–107.
3. E.g. the Lives of *St. Magdalena* (from Bodley MS Laud Misc. 108) and *St. Marina* (from B.M. MS Harley 2253) printed in *Sammlung Altenglischer Legenden*, ed. C. Horstmann (Heilbronn, 1878), pp. 148, 171 (the former also in *The Early South-English Legendary*, ed. C. Horstmann, EETS, OS 87, 1887, p. 462), and *St. Eustace* (from Bodley MS Digby 86) printed in *Altenglische Legenden, Neue Folge*, ed. C. Horstmann (Heilbronn, 1881), p. 211. In other genres, there is a long prologue in the *Cursor Mundi* (ed. R. Morris, EETS, OS 57, 59, 62, 66, 68, 99, 101, 1874–1893) which assumes an extensive familiarity with the romances and makes a deliberate attempt to capture their audience, while in a fifteenth-century lyric of complaint, the Virgin herself adopts the "minstrel's" form of address: "Listyns, lordyngus, to my tale" (*Religious Lyrics of the XVth Century*, ed. C. Brown, Oxford, 1939, No. 10). Rosemary Woolf criticises the "impropriety" of this opening (*The English Religious Lyric in the Middle Ages*, Oxford, 1968, p. 260), but there seems no good reason to attribute it, as she suggests, to textual confusion.
4. *The South English Legendary*, ed. Charlotte d'Evelyn and Anna J. Mill (EETS, OS 235–6, 244, 1956–9), *Prologue*, lines 59–64.
5. See W. F. Schirmer, *John Lydgate: A Study in the Culture of the XVth Century*, trans. Ann E. Keep (London, 1961; first published in German, 1952), p. 150; T. Wolpers, *Die englische Heiligenlegende*, pp. 301–8.
6. See e.g. D. Pearsall, *John Lydgate* (London, 1970), p. 277–8.
7. I first made this suggestion in an essay on "The English Chaucerians" in *Chaucer and Chaucerians*, ed. D. S. Brewer (London and Edinburgh,

1966), p. 234. It is the business of this paper to offer substantiation for that suggestion.

8. The fullest biography of Capgrave is that of A. de Meijer, O.E.S.A., "John Capgrave, O.E.S.A." in *Augustiniana*, 5 (1955), 400–40. The same writer gives a bibliography of primary and secondary sources in *Augustiniana*, 7 (1957), 118–48, 531–75.

9. For the history of the order in England, see A. Gwynn, *The English Austin Friars in the Time of Wyclif* (London, 1940); F. Roth, O.S.A., *The English Austin Friars 1249–1538*, 2 vols. (New York, 1958–61).

10. The library of the Austin friars at York was of exceptional range and quality. The catalogue (1372) survives, and is printed by M. R. James, in *Fasciculus J. W. Clark dicatus* (Cambridge, 1909), pp. 2–96.

11. Including the two that survive, on Genesis (Oriel College, Oxford, MS 32) and Exodus (Bodleian MS Duke Humphrey b.1, SC 32386).

12. Corpus Christi College, Cambridge, MS 408 (autograph) and B.M. MS Cotton Tiberius A.viii. Edited by F. C. Hingeston, Rolls Series 7 (1858).

13. Huntington Library MS HM 55 (autograph), formerly Phillipps MS 24309, not yet edited. An edition by C. Smetana is promised in the article by E. Colledge, O.S.A., and C. Smetana, O.S.A., "Capgrave's *Life of St. Norbert*: Diction, Dialect and Spelling," *Mediaeval Studies*, 34 (1972), 422–34.

14. B.M. MSS Arundel 20, 168, 396, and Bodley MS Rawlinson poet. 118 (SC 14611). Edited by C. Horstmann, with Forewords by F. J. Furnivall, EETS, OS 100 (1893).

15. It is mentioned as "newly compylyd" by Osbern Bokenham, in the prologue to his own life of St. Katharine (*Legendys of Hooly Wummen*, ed. M. Serjeantson, EETS, OS 206, 1938, line 6356), written soon after 1445, the date of the preceding legend (see line 4982).

16. Bodley MS 423 (SC 2322E, holograph), also fragments in the MSS of *De Fidei Symbolis*, below. Edited by C. A. Mills (London, 1911).

17. G. B. Parks, *The English Traveler to Italy, vol. I: The Middle Ages (to 1525)*, Rome, 1954, p. 350; see also pp. 588–600.

18. C. A. Mills, "Ye Solace of Pilgrimes," a lecture given to the British and American Archaeological Society of Rome, *Proceedings* (1911), pp. 440–65 (p. 447).

19. See the edition of J. J. Munro (cited below), p. 61.

20. All three in B.M. MS Add. 36704 (holograph), and a fire-damaged copy of *St. Gilbert* in B.M. MS Cotton Vitellius D. All three edited by J. J. Munro, EETS, OS 140 (1910). The *Sermon* was one originally delivered by Capgrave at Cambridge in 1422.

21. A well-publicized program which did not, however, inhibit Capgrave from making it clear that the order of Austin friars had the strongest claim to priority of foundation. See G. Sanderlin, "John Capgrave speaks up for the Hermits," *Speculum*, 18 (1943), 358–62; R. Arbesmann, O.S.A., "Jordanus of Saxony's *Vita S. Augustini*: the Source for John Capgrave's *Life of St. Augustine*," *Traditio*, 1 (1943), 341–53. See also *St. Katharine*, iii. 84–90.

22. Balliol College, Oxford, MS 189 (autograph).

23. Balliol College, Oxford, MS 190 and All Souls' College, Oxford, MS XVII.

24. C.U.L. MS Gg. iv.12 (autograph) and Corpus Christi College, Cambridge, MS 167. Edited by F. C. Hingeston, Rolls Series 1 (1858).

25. This has been demonstrated by P. J. Lucas in a series of articles to which

I am much indebted: "John Capgrave, O.S.A. (1393–1464), Scribe and "Publisher"," *Transactions of the Cambridge Bibliographical Society,* vol. V, part 1 (1969), 1–35; "Sense Units and the use of Punctuation Markers in John Capgrave's *Chronicle,*" *Archivum Linguisticum,* new series, 2 (1971), 1–24; "Consistency and Correctness in the Orthographic Usage of John Capgrave's *Chronicle,*" *Studia Neophilologica,* 45 (1973), 323–55. Lucas has also unburdened Capgrave of the massive Latin legendary long associated with him: "John Capgrave and the *Nova legenda Anglie:* A Survey," *The Library,* 5th series, 25 (1970), 1–10.

26. In the EETS edition, MSS Rawlinson and Arundel 396 are printed parallel as far as the end of book III, thereafter the Arundel MS alone. This was the result of a last-minute attempt by Furnivall to make good Horstmann's mistake in accepting Arundel 396 as copy-text: his reproof to Horstmann (p. xxviii) is the liveliest part of one of Furnivall's most endearingly idiosyncratic Forewords. In this essay I quote from Rawlinson (with expansion of final *r* contraction) as far as it is printed, elsewhere from Arundel 396.

27. In Book V (line 62) he reverts of necessity to the Latin. In his sidenotes to the Prologue, and in his Forewords (p. xxiii), Furnivall confused the English priest with 'Arrek' (and consequently spent some fruitless time searching for Arrek in the St. Pancras records). He is followed in this error by A. de Meijer, *art. cit.* (*Augustiniana* 7), p. 565; by Roth, *English Austin Friars,* i. 420; and by A. Kurvinen, "The Source of Capgrave's *Life of St. Katharine of Alexandria,*" *Neuphilologische Mitteilungen,* 61 (1960), 268–324. "Arrek" is presumably "Arechis," who is named in some MSS of the early Latin translation of Athanasius: Kurvinen notes this (p. 275), but explains that Capgrave must have been confused. Wolpers (*Die englische Heiligenlegende,* p. 332) makes the distinction clear.

28. See the valuable discussion of the poem in Wolpers, *op. cit.,* pp. 330–42.

29. E.g. i. 155–75, iii.365–71, v.1368–74, and cf. Chaucer, *Man of Law's Tale, Canterbury Tales,* II. 470–504, 932–45. The edition of Chaucer used here is that of F. N. Robinson (2nd ed., Cambridge, Mass., 1957).

30. *Katharine,* Prol. 139, and *Troilus and Criseyde,* ii. 1622 (also *Man of Law's Tale,* II. 374). See also *Katharine,* i. 469, iii. 180, and cf. *Canon's Yeoman's Tale, CT,* VIII. 1221.

31. Other examples are *Katharine,* v.553, cf. *General Prologue,* 737, *Parl. of Foules,* 566, *Troilus,* ii.1620; and *Katharine,* v.1395, cf. *Knight's Tale,* I. 1870.

32. *Katharine,* ii.1046 and *Manciple's Tale, CT.*IX.5; *Katharine,* iv.1449 and *Franklin's Tale, Ct.*V.1131–2 (cf. *Reeve's Tale, CT.*I. 4192, *Canon's Yeoman's Tale, CT.*VIII.1150, *Parl. of Foules,* 501). See B. J. Whiting, *Proverbs, Sentences and Proverbial Phrases from English Writings Mainly before 1500* (Cambridge, Mass., 1968), nos. D434 and F345.

33. For some extreme examples, see i.819, 889, ii.518.

34. E.g. i.197–203, 589–602, iii.1275–81. Capgrave is evidently little concerned with poetic form as such.

35. C. S. Lewis, "The 15th Century Heroic Line," *Essays and Studies,* 24 (1938), 28–41.

36. Both *meke as a mayde* and *stable and stedfast* appear in Chaucer, the former in *CT, Gen. Prol.* 69, the latter in *Lak of Stedfastnesse,* line 1, and thrice in the prose works (see the *Chaucer Concordance* of J. S. P. Tatlock and A. G. Kennedy, Washington, 1927).

37. *The Lay of Havelok the Dane*, ed. W. W. Skeat; 2nd ed., rev. K. Sisam (Oxford, 1915; rev. 1956), lines 5–6. Cf. 898, 2286–9. It is hardly necessary to multiply examples of such a common feature of the popular romances.

38. i. 559–60. Cf. i. 747, v. 843; also (*ten or twelue*) i. 47, ii. 991, 1167, iii. 858.

39. Like the clerks' bed "ten foot or twelve" from the miller's in the *Reeve's Tale* (CT I.4141) or Criseyde with "nyne or ten" of her women (*Troilus*, iii. 598). For study of Chaucer's use of the phraseology of the romances, see D. S. Brewer, "The Relationship of Chaucer to the English and European Traditions," *Chaucer and Chaucerians*, pp. 1–38; P. M. Kean, *Chaucer and the Making of English Poetry*, 2 vols. (London, 1972), i. 6–10; also J. A. Burrow, *Ricardian Poetry* (London, 1971), pp. 12–23.

40. See the note to *blac and brown*, line 1008, in the edition of Skeat-Sisam, which gives a list of such formulae in *Havelok*. There are extensive lists of these and other romance-formulae in the earlier German editions of romances, e.g. *Sir Orfeo*, ed. O. Zielke (Breslau, 1880), pp. 7–21; *Amis and Amiloun*, ed. E. Kölbing (Heilbronn, 1884), pp. xxxvii–lxx; *Libeaus Desconus*, ed. M. Kaluza (Leipzig, 1890), pp. xcviii–cxxii.

41. See 2025, 2175, 2623, 2885, and variants in 2049, 2083, 2697.

42. Lines 30–33. Cf. 261, 273, 1326, 2183, 2194, 2465.

43. Cf. *Havelok* 955–6: "Him loueden alle, stille and bolde, / Knihtes, children, yunge and olde." For the formula *styll and lowde*, see *Guy of Warwick* (15th c. version, ed. J. Zupitza, EETS, ES 25–6, 1875–6), 792, 2524, 2615, 3214, 3466, 5758, 5862, 8440, 8492, 8570, 10739; *King of Tars* (ed. F. Krause, *Englische Studien*, 11, 1888, 1–62), 230, 290, 467; *Richard Coeur de Lion* (ed. K. Brunner, Vienna, 1913), 748. The formula in Capgrave is introduced with more than usual crudity.

44. *Katharine*, i.10–12. Cf. i. 479.

45. *Havelok*, 2034–5. Cf. 2911; *Sire Degarre* (ed. G. Scheich, Heidelberg, 1929), 168 ("bi sti and strete"), *Horn childe* (ed. J. Hall, Oxford, 1901), 609 ("bi way no bi strete"), *Richard Coeur de Lion*, 4600 (Boþe in hous and eke in ȝerde").

46. *Katharine*, iii. 374–5. Cf. *Beues of Hamtoun* (ed. E. Kölbing, EETS, ES 46, 48, 65, 1885–94), 1829, 3755 ("ouer dale and doun"), *Guy of Warwick*, 8500, 10020 ("be dale and downe"), *Kyng Alisaunder* (ed. G. V. Smithers, EETS, OS 227, 1952), 1766, 3125, 5892, 6059, 7017, 7536, 7769 ("dales and dounes"), *King Horn* (ed. J. Hall, Oxford, 1901), 154, 210 ("bi dales & bi dunes), 208 ("bi dales & bi hulle").

47. Kurvinen, "Sources of *St. Katharine*," p. 317, draws attention to this striking passage (i.768–74) as a specific addition to the source.

48. E.g. ii. 250, 253, 819, iv.21 (Kurvinen notes this point, "Sources of *St. Katharine*," pp. 318–19). Cf. *Havelok*, 307, 648, 1338, 1352, 1635, 1693, 2461, 2983. Again, Chaucer also uses proverbs and homely sayings, but always in such a way as to embed them in a meaningful dramatic context, just as his use of the romance similes (e.g. *Knight's Tale*, CT I 2692, *Troilus*, ii.926) makes them part of the *sense*.

49. For the corresponding passage in the near analog to his presumed source quoted by Kurvinen, see "Sources," p. 296. Kurvinen's careful discussion of the sources of *St. Katharine* is extremely valuable, but it does not bear upon the present argument about style.

50. See Judith Weiss, "Structure and Characterization in *Havelok the Dane*," *Speculum*, 44 (1969), 247–57.

51. See the note in Skeat-Sisam to lines 87–90, and lines 245–6 (especially

A.1063f) in the *Anonymous Short English Metrical Chronicle*, ed. E. Zettl (EETS OS 196, 1935), p. 11; see also pp. 58–9, lines 651–90, also from Auchinleck.

52. See lines 430 (p. 18) and 729 (p. 31) in Zettl's edition, and also his Introduction, pp. lxxvi, lxxxv.

53. See the Introduction in Skeat-Sisam, pp. xv–xxv. For detailed information on the use of the English poem by Latin and French choniclers, see the earlier edition of *Havelok the Dane* by W. W. Skeat (EETS, ES 4, 1868), Preface, pp. iv–xix.

54. For "putting (at) the stone", OED (s.v. *put, v*¹, B. 2) gives only the *Havelok* and Capgrave references before Skelton and Coverdale, whilst Coverdale is the only other writer to link wrestling with stone-putting (s.v. *wrestle, v.*I.1.a.), apart from the couplet quoted in a sermon of the thirteenth century which associates "wrastlynge" with "ston-kasting" (referred to in *Early Middle English Texts*, ed. B. Dickins and R. M. Wilson, London, 1951, note to *Havelok*, p. 179).

55. This is not to suggest that he did not know others. There are a variety of ways in which a knowledge of popular vernacular literature could readily have been acquired by a member of a religious house. Romances of the more pious kind were often associated with religious texts in MSS, and *Havelok* itself is bound up with a version of the *South English Legendary* in Bodley MS Laud Misc. 108 (and called the "Vita Hauelok," as if it were a saint's legend).

56. Ed. Skeat-Sisam, Introduction, pp. xi–xxv.

57. W. W. Skeat, "A New *Havelok* MS," *Modern Language Review*, 6 (1911), 455–7.

58. This opinion (cf. also H. Hupe, "Havelok-Studien," *Anglia*, 13, 1891, 186–200, where the Laud text is placed in Norfolk) has been communicated to me by Professor Angus McIntosh, whose readiness to make available the results of his dialectological researches is, as always, most generous.

59. For accounts of the Laud MS, see *Bodleian Library Quarto Catalogues, II: Laudian MSS* (1858–85, repr. 1973), Codices Miscellanei, no. 108; C. Horstmann, "Die Legenden des MS. Laud 108," *Archiv*, 49 (1872), 395–414; Skeat-Sisam, Introduction, pp. viii–ix.

60. Ed. C. Horstmann, EETS, OS 87, 1887.

61. Viz. Blaise, Cecilia (ed. Horstmann, with the *South English Legendary*) and Alexis (ed. F. J. Furnivall, EETS, OS 69, 1878).

62. For the fifteenth century dating of this poem, see T. Turville-Petre, " 'Summer Sunday,' 'De Tribus Regibus Mortuis,' and 'The Awntyrs off Arthure': Three Poems in the Thirteen-Line Stanza," *Review of English Studies*, n.s. 25 (1974), 1–14.

63. In his note to line 2521 in his Roxburghe Club edition of *Havelok the Dane* (London, 1828), p. 207.

64. F. Roth, *The English Austin Friars*, ii. 64.

65. Austin friars wore a black habit, but it was the Dominicans (who wore a white habit with a black mantle) who were conventionally called "Black friars." There could have been confusion with the Austin or "black" canons, who were often termed "monks."

66. There is at least one very remarkable example of stanzaic enjambement: 'He helde it fast ȝet at þe last he / Loked wisely and sey it was an asch' (ff. 39–39v). *Norbert* is quoted here, with conventional expansion of abbreviations, from a microfilm of Huntington Library MS HM 55. I am grate-

ful to the Librarian and Trustees of the Huntington Library for permission to quote from this manuscript.

67. The only feature of those listed above that appears with any frequency is the numerical tag, *nyne or ten, ten or twelue,* etc. There are examples on ff. 29v, 31, 33v, 37, 38v, 45v. There are odd examples of the 'inclusive' formula: "Go þi wey and ley thi boost adown / Thou may not noye neythir in feld ne toun" (f. 40v), "There schuld no man witʒ hood ne witʒ hat / Take a wey fro hem here possessioun" (f. 44v). The influence of Capgrave's presumed Latin source, the *Vita S. Norberti* (PL 170: 1254–1358), is not significant in the present discussion of style.

68. The circumstances of the commission are, in fact, very similar to those of Lvdgate's *Life of St. Albon* (1439), which was likewise written for the abbot of a nearby religious house (see Amundsham's *Annals of St. Albans,* ed. T. T. Riley, Rolls series 28, 1870–1, vol. II, pp. 256, lxiii) and dignified with the full apparatus of the high style. Capgrave's *Life of St. Gilbert,* commissioned in a similar way, was written in prose, probably because it was intended for the "the solitarye women of ʒour religion which vnneth can vndyrstande Latyn" to read "at vacaunt tymes" (ed. Munro, p. 61). The *Life of St. Augustine,* written for an unnamed "gentll woman" (ed. Munro, pp. 1, 60), is likewise in prose. The inference is that these were less significant "occasions." It would be interesting to examine the punctuation of *St. Norbert,* in relation to that of the prose lives (all, according to Lucas, are in autograph, "John Capgrave, Scribe and 'Publisher,'" pp. 2–3), to determine whether its function is "elocutionary" or "structural and expository" (Lucas, "Sense Units and Punctuation Markers," p. 4), i.e. whether or not it is designed to aid reading aloud.

69. Cf. ii.71: "Now is not ellys but ryde, go & ren."

70. It is probable that Capgrave's original, if we are to judge from the analog quoted by Kurvinen ("Sources," pp. 295–310), was indeed excessively wordy.

71. Cf. also i.558, 567, 576, 585, 608, 1042, iv.839, 944.

72. Quoted in the EETS edition of *Katharine,* p. 450.

73. E.g. i.365, 685, iii.1053 (Kurvinen, "Sources," p. 317). For some of those presumed to be from his source, see i.106, 125, 804, ii.734, iii. 798, 825, v.896. Compare Capgrave's handling of his Latin sources in the *Life of St. Gilbert* (see Jane C. Fredeman, "John Capgrave's *Life of St. Gilbert of Sempringham,*" *Bulletin of the John Rylands Library,* 55, 1972, 112–45) and in the *Life of St. Augustine* (see R. Arbesmann, *art. cit.* in note 21 above).

74. For the contrast of a truly popular work, see the Life of St. Katherine in the *South English Legendary* in MS Laud 108, ed. C. Horstmann, pp. 92–101.

75. See above, note 14. The texts of *De Fidei Symbolis* and of the Commentaries on Genesis and Exodus, though not Capgrave's holograph, have notes of textual revision and annotation in his own hand: in other words they are from his "publishing house" (see Lucas, "John Capgrave, Scribe and 'Publisher,'" p. 4).

76. *Index of Middle English Verse,* ed. C. Brown and R. H. Robbins (New York, 1943), nos. 2052 and 1762. In MSS Arundel 20, 168 and 396 the other contents are miscellaneous religious verse, mostly Lydgatian: see *Catalogue of Manuscripts in the British Museum,* vol.I (1840), Part 1: The Arundel Manuscripts. Two of the MSS have an explicit association

with East Anglia: the hand of the main scribe in Rawl. poet. 118 is that of William Gybbe (see *Bodleian Summary Catalogue*, ed. F. Madan *et al.*, 6 vols., Oxford, 1895–1953, no. 14611, iii.307: the EETS ed. of *Katharine*, p. 403, gives 'Tybbe'), who is probably to be identified with the William Sybbe of Wisbech who is responsible for a text of the *Fasciculus Morum* in Eton College Library (MS 34 in the *Catalogue* of M. R. James, Cambridge, 1895: I should like to thank Mr. Richard Beadle, of St. John's College, Cambridge, for bringing this MS to my notice, and for other help in the preparation of this paper), while Arundel 396 belonged to the Austin nunnery of Campsey Ash in Suffolk (*Katharine*, EETS ed., pp. xxix–xxx). All four MSS have the characteristics of the written East Anglian dialect of the fifteenth century; Arundel 168 presumably also belonged, judging from its contents (lives of St. Christina and St. Dorothea, Lydgate's *Life of Our Lady*, etc.), to a nunnery.

77. It is impossible to know whether the exceptional nature of the poem is in any way due to the parson of St. Pancras, who made the English version from which Cagrave worked (Prologue, 57, 204): he was a west-country man, judging from his language and style, says Capgrave (Prologue, 225).

Malory and the Ballad "King Arthur's Death"

ROBERT H. WILSON

"Kinge: Arthurs Death," in the Folio MS., was seen by Percy as a combination of two ballads, which he separated in the *Reliques*. Under the original title he printed the third person account of Arthur's last battle and disappearance, lines 97–247 as numbered later in the edition of Hales and Furnivall. Lines 1–96, the first person story of Arthur's whole career, he entitled "The Legend of King Arthur," and made an ending for it out of lines 248–51, changing them from third to first person.[1]

The separation and titles were adopted in Child's edition of 1857 and in the Billings and Wells manuals,[2] and have become standard. Percy's judgment of the independence of the "Legend" was confirmed by Millican's discovery of a text of it, including the last stanza in first person, in *A Briefe Discourse of . . . the Nine Worthies . . . Compiled by Richard Lloyd*, London 1584.[3]

For the remainder of the Folio text, "King Arthur's Death," Percy stated that "the old romance *Morte Arthur*," meaning Malory, was the primary source.[4] This inference, obvious as it may seem, is worth establishing in detail, because the issues have been obscured in some comments by medievalists. Furthermore, identifying the texts of Malory which could have been used as a source shows that the "Death" is not the medieval work it is commonly thought to be, but is as Mead suggested, "a sixteenth-century production."[5]

Of the numerous agreements between Malory and the "Death," many are also agreements with the Middle English stanzaic *Le Morte Arthur* (MS. B. M. Harley 2252). Sommer explained the relationship of the three versions by saying that the ballad "seems to go back to the same source as the accounts of Malory and of the poet of 'Le Mort Arthur.'" His view was reflected in the brief Billings references to the ballad.[6]

It is now recognized that Malory used *Le Morte Arthur* itself, and a common source need not be invented to explain his agreements with it.[7] Since inventing one to explain the "Death" would be even more gratuitous, recent accounts of the ballad have abandoned Sommer's explanation, but most are noncommittal about an alternative. Ackerman calls the ballad "a fairly straightforward synopsis of the version of the last battle given by the Stanzaic *Morte Arthur* and Malory," and he thinks of it as roughly contemporary with Malory: "late composition, possibly the end of the fifteenth century." Barber also dates it before 1500, says it "is from Malory, or one of his sources, *Le Mort Arthur*. The latter seems to present a closer version." Miss Newstead refers to "a ballad version . . . summarizing the story in a form similar to that in the stanzaic *Morte Arthur*." Only Fowler says, almost explicitly, that it "summarizes the most famous events of Malory's last book."[8]

In fact, the "Death" reproduces distinctive particulars of Malory's account, sometimes to the point of following word for word a printed text no earlier than Wynkyn de Worde's second edition of 1529. Use of Malory is clearest in two episodes where the ballad includes his expansions on the stanzaic *Le Morte Arthur*.

When the battle leaves Arthur with two companions and Mordred with none, Arthur sees the traitor and says only, "Shall we not brynge thys theffe to ground?" Later, when one of the King's companions has died trying to lift him, Arthur makes no comment but tells the other one to throw Excalibur into the water.[9] Malory has Arthur look over the field and finally observe Mordred, debate with his companions whether to attack him, and in the second scene, make a speech about his dead follower. The "Death," in which the two scenes have become consecutive, reproduces not only the action and the tenor of the speeches in Malory, but also the phrasing italicized below.

The ballad reads:

> *the King looked about him* there
>   & *saw his* Knights all *slaine* to bee;
>
> "*Alas!*" then sayd Noble King Arthur,
>   "*that euer this* sight *I see!*
> to see *all* my *good Knights* lye *slaine*,
>   & the *traitor* yett aliue to bee!
>
> "loe *where* he *leanes vpon his sword* hillts
>   *amongst* his *dead men* certainlye!
> I will goe slay him att this time;
>   *neuer att better advantage I shall him* see."
>
> "Nay! stay here, my Leege!" then said the Duke,
>   "for loue & charitye!
> for wee *haue* the battell *woone*,
>   for yett *aliue wee* are but *3:*"
>
> the King wold not be perswaded then,
>   but his horsse then Mounted hee;
> his Butler t[hat] helped him to horsse,
>   *his bowells* gushed *to his* knee.
>
> "*alas!*" then *said* noble *king Arthur*,
>   "that *this sight I* euer see,

> *to see this* good knight for to be slaine
> for loue *for to helpe mee!"*
>   ("Death," ll. 163–84)[10]

Compare Malory:

Then was king Arthur wroth out of measure, when he *saw his* people so *slaine* from him. Then *the king looked about him,* and then was hee warre that of all his hoost, and of *al* his *good knights,* were left no moe alive but two... *"alas! that ever I* should *see this* dolefull day... would to God that I wist were that *traitour* sir Mordred is, which hath caused all this mischiefe." Then was king Arthur ware *where* sir Mordred *leaned upon his sword among* a great heepe of *dead men.* "Now give mee my speare," said king Arthur to sir Lucan... "Sir, let him be... yee *have wonne* the field; for heere *wee* bee *three on live,* and with sir Mordred is none alive."... "Betide me death, betide me life," said the king, "now I see him yonder alone hee shall never escape my hands, for *at a better vantage shall I never* have *him."...* part of *his bowels* fell *to his* feete. *"Alas!"* said *king Arthur, "this* is unto me a full heavy *sight,* for *to see this* noble duke so to die for my sake... his heart was so set *for to helpe me."* (Malory, III, 333–35)[11]

After observing such evidence that the ballad copies Malory, we cannot be impressed by other portions of the story where *Le Morte Arthur* and Malory are much alike, and details of the ballad might be traced to either one. A few details are closer to *Le Morte Arthur,* and conceivably indicate that the author of the "Death" consulted it as well as Malory,[12] though coincidence is more likely. But the indebtedness to Malory remains unmistakable.

Compare the agreement with Malory for six consecutive words, in the first line of the ballad, with a barely possible borrowing from *Le Morte Arthur* in the second:

> but *vpon a Monday after Trinity sonday*
> this *battaile* foughten *cold bee.*
>   ("Death," ll. 97–8)

... they should meete... *upon a Munday after Trinitie Sunday.* (Malory, III, 330)

> Sone After the feste of the trynyte
> Was a batayle by-twene hem sette,
> That A sterne *batayle* ther *shuld be.*
>   (*Le Morte Arthur,* ll. 3160–2)

In three more passages, verbal identities between Malory and the ballad appear in close succession:

> but *vpon Sunday* in the euening then,
> when the King in his bedd did Lye,
> he *thought Sir Gawaine to him came.*
>   ("Death," ll. 101–3)

And so *upon* Trinitie *Sunday* at night... king Arthur *thought* that there *came sir Gawaine unto him.* (Malory, III, 330)

> *& when* these 2 *osts saw* they *sword drawen,*
> thé Ioyned battell certainlye.
> ("Death," ll.153–4)

And when the *hoosts* on both parties *saw* that *sword drawen...* both hoosts
dressed them together. (Malory, III, 332)

> *then* the Duke *to the* riuer *sid went,*
> *& then* Kings *sword* then *threw* hee:
> *a hand & an arme* did *meete* that sword,
> & flourished 3 times certainlye.
> he *came againe to* tell *the King.*
> ("Death," ll. 226–30)

Then sir Bedivere... *went to the* waters *side;* and... *threw the sword* into the
water... and there came *an arme and an hand* above the water, and *met* it and
caught it, and so shooke it thrise and brandished.... So sir Bevidere *came
againe to the king.* (Malory, III, 336)

To represent the cumulative alterations of the black letter texts, parallels in Malory have been quoted from Wright's reprint of the Stansby
edition. Of the readings in the quotations which stand closer to the ballad
than do their equivalents in the Winchester MS. of Malory, three first
appeared in Caxton: III, 336, *met* for Winchester *toke;* 333, *leaned* for
stood . . . leanyng; 330, the *a* of *on a monday after Trynyte sonday.*
The reading last cited is most obviously Caxton's error, further altered in
DeWorde's edition of 1498 by changing *on* to *upon.* The 1529 DeWorde
text kept this and originated other readings, mostly modernizations, which
the ballad follows. In the quotations we have: III, 334, *vantage* for *avayle;*
335, *bowels* for *guttes* and *king Arthur* for *the kynge;* 330, *king Arthur
thought* for *the kyng semed;* 332, *hoosts* for *oste.* In passages not quoted,
there are *to-morrow* for *to-morne,* if for *&,* *betweene* for *betwyxte.*[13]
For the appearance of these forms in the "Death," there can be no explanation except that its author was reading the 1529 DeWorde or one
of its reprints.

To determine whether it might have been one of these, there is no
convincing textual evidence. Copland, 1557, changed DeWorde's modernization *alyue* back to *on live,* but the ballad-writer might easily have
remodernized. *Vice versa,* the detail that Lucan's bowels *fell to his feete*
for *lay at hys fyete* did not appear until East, 1578 (?); but it is derivable
from the previous sentence. So either of these texts could have been the
source. Stansby, 1634, seems unlikely, since there are no textual agreements, and there would have been little time for oral transmission of the
ballad before it was copied in the Folio MS. of about 1650.[14] But if the
"Death" was not composed in the seventeenth century, it was in the
sixteenth.

Was the "Death," as Percy thought, originally an independent ballad, of which a "fragment" was patched together with the "Legend" by some later minstrel, scribe, or antiquarian? Belief in a once-independent ballad is perhaps shared by Millican, who refers to "partial fusion" with the "Legend." Miss Newstead, certainly, thinks of two works which were "mistakenly combined." Neither writer considers whether the "Death" was originally longer.[15] But its start with no introduction of the characters, in the middle of an account of Arthur's campaign in which the final battle has already been arranged, is so abrupt as narrative, and so different from a ballad-style opening with a dramatic scene, that this would seem to be a necessary part of the hypothesis.

Furnivall suggested that the "Death" was composed as an addition to the "Legend" (so that there was no loss at the beginning). This interpretation is followed tentatively by Ackerman, who assigns the addition to a late fifteenth-century scribe because he thinks it likely that the "Legend" was medieval writing, later used by Lloyd.[16]

However this may be – and there are arguments which cannot be detailed here, that the "Legend" was Lloyd's original composition – it has now been shown that the "Death" itself is a sixteenth-century creation. A date for it in one of the last decades would harmonize with the Arthurian revival near the end of the century,[17] with the availability of East's edition of Malory, and with use of Lloyd's newly published text. But earlier composition, and use of a "Legend" which Lloyd then merely reprinted, may also be conceived without altering the essentials of the problem.

The strongest indication of patchwork is the bad fit between the abrupt beginning of the "Death," which has been referred to, and the end of the "Legend": the narrative switching from first to third person, and from summary of Arthur's career, with three stanzas reporting his last battle as completed, to a detailed account of this battle introduced by *but*. Though the material from Malory could not plausibly have been put into first person, the inventor of a continuation might otherwise, it seems, have done better. Nor do the verse and most of the wording of the "Death" suggest the literary skill to be expected of a continuator. Yet some of this faulty style can be blamed on errors in memorial transmission, some on ballad conventions. And there are signs of originality and good craftsmanship to be noted.

In the handling of Malory's narrative in the "Death" there is more sophistication than has been indicated by references to "summarizing" or a "synopsis." The author's purpose, one can see, was not only to shorten the story but to tighten up the action by telescoping similar materials.

Thus, where in Malory the King has two dreams on the night before the battle, the "Death" omits his dream of Fortune's wheel but retains a few words, from its description of his going to sleep, to introduce his second dream, of Gawain warning him to postpone the battle. In Malory there are two meetings with Mordred. First, Lucan the Butler and Bedivere, with two bishops, go to ask for a delay, but end with an agreement for Mordred to take Cornwall and Kent now, all England after Arthur's death. The second meeting, of Arthur and Mordred between the armies, has nothing to do but ratify this draft treaty. In the single meeting in the "Death," two deputations of knights, and perhaps Arthur and Mordred themselves, confer between the armies, and a truce is agreed on just before the adder's bite precipitates fighting.[18]

In Malory, after Arthur kills Mordred on foot, Lucan and Bedivere help the King to go to a chapel. The chapel, however, is so close by that it is unsafe to stay there when pillagers appear on the battlefield. The knights try to lift Arthur up to take him to town, but Lucan dies from the strain; then, after Bedivere has thrown away Excalibur, he manages to carry the King, on his back, the shorter distance to the waterside scene of his "passing." The "Death" eliminates both of these trips with the King. A river beside the battlefield is where Excalibur is thrown, and where presumably the barge appears. But the author saw the drama in Lucan's death and Arthur's lament for him, and salvaged this part of the chapel scene by having the Butler, earlier, lift Arthur onto his horse to attack Mordred. As a result, in the passage which has already been quoted for verbal parallels, Arthur's sorrow for the knight who died helping him is juxtaposed with his almost identically phrased lament for his army, and his words about risking his own life to punish the traitor who caused the death of so many.[19]

Craftsmanship is also visible in the ways the "Legend" and the "Death" are not just attached one at the end of the other, but adapted to the combination. Millican points out in the "Death" some verbal borrowings from the "Legend," and apparently attributes both them and the combination of the two poems to oral transmission. In couplet 31 of the "Legend" the King says:

> And *afterwards* was *neuer séene*, nor what became of mée
> Was neuer *knowen* vnto this day, for anie *certaintée.*

In the "Death," lines 232–7, Lukin (who is made Arthur's final companion, while Bedivere is the Butler) does not know where the King has gone, for *"neuer after* hee did him *see."* Even after glimpsing the barge, he *"knew* not *certainlye."* A similar parallel, which Millican does not note, exists between couplet 26,

> That *of an hundred thousand men* scarce one *was left* on liue

and the "Death," lines 155–6

Till *of a 100:1000: men*
of one side *was left* but 3.[20]

Since the statement about the casualties exists also in the Folio form of the "Legend" (lines 87–8), repetition in the "Death" through oral transmission of the combined work is a possible explanation for this agreement by itself. But in the Folio "Legend" the *neuer séene* couplet 31 is missing, along with couplets 29–30, which describe Arthur's hand-to-hand combat with Mordred and his going to Avalon.[21]

The Millican interpretation would therefore require us to believe that couplets 29–30, which the "Death" either repeats or contradicts, were cancelled first; couplet 31 was retained long enough to have its phrasing transferred in oral transmission, and then was "cancelled" by accident. But the logical connections between the changes make it much more likely that all the cancellation and borrowing occurred while the "Legend" was still before the eyes of the author of the "Death."

The author eliminated couplet 29 to make room for the longer version of this combat in the "Death." Couplet 32 he moved to the end for a conclusion, and changed it to third person to match the rest of the "Death." From couplet 31 he derived not only some words but the basic idea of Arthur's uncertain fate, which he developed in the "Death" by changing Malory's narrative. In Malory, Arthur's last companion Bedivere comes back to the King and reports on the hand in the lake grasping Excalibur; they talk, and Bedivere carries the king to the waterside; then the barge of wailing ladies arrives and takes Arthur away. But in the "Death," at Lukin's return, the King already "was gone from vnder the tree." Whether he was on the departing barge is not sure. Since the author wished to present this view of the story, he found that couplet 30 of the "Legend," to which the omitted couplet 31 refers in "afterwards," was not uncertain enough. What couplet 30 tells, and what Malory tells, about Arthur's going to Avalon, is therefore omitted from the "Legend"-"Death" combination. Also omitted is the scene in Malory in which Bedivere finds a newly-made tomb which is apparently Arthur's. Thus the King's being simply "gone" produces the utmost strangeness.[22]

It might still be imagined that we have the work of two craftsmanlike balladeers. One composed a telescoped version of Malory, now lost. Another took a portion of this version, made changes from it which have just been discussed as changes from Malory, and effected the combination with the "Legend." If this is indeed what happened, the portion or "fragment" was probably almost the whole of the lost ballad. For to continue in Malory much beyond Arthur's departure would have meant starting on the different story of Lancelot and Gueneuere. At the beginning, a very few stanzas introducing Mordred's revolt and Arthur's return seem more balladlike than a long retelling of the war on the Continent.

A conclusive argument against such a two-stage development of the "Death" is probably impossible to formulate, but the hypothesis seems unnecessary when one continuator could have done everything that has been observed, and the lost ballad need have been so little different from what we now have. Moreover, there are a few details in the "Death" which can be better understood on the assumption that someone wrote it afresh while looking at both the "Legend" and Malory.

In the middle of the "Death," the stanza of lines 153–6 follows Malory (III, 332–3) in reporting that when the armies see a sword drawn, they join battle and a hundred thousand die. There are verbal parallels, already noted, between the first two lines of the stanza and Malory, between the last two and couplet 26 of the "Legend." Insertion or rewording of this last half-stanza as part of a revision of an earlier ballad is not easy to credit.

Near its end the "Death," as has been discussed, lacks the Malory episode in which Arthur's last companion tells him what has happened to Excalibur and helps him toward the barge. The omission of this scene resembles the other telescoping of Malory, yet it is done to develop the conception of the "Legend," that what happens to the King is a mystery. Finally, the two-and-a-half stanzas which conclude the "Death" by following the companion (Lukin) to his own fate are appropriate as an epilogue to Arthur's story *if* it ends with his "passing." But it is hard to see that this small point about Lukin would have been given so much space in a ballad where, like Bedivere in Malory, he found Arthur's tomb; or that a reviser would have gone to the trouble of adding lines about Lukin while he cancelled some about Arthur.

It seems most likely, then, that the "Death" as we have it (with a little allowance for oral transmission) was written as a continuation for the "Legend" by a single author who also revised the ending of the "Legend." It is the simplest hypothesis that this author used the text of the "Legend" published by Lloyd in 1584, and used the East edition of Malory, though it is possible that he worked from older texts.

The "Death" would not, then, be a separate poem, as Percy treated it. But it stands well enough alone, and is so different in literary qualities from the piece it was designed to expand, that there are critical advantages in continuing the tradition of calling it separate. Neither would it be a medieval poem, unless it was written so soon after 1529 that it might loosely be so considered. A piece of archaism in the ballad style, it reproduces from Malory the precipitation of the final battle by what line 147 calls a "woefull chance," though it does not retain the dream of Fortune. It reproduces likewise the timeless appeal of Arthur's self-sacrificing determination to fight Mordred, and his guilt feelings at the death of his Butler. But it is most original when it sees in the traditional narrative a source of romantic strangeness.

NOTES

1. Thomas Percy, *Reliques of Ancient English Poetry* (London, 1765), III, 28–36 (the "Death"), 37–41 (the "Legend"): Book 1 [Book 7 of the whole work in some later editions], nos. 4, 5. *Bishop Percy's Folio Manuscript*, ed. John W. Hales and Frederick J. Furnivall (London, 1867–68 [reprinted Detroit, 1968]), I, 497–507, including quotations of Percy's notes in the MS. The Hales and Furnivall text of the "Death" is reprinted, with a few variations and without its commentary or notes, in *The Percy Folio of Old English Ballads and Romances* (London, 1905–10, limited edition, The King's Library, ed. I. Gollancz), II, 72–78, and the Reliques, ed. Henry B. Wheatley (London, 1886 [reprinted New York, 1966], 1889), III, 35–9.

2. Francis James Child, ed., *English and Scottish Ballads* (Boston, 1857–1859), I, 106–15 (the "Death"), 116–20 (the "Legend"); revised, Boston, 1864, 1880, I, 40–9, 50–4. These two pieces were dropped in *English and Scottish Popular Ballads* (Boston, 1883 [c. 1882]–1898). Anna Hunt Billings, *A Guide to the Middle English Metrical Romances* (New York, 1901; Yale Studies in English, Vol. IX), p. 208n. John Edwin Wells, *A Manual of the Writings in Middle English* (New Haven, 1916), chap. I, nos. 30, 22. The new edition of the *Manual*, ed. J. Burke Severs, Fascicule I (New Haven, 1967), section on Arthurian Legends by Helaine Newstead, nos. 24, 17, follows Wells in titles (and in mistaken page references to the 1857 Child).

3. Charles Bowie Millican, "The Original of the Ballad 'Kinge: Arthurs Death' in the Percy Folio MS.," *PMLA*, XLVI (1931), 1020–4. The *Worthies* is in University Microfilms, English Books 1475–1640, Reel 475.

4. *Reliques*, III, 37, 28 (italics and Roman type reversed in the quotation). Evidence for Percy's meaning of *Morte Arthur* is on I, 181 [1767 edition, 198; 1794 edition, 214], a note on the ballad "Sir Lancelot du Lake" which is obviously Malory versified; III, 25, where Malory is quoted; III, 343 [1767 and 1794, 28], a note on his own additions, some of them recognizably from Malory, to the "Death."

5. William Edward Mead, ed., *The Famous Historie of Chinon of England by Christopher Middleton* (London, 1925; EETS 165), p. xxxiii.

6. H. Oskar Sommer, ed., *Le Morte Darthur by Syr Thomas Malory* (London, 1889–1891), III, 269n. *Guide*, pp. 204n, 208n.

7. See Eugène Vinaver, ed., *The Works of Sir Thomas Malory*, 2nd ed. (Oxford, 1967), pp. 1585, 1615–1616, and for a bibliography including treatments of this source problem, 1627–1628.

8. Robert W. Ackerman, in *Arthurian Literature in the Middle Ages; a Collaborative History*, ed. Roger Sherman Loomis (Oxford, 1959), p. 484. Richard Barber, *Arthur of Albion; an Introduction to the Arthurian Literature and Legends of England* (London, 1961), p. 121. Newstead in the Severs *Manual*, p. 53. David C. Fowler, *A Literary History of the Popular Ballad* (Durham, N.C., 1968), p. 133.

9. *Le Morte Arthur; a Romance in Stanzas of Eight Lines*, ed. J. Douglas Bruce (London, 1903; EETSES 88), ll.3380–3450, quotation l.3389. Subsequent references to *Le Morte Arthur* are to this edition. Any italics will be for emphasis.

10. All quotations from the "Death" are from Hales and Furnivall; italics will be for emphasis. The Duke (of Gloster) is Lukin.

11. Malory quotations here and later (with italics for emphasis) are from *La*

Mort d'Arthure. The History of King Arthur and of the Knights of the Round Table...from the Text of the Edition of 1634, ed. Thomas Wright (London, third edition, 1889, reprinted from the second edition, 1866 [some copies 1865]; the first edition, 1858 [not 1856] has slightly different paging). Caxton's Book XXI, chaps. iii–vii (these numbers providing reference to the early texts and most modern editions, including Vinaver's *Works of Sir Thomas Malory*) include the quoted passage and the text of Malory paralleling all of the "Death."

12. "Death," ll.121, 130, Mordred and Arthur each take twelve companions to the final conference, matching Mordred's suggestion in *Le Morte Arthur*, ll.3280–1, that Arthur bring "xij knyghtis or fourtene," whereas in ll.3332–7 and Malory, III, 332, fourteen attend. Verbal parallels which, if they are not accidental, would mean that the author of the "Death" kept his eyes on two almost identical sources, exist between l.145, "an Adder came forth of Bush," and Malory, III, 332, "came... out of a little heath *bush,* "Le Morte Arthur,* l.3341, "glode *forth* vpon the grownde"; l.192, "& gaue his father a wound certainlye," and Malory, III, 334, "smote *his father* Arthur," *Le Morte Arthur,* l.3397, "*yaff* Arthur *A wound.*" In l.239, and in *Le Morte Arthur,* ll.3524–5, Arthur's companion *found* a chapel, whereas in Malory, III, 337, he *was ware* of it. In the "Death," l.217, and *Le Morte Arthur,* l.3471, Arthur's last companion, on his second trip to throw Excalibur into the water, throws its scabbard, whereas in Malory, III, 336, he throws nothing. But if there is borrowing here, rather than coincidental agreement, the more probable source would seem to be the original of both *Le Morte Arthur* and Malory, the prose romance *La mort le roi Artu,* ed. Jean Frappier (Geneva, 1954), sec. 192; compressed version, *Histoire, contenant les grandes provesses.. . . de Lancelot du Lac* (Lyons, 1591), p. 163. For in the *Mort Artu,* the knight not only throws the scabbard on the second trip; on the first, he throws his own sword, as in the "Death," l.205, but not either *Le Morte Arthur,* l.3460, or Malory, III, 336. The ballad's author, as distinguished from an uncultivated reteller, might conceivably have read this French work, or might have heard its story line reported.

13. On Wright and the early texts, see Eugène Vinaver, *Malory* (Oxford, 1929), pp. 190–3. DeWorde 1498 has been collated in the reprint ed. A. S. Mott, *The Noble & Joyous Boke Entytled Le Morte Darthur* (Oxford, 1933), and in microfilm of the surviving copy by kindness of the John Rylands Library, Manchester; DeWorde 1529 in University Microfilms, English Books 1475–1640, Reel 16. All readings cited in this paragraph fall within Caxton, XXI, iii–v. Variants are quoted in the spelling of Winchester (ed. Vinaver, *Works*) for the earlier form, or of Wright for the later. Here, "on a monday..." is from Sommer's edition, a type facsimile of Caxton, III, 843; "&" in Caxton, where it too first appeared, is from Vinaver's textual appartus, p. 1234. Vinaver also records "mette" and "lenyd," pp. 1240, 1236. "As to-morrow day," in the "Death," l.107, corresponds to Wright, III, 331, "and yee fight as to morrow"; "to parle... if itt might bee," l.120, to III, 331, "if they might take a treatise"; "betweene those 2 hosts," l.132, to III, 332, "betweene both their hoosts." Sommer, II, 43ff., gives an incomplete collation of DeWorde 1529, with the generalization that modernization of language and uniform use of the full name "King Arthur" are characteristic of 1529.

14. "Death," l.176, "yett aliue wee are but 3"; Caxton, XXI, iv; Wright, III,

333. Line 180, "his bowells gushed to his knee"; Caxton, XXI, v; Wright, III, 335. The Copland, East, and Stansby texts have been collated in English Books 1475–1640, Reels 521, 194, 949. See n. 13, and for the dating of East, Josephine W. Bennett, *The Evolution of "The Fairie Queene"* (Chicago, 1942), p. 76, n. 46. Instead of the misprint in DeWorde 1498, "alyue" is quoted from 1529.

15. *Reliques*, III, 28 (also, in 1765, 343); opinions repeated in Billings, p. 208n, and Wells, p. 51. *PMLA*, XLVI, 1023. Newstead in the Severs *Manual*, p. 53.

16. *Bishop Percy's Folio Manuscript*, I, 497 (for Furnivall's authorship of this introductory note, see I, v). Ackerman in *Arthurian Literature in the Middle Ages*, pp. 484–5.

17. Bennett, *Evolution of "The Fairie Queene,"* pp. 68, 77–9.

18. Malory: Wright, III, 330–2; Caxton, XXI, iii–iv; "Death," ll.101–44.

19. Malory: Wright, III, 334–7; Caxton, X[I, iv–v; "Death," ll.165–231.

20. *PMLA*, XLVI, 1022–4: Millican's opinion, and Lloyd's text of the "Legend" reprinted from *Worthies*, fol. F 1 (italics added in the quotations). Malory (Wright, III, 333; Caxton, XXI, iv) has the fact of the casualties but not the verbal tags: "by that time was there an hundred thousand laid dead upon the doune."

21. Folio "Legend" in Hales and Furnivall; reprinted in Gollancz, II, 69–72, and in Wheatley, pp. 39–43, with Percy's variations, which include changing the first word of l.87 from *that* to *till* and thus increasing the resemblance to the "Death" (change not noted by Wheatley).

22. "Death," ll.228–39; Malory: Wright, III, 336–9, Caxton, XXI, v–vi.

bi lag mon: *A Crux in*
Sir Gawayn and the Grene Knyȝt

WILLIAM MATTHEWS

In *As You Like It,* Touchstone sings a song which contains a gay, mocking refrain:

> And if it come to pass
> That any man turn ass,
> Leaving his wealth and ease
> A stubborn will to please,
> *Ducdame, ducdame, ducdame.*
> (Act II. Sc.v.)

Furness in his Variorum edition of the play cites an abundance of commentary on the problems that innocent gaiety raises: what does it mean, where did it originate? The many answers are heavy with learning, fascinating in their irrelevant detail, and provide not one single satisfying solution. And at the close, Furness quotes Touchstone's reply to Amiens's query about the phrase – " 'Tis a Greek invocation, to call fools into a circle."

In *Sir Gawayn and the Grene Knyȝt,* in the middle of the great fox-hunt, when Reynard is leading Bertilak and his meiny a merry chase, this line occurs (1729): "and ȝe he lad hem bi lag mon, þe lorde and his meyny". The problem of what "bi lag mon" means has proved a pretty one and raised much discussion; not so much as *ducdame,* but enough. In her rather nice translation, Marie Boroff renders it "merrily tormenting them"; in his better one, Brian Stone gives "Yes, he led the lord and his liegemen a dance"; and Emil Pons in his neat French version renders it: *"il les menait, tout crottés"* ("he led them, all covered with mud").

Sir Frederic Madden (*Sir Gawayn,* 1839) bound up the two words into a compound, "bi lagmon"; but in his notes he is silent and in his glossary he ventured no more clarification than a question mark. Richard Morris, in his 1864 edition of *GGK* for the EETS, repunctuated "lad hem bi lag, mon, þe lorde and his meyny." In the margin he sensibly glossed "led them astray"; but in his glossary, like Reynard, he shifted his tack: "Lag = lagh = law = low(?)." Israel Gollancz, who fancied his skill in bringing old texts into good sense – he almost rewrote *Death and Life* – revised Morris' edition in 1897. There he most ingeniously misemended to "bilagged

151

men," a change, it seems, that A. S. Napier had independently proposed in his lectures. In Middle English, *bilag* is recorded as meaning *esclaté*, *madidatus*, clogged with wet mud (Bibbesworth c. 1300, *Prompt. Parv.* c. 1440: cf. OED, *belag*). By this change a new *aperçu* was brought in: the poet's and the reader's eye was now not on the fox but rather on his muddy chasers. The emendation has since been dropped, and very rightly so; but its point of view lingers on. In the Tolkien and Gordon edition of 1925 (whether out of deference to Gollancz or out of that abiding Oxford devotion to the memory of Napier it is hard to say), this emendation was accepted, "bilagged men;" and it was presumably from there that Emil Pons in 1946 derived his *tout crottés*. The emendation, however, must have been removed later, for the 1936 reprint has "bi lagmon" (I have not seen the 1930 reprint). Tolkien and Gordon in this edition state: "the sense can only be guessed at: perhaps 'led them by devious ways.' "

In 1931, the late great Robert J. Menner published a new insight that he had gained as he supervised Miss Whiting's dissertation at Yale University. (Menner, "Middle English 'Lagmon' [*Gawain* 1729] and Modern English 'lag' " [*PQ* 1931, 163–8]; the dissertation was published as: Ella Keats Whiting, ed., *The Poems of John Audelay*, EETS 184, 1931.) Menner noticed that in poem No. 54 Audelay used the same phrase as in *GGK* – the only other known instance. He made the most of the observation. I will briefly restate what he says and add some little things of my own.

Audelay's fine poem is similar to the first part of *Awntyrs of Arthur*. Three kings, out hunting, are greeted by three ghostly figures, who prove to be the ghosts of their fathers. These ghosts warn the living kings of their various sins and then disappear. The second king's warning includes these lines:

> And ȝif ȝe leuyn vpon Crist and on His lore lerys,
>   Leuys lykyng of flesche and leue not þat lare
> For warto schuld ȝe leue hit, hit lyus: [i.e. "lies"]
> Hit ledys ȝoue be lagmon be lyus
>
>   (111–4)

Menner deduces from the two uses that the true meaning is the same as that of Modern English *lagman* (derived from *lag*), the hindmost person. Under "lag" – "slow, tardy, sluggish" – the *English Dialect Dictionary* cites "lagman": "an epithet applied to the last of a gang of reapers or mowers," its authority being C. H. Hartshorne, *Salopia Antiqua*, London, 1841. Menner also declares that the *EDD* has other western dialect usages of the word; but if it has they escape my own wandering eye. Menner thinks it probable therefore that a lagman was a man who lingered or stayed behind. He admits that Morris' suggestion, "led astray," makes sense for both contexts in which "bi lagmon" is used; but somehow he feels there is something fishy about a meaning that is merely suggested by context. Somehow, even the last man in a line does not quite appease his hunger for full apprehension: the true meaning he suspects is something more lively. Evidently "bi lagmon" is a colloquial idiom – it may be a proverbial idiom, or it may relate to a game. There Menner cries quits and leaves the problem to the folklorists. Having thus left his last reaper or last mower dangling in midair, he trants off like Reynard to etymology. The word "lag" is often said to be Celtic in origin (cf. Welsh *llag*, slack, loose, sluggish). But according to the Oxford English Dictionary this is highly improbable, and Menner thinks the word more likely comes from Old Norse. He cites *lagga* as used in the Borgholm dialect of Swedish, where it means "to wander aimlessly about; to become sluggish"; and he notes too that in the Shetlands "lag" means "to loiter."

The next (1940) EETS edition of *GGK* has a note by one of its editors (my guess is that it was Mabel Day rather than either Mary Serjeantson or Sir Israel Gollancz) that "*E.D.D.* gives 'Lagman' as last of a gang of reapers in Shropshire, so that the true meaning may be 'leads you so that you come out last.' He [Menner??] suggests a derivation from Norw. dial. *lagga*, to go slowly and evenly." In his little revision of Tolkien and Gordon's edition (1967), Norman Davis states: "The only known parallel is 'Hit [*sc.* lust] ledys ʒou be lagmon' in the fifteenth-century Shropshire poet Audelay (ed. E. K. Whiting, E.E.T.S. 184 (1931) p. 232, l. 114). *Lagman* was used in western dialects for the last of a line of reapers. The picture intended is evidently of the lord and his company strung out after the fox – 'at his heels.' See Menner, *P.Q.* x (1931) 163–8."

Concerning this most recent interpretation of *bi lag mon*, however, there is the question of date and there is the question of likelihood. The *EDD*'s citation for the meaning "the last of a gang of reapers or mowers" comes from a book dated no earlier than 1841. To that I can throw in an earlier citation taken from the *OED*. It comes from the burlesque panegyric of the red herring, Thomas Nashe's *Lenten Stuffe*, 1599: "The Essex calfe, or lagman, who had lost the calues of his legs by gnawing on the horslegs." In simpler form, "lag," meaning the last person in a game, occurs in one of Barclay's eclogues in 1514, and the related verb, meaning to fail to maintain a desired rate of progress, is recorded first from Palsgrave 1530. The weight of the evidence is that "lag" and "lagman," with these meanings, may be pretty much latecomers, too late to be applied in explanation of "bi lagmon" in either *GGK* or Audelay's 54th poem.

As for likelihood, the new reading proceeds from the same *aperçu* that Gollancz needed when he amended to *bilaggid* "muddy," namely that the reference of the phrase is to Bertilak and his meiny. About the kings and lust in Audelay's poem, which is follower and which followed raised no man's curiosity – a sorry slight to a good alliterative poem, whose poet may well have read *GGK*. Yet from any straightforward reading it seems crystal clear that in the one poem the reference is to Reynard and that in the other it is to lust: "And ȝe he [Reynard] lad hem bi lagmon, þe lorde and his meyny"; "Hit [lykyng of flesche] ledys ȝoue be lagmon be lyus." With all due respect to several old friends, some dead, some still kicking, I would suggest that in both good grammar and good sense the phrase attaches to the leader and not to the led, and that the last man in a line of Shropshire reapers or an Essex sheep that has lost the use of its legs by gnawing on a horseleg or with Audelay's sadly disturbed kings as the dappled cow that jumped over a green Wiltshire moon in 1097.

From living and linguistic contexts, the meaning of "lad by lagmon" seems as plain as the back of your hand – "led astray." But what is its connotation? Is it to be sought from speirs and nitzes, or groped for in the foggy branches of the golden bough? Or is it something simpler, more familiar? And here, as one who prefers plain mutton in scholarship (with occasional caper sauce), I would venture a suggestion. Norman Davis, of all people, as Director of the EETS, must be more familiar than most with a book the nonprogress of which he has been watching for some eleven long years – years while the EETS has tapped its foot with still more reiterations of the *Ancrene Riwle*, feeble flickers of an inspiration long since spent.[1] I refer to the *Brut*, by a western poet named Laȝamon. Laȝamon's name, as every schoolboy knows, is the old form of "Lawman." The Anglo-Latin form, *lagamannus*, first recorded by the *OED* for the year 1000, was current among lawyers well into the seventeenth century and was often anglicized as *lageman* (see *OED*, *lawman*). The *OED*'s citations are solemn; but no medievalist needs any instruction or any exempla as to what a lawman meant in the way of trickery, guile, deceit to a medieval man, nor as to how closely he was associated with the fox and with the deadly sins:

> Santus Yvo erat Brito
> Advocatus et non latro,
> Res mirando populo.[2]

With the temerity that may go before a fall, I therefore propose that "lad bi lagmon" means simply "cunningly led astray," and that if the idiom were still fresh at the time the two poems were written that it carried the implication, "like a lawyer." An appropriate annotation for yet a further edition of *GGK* might therefore be:

1729. lad hem bi lagmon. Variously interpreted: "led astray" (Morris 1864); amended to *bilaggid* 'muddy' (Gollancz 1897; Tolkien and Gordon 1925); connotes last man in a line, referring to Bertilak (Menner, *PQ* 10, 1931), cp. "to lag"; "led to come out last" (Gollancz, Serjeantson, Day, 1940); "at his heels" (Davis, 1967). Probably, however, simply "cunningly led astray" with possible connotation "like a lawyer" (cp. "lawman" *OED*; cp. Book and Leslie, *Laȝamon, Brut*, I, EETS 250, 1963).

NOTES

1. It is good news that Roy Leslie, frustrated for several years, is now putting the finishing touches to Volume II of the *Brut*.
2. Cited from David Mellinkoff, *The Conscience of a Lawyer* (St. Paul, Minn., 1973), p. 13. The introduction to this fine book, "Love all the lawyers," is a lively survey of popular thinking about one of the world's oldest professions – "in close order after whoring and pimping."

Isolt's Trial in Béroul and La Folie Tristan d'Oxford

ERNEST C. YORK

In the *Tristan* of Thomas and its derivative versions, Isolt clears herself of the charge of adultery by undergoing the ordeal by hot iron. After going through the prescribed legal preliminaries, she carries the glowing iron without getting so much as a single blister on her queenly hands. She is thus proved innocent.[1] In Béroul a different kind of trial takes place. It is the trial by oath. Standing between Mark and Arthur, Isolt swears her well-known equivocal oath on the holy relics. All declare "si fiere en jure/Tant en a fait aprés droiture."[2] And Arthur pronounces her innocent.

In this type of trial the defendant must swear an oath denying the charge made by the plaintiff. In most instances the accused must also have a number of oath helpers who swear that he is oathworthy, that is, that he has a reputation for telling the truth. Under the influence of the church, this type of trial came to be known as compurgation, and the oath helpers were called compurgators. During the centuries in which the Tristan legend developed, the trial by compurgation was practiced by all the nations to whom the legend was known. It was the usual mode of procedure in France, England, and Germany. In the earlier centuries of the Middle Ages, it was employed by the Franks, the Celtic nations, and the Anglo-Saxons. Down to the thirteenth century, compurgation was used for both criminal and civil cases. It was competent for all types of crimes provided that the accused was not caught in the act or that there was no clear presumption of guilt. The number of compurgators required in a given case varied widely among the different codes. It depended in part on the gravity of the charge and on the rank and reputation of the defendant. From fewer than six to over a hundred might be required.[3]

In Isolt's case, no oath helpers are employed. The queen clears herself by her own oath. This variation from the more normal use of compurgators is also historical legal procedure. There were many instances in which the single oath of the defendant was sufficient. It was common usage under the old Norman customary law, in which it was known as *deraisne*. This was still employed in France in the thirteenth century in civil cases or for minor offenses at a time when the use of oath helpers was becoming rare. The use of the single oath is recorded among the French in the twelfth century and among the northern and southern Germans. Historians of Anglo-Saxon law frequently cite cases in which it was used, and in later English law it was sufficient for the person of high rank. In Welsh law, however, the single oath hardly prevailed. The Welsh laid great stress on oath helpers and employed two classes of them. The single oath was used only under very limited conditions.[4]

From all of this we can draw two conclusions. In depicting Isolt's trial, Béroul is reflecting historical legal custom as it was practiced in his own day and earlier. In spite of several Celtic analogues, he can hardly be reflecting a Welsh procedure.

In a recent study of Isolt's equivocal oath, the author's chief concern is to point out Oriental analogues. According to this view,

Béroul's emphasis upon the successful trick and the cruder elements of Isolt's behavior closely resembles the treatment of the story in the Oriental versions, despite the omission of the ordeal that verifies the ambiguous oath. In Thomas, the ordeal rather than the ruse is stressed, so that the scene of Isolt's public trial strongly suggests similar ordeals in which falsely accused queens are vindicated.[5]

But the passage also implies that Béroul intentionally omitted the ordeal in order to emphasize the equivocation of the oath. It is with this that I disagree. The oath played a part in the ordeal just as it did in the trial by compurgation. In the ordeal by hot iron, the accused was required to take an oath denying the charge made by the plaintiff. This was part of the preliminary procedure before the defendant actually carried the iron.[6] Now, in the versions of the Tristan story which describe a trial, Isolt's equivocal oath serves both as the preliminary oath in those versions which depict the ordeal and as the exculpatory oath in the trial by compurgation. In Béroul's version of the trial, the equivocation of the procedure – the great hoax of it all – gets more emphasis than it does in those versions depicting the ordeal. But the emphasis on equivocation in Béroul is due rather to the nature of the trial itself. In this type of trial the oath is the central feature rather than a preliminary part of the procedure.

Nor is there any reason to trace the equivocal oath to the "ancient Hindu ritual known as the Act of Truth, which rests on the belief in the magical power of a truthful statement. . . . When this story [the typical Oriental version] reached the Occident, the European version, of course, substituted for the Act of Truth a Christian oath and an ordeal."[7] I do not believe the twelfth-century French writer needed to know about the Hindu ritual any more than he needed to know of the biblical fidelity test, the Waters of Bitterness (*Numbers* 5: 11–31), to which another recent critic has traced Isolt's trial.[8] The fact is that both the trial by oath and the ordeal were practiced by most of the nations of the Western world long before the Tristan legend developed, and at the time the trial was first included in the story, both forms of trial had long been under the jurisdiction of the church and were administered by ecclesiastics. If the medieval writer knew some Oriental analogues, though it is not at all certain how he would get them, all the better for him.[9] What I wish to emphasize here is that the authors of both types of trials are depicting historical legal procedure of their own periods. They could as well have witnessed such trials as read of them in contemporary romance or Oriental tales. Thomas chose the ordeal; Béroul the trial by oath. Both were contemporary procedures.

The short poem known as *La Folie Tristan* has come down in two versions, the Oxford and the Berne. The Berne makes no reference to Isolt's trial; the Oxford does. In the Oxford version, Tristan, disguised for his own protection, meets with Isolt, and in order to get her to recognize him, recalls a number of incidents in their life together before he went into exile. Among others, he refers to her trial by asking her if she remembers the oath that she took:

> Isolt, membre vus de la lai
> Ke feïtes, bele, pur mai!
>
> . . .
>
> Par tant fustes, ce je l'entent,
> Ysolt, guarie al jugement
> Del serement e de la lai
> Ke feistes en la curt le rai.[10]

From this passage it is clear that Tristan supposed that she would surely remember taking the oath. He does not mention the ordeal. Of course, the equivocal oath was part of a great hoax, a hoax in which Tristan himself had taken part, which from their present distance both he and the queen might well find amusing. But surely if he were referring in these lines to the ordeal, he would have asked her to remember her precarious walk with the hot iron, an incident not likely to be forgotten, and one to which the oath was only a preliminary procedure. Certainly, the ordeal by hot iron would have a lasting impact on the participant. It was no small moment in the life of the accused. Anxious to be acquitted of a serious charge, fearful of having her hands burned to a crisp, the defendant had to carry the glowing iron at least three feet before dropping it, and all of this in public before the mightiest of the land and after a rigorous formal ceremony which alone must have put every nerve on edge. If Tristan had this terrifying experience in mind, then simply asking Isolt to remember the oath preliminary to the ordeal is, indeed, a very strange way to prod her memory. It is simply not realistic. Furthermore, the terminology Tristan uses is significant when he says to Isolt, "membre vus de la lai/Ke feïtes" (ll.817–8). The expression "to make one's law" is the way the trial by oath is regularly referred to in the legal literature of the period. It is the standard terminology for the procedure.[11] And the expression is repeated in lines 833–4. In all probability, then, Tristan is referring to the trial by oath as depicted in Béroul.

This means that the author of the Oxford *Folie* drew on the same version of the story as Béroul, since Béroul is the only one to depict the trial by oath. One poem depicts, the other refers to, this very unique plot incident. The fact that the author of the *Folie* evidently did not know of the ordeal by hot iron raises a question about the validity of the traditional theory that the poem derives from Thomas. This theory was set forth by Bédier, and has been accepted by all subsequent editors and critics.[12] Bédier assumed that the episode was in Thomas, but, more to the point at hand, he did not at all distinguish between the two types of trials. It was the courtly tone of the Oxford *Folie* which he thought chiefly allied it to the *Tristan* of Thomas. The present study indicates that it more likely derives from Béroul, and that the anonymous author himself gave it the courtly tone.

NOTES

1. The ordeal by hot iron is not in the extant fragments of Thomas but is known from Bédier's reconstruction. It is in Gottfried's *Tristan and Isolt*, the *Tristrams saga*, and *Sir Tristrem*.

2. Béroul, *Le Roman de Tristan*, ed. Ernest Muret, 4th ed., rev. (Paris: Libraire Ancienne Honore Champion, 1957), 4219–20. The trial in Béroul (ll.3032–4268) is in that portion of the work which some scholars attribute to a continuator.

3. Henry Charles Lea, *Superstition and Force*, 4th ed. (Philadelphia: Lea Brothers & Co., 1892), Chaps. 2–7; A. Esmein, *History of Continental Criminal Procedure*, trans. J. Simpson (London: J. Murray, 1914), p. 57; W. S. Holdsworth, *A History of English Law*, 3rd ed., rev. (Boston: Little, Brown, 1922), I, 396, II, 109; Sir Frederick Pollock and F. W. Maitland, *The History of English Law*, 2nd ed. (Washington, D.C.: Lawyer's Literary Club, 1959), II, 600; J. B. Thayer, *A Preliminary Treatise on Evidence* (Boston: Little, Brown, 1898), pp. 16, 24–25; *Essays in Anglo-Saxon Law* (Boston: Little, Brown, 1876), p. 298; T. P. Ellis, *Welsh Tribal Law and Custom in the Middle Ages* (London: Oxford University Press, 1926), II, 303, 306–7; *Ordeals, Compurgation, Excommunication, and Interdict*, ed. Arthur C. Howland (Philadelphia: University of Pennsylvania Press, 1898), p. 3.

4. Esmein, p. 57; Lea, pp. 22–4; *Essays in Anglo-Saxon Law*, p. 297; Thayer, p. 24; Ellis, II, 306–7. In Marie's *Lanval*, where we might expect a Welsh procedure, the hero clears himself with oath helpers, although the trial is not actually for a legal issue (Ed. J. Rychner, Textes littéraires français, No. 77, Paris, 1958, ll.416–25).

5. Helaine Newstead, "The Equivocal Oath in the Tristan Legend," in *Mélanges offerts à Rita Lejeune* (Gembloux: Duculot, 1969), II, 1082.

6. Holdsworth, II, 106–7; Esmein, pp. 56–7.

7. *Mélanges*, II, 1081.

8. *King Artus*, ed. and trans. Curt Leviant (New York: Ktav, 1969), p. 102.

9. Helaine Newstead admits that "it is difficult to determine exactly how [the Oriental story] reached the Tristan legend." See her article "The Origin and Growth of the Tristan Legend" in *Arthurian Literature in the Middle Ages,* ed. Roger Sherman Loomis (London: Oxford University Press, 1959), p. 131.

10. *La Folie Tristan d'Oxford,* ed. Ernest Hoepffner, 2nd ed., rev. (Strasbourg: Publications de la Faculté des Lettres, 1943), ll.817–8, 831–4.

11. M. M. Bigelow, *History of Procedure in England* (Boston: Little, Brown, 1880), p. 303. The fact that in the Norman period this terminology was also used for the ordeal hardly weakens the point.

12. *Le Roman de Tristan par Thomas,* ed. J. Bédier, *SATF,* No. LIII (Paris, 1905), II, 282–96, 372–9; *Deux Poèmes de la Folie Tristan,* ed. J. Bédier, *SATF,* No. LIV (Paris, 1907), p. 2; *La Folie Tristan d'Oxford,* pp. 7–12; Frederick Whitehead, "The Early Tristan Poems," in *ALMA,* p. 144; Sigmund Eisner, *The Tristan Legend* (Evanston: Northwestern University Press, 1969), p. 31.

The Heavenly Letter in Medieval England

W. R. JONES

One of the most famous medieval forgeries was the mysterious letter from Christ admonishing Christians, under threat of divine punishment, to preserve the sanctity of Sunday and the saints' days by avoiding servile labor and other demeaning secular activities at these holy times. The letter claimed to have fallen from heaven or else to have been brought to earth by the Archangel Michael, who deposited it on the altars of such illustrious churches as St. Peter's Sepulchre in Jerusalem or St. Peter's, Rome. Various editions of the letter differed as to the means of its transmittal and the place or circumstances of its reception. Reference to the Archangel Michael was sometimes omitted; its point of descent was identified variously as Jerusalem, Bethlehem, or Rome; an assembly of clergy, which was said to have examined it, was located in Cappadocia, Armenia, Arabia, or Palestine; and some copies said that it had been sent to Rome for the pope's consideration. Similarly, the texts of different versions of the letter varied in detail – the product of the tastes or interests of successive editors and copyists. Some added to the requirement of honoring the Lord's Day such supplemental Christian duties as paying tithes, avoiding vice, helping the poor, and maintaining the decorum of divine services. Parish priests were occasionally ordered to read it to their congregations; and some editions contained the archaic definition of the Sabbath as extending from nones on Saturday to sunrise on Monday – the sanctity of which period was protected even to the extent of forbidding the performance of acts of personal hygiene. All versions of the letter, however, were characterized by an ardent sabbatarianism, which was couched in Old Testament rhetoric and enforced by anathemas and horrendous threats of retribution pronounced against violators.

The letter's history, most thoroughly explored by the Bollandist hagiographer Delehaye, is an extraordinarily lengthy and colorful one.[1] It first appeared in the sixth century A.D., and spread throughout the Christian world. As popular among eastern Christians as in the Latin West, versions of the letter in Latin, Greek, Syriac, Arabic, Ethiopic, Old Norse, Anglo-Saxon, Gaelic, French, Spanish, German, and the various Slavic languages circulated among Christians from Iceland to Malabar during the long period extending from late antiquity to the modern era. On the basis of the chronological distribution of surviving copies, Delehaye has identified three periods of its exceptional popularity in medieval Europe: the first, in the eighth and ninth centuries, from which time the earliest Latin text of the letter may derive; the second, during the twelfth and thirteenth centuries, when its apocalyptic style and message were probably appealing to Christians of the crusading era; and the third, during the fourteenth century, when it became the emblem of certain flagellant sects.[2] On the other hand, the letter retained its popularity during the early modern and modern periods, when manuscript or printed copies of it were employed for such diverse purposes as talismans protecting seventeenth-century Icelandic peasants against misfortune, as "seditious" propaganda circulated against the French occupiers of Belgium during the Revolutionary wars, and as pious souvenirs cherished by modern Greek tourists in the Holy Land.

The earliest verifiable reference to the letter dates from the late sixth century and is contained in a letter from Licinianus, bishop of Cartagena in Spain, to Bishop Vicentius of Ibiza, who was warned of its apocryphal origin and heretical argument.[3] Probably composed originally by an anonymous Christian cleric in northeastern Spain or southern Gaul shortly after A.D. 584, the letter seems to show the "judaizing" sentiments of Christian communities of that region, which are also reflected in the writings of Caesarius of Arles and Martin of Bracara and certain local ecclesiastical legislation. After its initial appearance, however, there is no further evidence of it in Europe until the eighth century, when it experienced a revival of popularity.

Two hostile references to the letter in Frankish sources and a copy of it, which may date from this period, indicate its notoriety in eighth-century *Francia*. In the first instance, a "Christian eccentric" named Aldebert, who was a self-proclaimed evangelist and faith-healer among the countryfolk near Soissons, claimed as his mandate a letter from Christ brought to earth by the Archangel Michael.[4] Aldebert, who preached a strange blend of apostolic Christianity, antipapalism, angelology, and self-worship, was eventually condemned by a church council in his homeland presided over by the great English missionary-reformer, Boniface. Boniface sent a report of Aldebert's heretical teachings and a copy of his heavenly letter to Rome. Although the text of the letter has not survived, its preface, as quoted in Pope Zachary's condemnation of 745, is virtually identical with the introductions to other versions of the letter. Aldebert himself may have edited an older copy of it in order to acquire proof of God's endorsement of his activities; and it has been suggested that a version of the letter preserved in a tenth- or eleventh-century English manuscript and a fourteenth-century Austrian one may represent the letter actually used by Aldebert.[5] The second allusion to the Christ-letter in Frankish sources was likewise highly skeptical of its pretended origin and critical of its point of view. This occurs in a capitulary of Charlemagne dated 789, which denounced and ordered to be burned a false and heretical letter on the observance of Sunday said to have descended from heaven in Jerusalem.[6]

One of the oldest surviving Latin texts of the letter, a twelfth-century transcript of a lost manuscript of the cathedral of Tarragona in Spain, has been ascribed by its seventeenth-century editor to the time of Charlemagne and by its twentieth-century editor to the sixth century.[7] Whatever its exact date of origin, however, the antiquity of this text is clearly demonstrated by its references to such apparently contemporary superstitions as the veneration of springs, trees, and stones, incantations to the dead, and belief in the powers of "sorcerers, diviners, enchanters, and augurers" – implying its composition at a time when the church was still struggling to root out the old pagan customs. It is noteworthy that later editions of the letter substituted for these archaic sins the more prosaic modern ones of adultery and perjury, although the prohibition of sorcery was frequently kept. Yet this obviously early version of the letter contains most of the elements present in later copies. Its preface, which is very similar to the introduction to Aldebert's letter, identifies the Archangel Michael as its transmitter, Jerusalem as its place of descent, and Cappadocia as the scene of the church council which received it. The letter's text admonishes Christians to avoid secular activities on the Lord's Day and, instead, to devote themselves to prayer and good works. It adds to the obligation to honor Sunday, the duties of paying tithes, and of behaving respectfully in church, and it defines the Sabbath in almost Judaic fashion by forbidding all secular activities, including the washing of clothes and the cutting of hair and beards, on this sacred occasion. Priests were ordered to read the letter to their parishioners, and, as in later versions of it, these exhortations were reinforced by threats of mundane and supernatural punishments. Whether this copy of the letter was the one known to Licinianus and Vincentius in the sixth century or was the one used by Aldebert in the eighth, it evidently derives from the period of the Christian conversion of Europe and constitutes one of the earliest surviving copies of this famous forgery.

The letter continued to spread through Europe. It was known in Gaelic translation to Irish Christians of the ninth century, among whom it circulated in conjunction with an old Irish law tract on the observance of Sunday.[8] From both Ireland and the continent it passed into England, where it was denounced as heretical by a ninth-century English bishop and constituted a source for an eleventh-century Anglo-Saxon homily mistakenly attributed to Archbishop Wulfstan of York.[9] By the twelfth or early thirteenth century the letter had reached Iceland, where it was paraphrased in an Old Norse religious lyric.[10] Viewing the manuscript evidence as a whole, however, Delehaye has argued that its second revival came in the period of the early crusades.

During the twelfth and thirteenth centuries, manuscript copies of the letter seemed to multiply significantly, and it is indicative of its renewed popularity that it was during this period that an older version of it – the Tarragona text described above – was recopied by a Christian cleric in Spain. The letter's apocalyptic character agreed with the wave of eschatological fervor accompanying the crusades, and this aspect of it probably recommended its use by those prophets and seers who voiced the religious enthusiasms of that age. The most explicit account we have of the actual pastoral use of the Christ-letter in late medieval Europe dates from the early thirteenth century and is closely associated with the preaching of the fourth crusade to the English.

Most surviving copies of the letter appear in isolated form or in disparate contexts in various manuscript sources, which provide little information concerning the origin, purpose, or use of particular letters. Copies are sprinkled through sermon collections, saints' lives, theological treatises, and even books of medicine and magic dating from the tenth to the fifteenth centuries; and the authors or copyists of these works seldom showed a desire to speculate about the letter's use or to assess its authenticity and orthodoxy. Very exceptional and helpful, therefore, for understanding its value as an accessory of medieval folk religion and as an instrument of popular devotionalism, is the story of its use by a religious reformer and preacher of the crusade contained in certain thirteenth-century English chronicles.

Prophecies, visions, and apocalyptic dreams flourished in Europe during the era of the third and fourth crusades, and Norman Cohn has commented on the unusual susceptibility of England at that time to eccentric forms of religious excitement.[11] Roger of Hoveden, the chronicler of the reigns of Richard I and John, has preserved several literary testimonials to the prophetic strain in English Christianity at the end of the twelfth and the beginning of the thirteenth centuries. One of the most striking of these is his story of the two visits to England of Abbot Eustace of Flay, a preacher of repentance and miracle worker, who claimed as divine authorization for his mission a letter from Christ in heaven.[12] According to Roger, Abbot Eustace visited England twice – in 1200 and, again, in 1201 – to preach the fourth crusade and a distinctive message of righteousness, charity, and the need to preserve the sanctity of churches and the holiness of Sunday and the saints' days. Roger was the first of several English chroniclers (all of whom were indebted to him for the story of Abbot Eustace) to report the gist of the abbot's sermons, the swath of miracles he worked from Kent to York during his two visits, and the text of the heavenly letter which publicized his teachings and authenticated his private revivalistic campaign.[13] Because Abbot Eustace's letter was a version of the famous sabbatarian letter from Christ, Roger of Hoveden's transcript of it and his account of the abbot's activities in England constitute a unique source of information concerning the use of one of the middle ages' most popular forgeries.

Eustace of Flay was a colleague of the noted "ascetic thaumaturge," Fulk of Neuilly, who was a corrector of morals and a preacher of the crusade in northern France.[14] Fulk's brief public career extended from 1195, when he began to win a reputation as an eloquent preacher of Christian virtue, a stern critic of public morals, and a prodigious *mirabilium operator*, until his death in 1202, at the height of his fame as an advocate of the crusade.[15] As a Christian reformer, Fulk attacked the vices of avarice, usury, prostitution, and clerical marriage. He was outspoken and intolerant of sin, and once offended Richard I of England by excoriating the king's devotion to *superbia, cupiditas,* and *luxuria*.[16] In 1198 Pope Innocent III drew him into the service of the crusading movement by commissioning him to preach the fourth crusade to his countrymen. Fulk seemed to have addressed himself especially to the Christian poor of France, who, as Cohn has suggested, may have felt alienated from an enterprise which was becoming increasingly subordinated to the interests of the rich and powerful.[17] To assist him in his new mission, Fulk enlisted a small band of disciples, one of whom was the Benedictine monk Eustace of Flay. Although contemporary continental sources do not mention Eustace in connection with Fulk's preaching of the crusade, the thirteenth-century English chronicler, Ralph of Coggeshall, listed the abbot, together with certain French prelates, as associates of Fulk; and Roger of Hoveden, who was the best informed of all the English chroniclers, specifically stated that the abbot had been assigned the task of preaching the crusade to the English.[18]

The evidence for Eustace's life prior to and following his English visits is sketchy. As a monk of the Benedictine house of St. Germer de Flay in Normandy, he served as secretary to his diocesan, Philip of Dreux, bishop of Beauvais, immediately before his elevation to the abbacy of his monastery.[19] Upon the death of Abbot Hugh III on October 26, 1200, or possibly even after his first visit to England, Eustace, who was noted for his piety, was elected abbot of St. Germer de Flay. After his spectacular English mission Eustace returned to Normandy, where he devoted himself to serving the interests of his house until his death in 1211. Generally speaking, Eustace of Flay seems to occupy a more important position in English religious history than in that of his native France.

Although Roger of Hoveden was occasionally muddled in his chronology, he was quite positive about the fact that Eustace had visited England twice.[20] During his first stay in the year 1200, the abbot was said to have preached and performed miracles at the Kentish village of Wye, where a fountain which he blessed had exorcised a demon from a dropsical woman, and at another Kentish town, Romney, where he caused water to flow from a stone struck by his staff. During this same visit Eustace labored to reform the lives of the Londoners, whom he urged to abandon usury, join the crusade, honor the sacraments with lights, give alms to the poor, and keep holy the Lord's Day. Like his colleague, Fulk of Neuilly, Eustace stirred up opposition to himself, especially among the English clergy, who accused him "of putting his scythe in another's harvest." Although he managed to avoid imprisonment, which had been Fulk's misfortune at Lisieux and Caen in Normandy, Eustace's abrupt departure from England was doubtlessly due to the hostility he had aroused.[21]

The next year, however, the abbot was back in England, preaching and working miracles from Lincolnshire to York. It appears that on the occasion of his second visit he tried to heighten his appeal and dramatize his message by bringing with him the letter from Christ which Roger transcribed under the year 1201. Roger said that Eustace was enthusiastically received by Archbishop Geoffrey and the clergy and people of York, to whom he preached his sabbatarian doctrine and gave penance and absolution on condition they honor Sunday and the saints' days. In addition to warning his audiences to avoid secular activities on the Lord's Day, he counseled merchants to devote a portion of their profits to the illumination of altars and the burial of the poor, ordered receptacles called "alms-trunks" to be placed in parish churches to receive pious donations, taught the people the custom of keeping alms-bowls in their homes so that the poor might be fed from the tables of the more fortunate, and denounced the use of churches as markets and places of exchange. The miracles he was said to have worked at Beverley, Nafferton, Wakefield, and various places in Lincolnshire were all designed to stress the sanctity of Sunday and to exalt the Lord's Day in the eyes of the people, and this was also the intent of the heavenly letter which Roger said the abbot had brought with him into England. But Eustace's individualistic program of reform and his aggressiveness in enforcing it again provoked resentment, and Roger reported that certain great men, including the king himself, forced the abbot to abandon his mission for a second time. The story ends with Roger complimenting the abbot's piety and miraculous powers but confessing that the effects of his efforts were transitory.

Roger of Hoveden transcribed in full (as did Walter of Coventry, Roger of Wendover, and Matthew Paris, who followed him in recording the visits of Eustace of Flay) the letter from Christ which seemed to serve as his warrant.[22] According to the preface accompanying Roger's copy of the letter, it had descended above the altar of the church of St. Simeon on Golgotha in the Holy Land, where for three days and nights it hung suspended beyond reach of an admiring congregation. Finally, the patriarch of Jerusalem, identified as a certain Archbishop Akarias or

Acharias, succeeded in pulling it down to earth, using his pallium as a sort of rope.[23] In the preface quoted by Roger of Hoveden, no mention is made of the Archangel Michael, of the letter's examination by a clerical assembly, nor of its dispatch to Rome. Writing later, however, Roger of Wendover and Matthew Paris embellished the story of the letter's reception. Although they telescoped Eustace's two visits into one, they added the important new details of the letter's transmittal to Rome following its examination by a church council in Palestine.[24] They went on to say that the pope, equally impressed by it, had created a special corps of preachers to convey its message to the world at large. The English mission had fallen to Eustace of Flay, whose preaching throughout the English countryside had been attended by a large number of miracles – irrefutable proof of the divine sanction he enjoyed. It would appear that this expanded story of the letter's reception was the result of confusion on the part of later chroniclers, who attributed to Eustace the legatine powers of a crusade-preacher which the pope had given to Fulk of Neuilly.

Eustace's letter, as quoted by Roger of Hoveden, is distinguished by the same sabbatarian point of view characteristic of other versions of it. After the brief preface detailing the circumstances of its earthly appearance, it begins:

I, the Lord, who commanded you to observe my Holy Lord's Day, which you do not keep nor do penance for your sins, said through my Evangelist: "Heaven and earth shall pass away: but my words shall not pass away." [Mark 13: 31]

Reminding sinners of promised retribution, the letter continues:

I caused to be preached unto you repentance of life, but you did not believe; and I sent among you pagan peoples, who shed your blood throughout the land, yet still you did not believe; and because you do not keep the Holy Day of the Lord, in a short while you shall suffer famine; but I will quickly send abundance again, although thereafter you will do even worse.

Eustace's version of the letter contains the archaic definition of the Lord's Day as extending "ab hora nona Sabbati usque ad solem surgentem diei Lunae," which appears in several other editions of it, and also the distinctive invocation, "Amen, dico vobis," which was a standard rhetorical component of the Christ-letter. It expresses outrage that an unrepentant people persists in ignoring God's Commandments, and it threatens the ungodly with a variety of apocalyptic woes – assaults by "pagan peoples," blizzards of "stones," "firebrands," and "scalding water," the terrors of "famine," "thirst," and "darkness," and torments by monstrous creatures "with the heads of lions, the hair of women, and the tails of camels." "Abandon the path of wickedness," it exhorts, "and do penance for your sins." In the event its warning is unheeded, the letter repeats its roster of punishments:

I swear to you by my right hand, that, unless you keep the Lord's Day and the days of my saints, I will send pagan peoples to slay you . . . and even worse beasts to devour the breasts of your womenfolk.

Concluding with a series of curses, it denounces "those who act unjustly toward their brothers" and those who mistreat the "poor and orphans." "Hear my voice and have mercy," the letter ends, "for unless you cease your wicked works, the works of the devil – the perjury and adultery you commit – you shall be engulfed by those people, who will devour you like beasts." Although Eustace's letter differs slightly from other versions in omitting any reference to the payment of tithes or the need for parish priests to read it in their churches, nevertheless, it conforms to the model of such letters by virtue of its strict sabbatarianism, its hortatory style, and its colorful threats of divine punishment.

Roger of Hoveden and other contemporary observers of Abbot Eustace, as Gerald of Wales and Jocelin of Brakelond, seemed to suggest that the abbot's principal goal was the abolition of Sunday markets and the reassertion of the absolute sanctity of Christian holy days, which should be kept inviolate from any sort of commercial activity or servile labor.[25] A modern scholar, J. L. Cate, who examined the possible motives for Eustace's mission, has concluded that the incidence of the abolition of Sunday markets during the years immediately following the abbot's visits implies that Roger of Hoveden was too pessimistic in assessing the effects of his campaign and that a temporary trend to abolish them can be ascribed to the abbot's efforts.[26] Viewed in this way, the teachings of Abbot Eustace represented a revolt, comparable to that typified by early Franciscanism or the Waldensian movement, against the morally corrupting effects of the new commercial capitalism which was transforming European society during the twelfth and thirteenth centuries. Fulk's denunciation of "avarice," like Eustace's attack on Sunday markets and the "usury" of the Londoners, signified a reaction on the part of advocates of an apostolic faith against the prosperity and the attendant moral laxity and spiritual indifference of an increasingly commercialized Europe. The interjection of monetary values into European social relationships seemed to constitute an affront to the perfect Christian life portrayed in scripture and to imperil even the sanctity of the traditional times and places of Christian worship, and contemporary Chrisitan moralists and reformers singled out this spirit of acquisitiveness for special denunciation. This is a phenomenon which Professor Lester Little found reflected in an interesting change of twelfth-century iconography, i.e., the substitution in church decoration of the symbol of the relatively new sin of "avarice" for that of the old vice of knightly "pride." [27] All of Eustace's miracles during his second visit conveyed the lesson that Sunday was a most inappropriate time for selfish labor and profiteering; and this was also the message of his heavenly letter. At an earlier time the Frankish prophet, Aldebert, had probably edited a copy of the Christ-letter for use in his campaign to convert rural Franks to his peculiar brand of Christianity, and Eustace doubtlessly recognized the same letter's value as a weapon in his war against the materialism, which, in his view, was debasing the most sacred sites and institutions of the Christian religion.

Despite their unpopularity with some of the clergy of Normandy and England, neither Fulk nor Eustace were, however, heretics of the kind represented by Aldebert, the Spiritual Franciscans, or those strange *propheta* whose antics have been described by Norman Cohn. Fulk's war with vice was implicitly condoned by Pope Innocent III, who saw his usefulness for promoting the crusade. If we accept Roger of Hoveden's characterization of the views of Eustace's servant, a certain Walter, as reflecting the abbot's own opinions, then Walter's criticism of King Henry II for having been remiss in not stamping out heresy in his French dominions surely implies Eustace's theological orthodoxy.[28] The abbot's difficulties in England were political, not theological – the result of his meddling in local ecclesiastical affairs, his independent preaching and granting of penance and absolution, his criticism of the rich and power-ful, and, doubtlessly, his attack on the Sunday markets which were profitable to clergy and laity alike. Further, none of the English sources which quoted it expressed any suspicion concerning the authenticity or orthodoxy of his heavenly letter. The criticism of the Christ-letter voiced earlier in the middle ages was notably lacking in this later period. Roger of Hoveden's strong taste for the occult did not encourage him to be skeptical; the later chroniclers seemed to have suspended judgment con-cerning this exotic and exciting document; and contemporary canonists and theologians apparently never thought it worthy of serious attention.

Both Fulk of Neuilly and Eustace of Flay were Christian moral re-formers, who had been drawn into the service of the crusades. The Christ-letter complemented the two aspects of Eustace's missionary role – the exhortation to preserve the sanctity of churches and holy days and the call to the crusade. The letter's repeated reference to the possible annihilation of backsliding Christians by unnamed "pagan peoples" drew attention to the desperate situation in the Christian East – an allusion which later versions of the letter made more explicit by substituting the word "Saracen" for the somewhat ambiguous term of Eustace's letter.[29] The Christ-letter's hortatory style and apocalyptic rhetoric coincided with that prophetic element which Roger of Hoveden showed was a dominant theme of English spirituality during the era of the third and fourth crusades. Among several occult works quoted or cited in his chronicle is another famous epistolary forgery – the "letter of Toledo."[30]

This appeared on the eve of the third crusade and expressed the anxiety evoked within Christian Europe by the conquests of Saladin. Attributed variously to Spanish or Sicilian astrologers or to a certain "Master John David of Toledo," the letter prophesied the triumph of Christianity over Jews and Muslims following a time of tribulation to be inaugurated shortly by a solar eclipse and a spectacular series of geological and meteorological catastrophes. Like the letter from Christ, the letter of Toledo called for repentance in order to assure the church's survival in the face of the divine wrath symbolized by its ancient adversaries; like Eustace's heavenly letter, it was periodically reedited during the later middle ages so as to accommodate its prophetic message to new historical situations.[31]

The letter from Christ also seemed to serve as Eustace's warrant – authenticating, as did the miracles he worked, his program of revivalism and reform. An earlier version of the letter had served a similar purpose for Aldebert, and during the middle ages a number of other self-appointed prophets and reformers claimed to have received direct revelations from God in the form of heavenly letters. Peter the Hermit, the leader of the savage mob accompanying the first crusade, insisted that his mandate was a letter from Christ delivered to him in the church of the Holy Sepulchre in Jerusalem.[32] The former carpenter and Christian pacifist, Durand of Le Puy, who appeared in the twelfth century, claimed to have had a vision in which the Virgin Mary gave him a parchment bearing a picture of herself with the infant Jesus in her arms on which was written the prayer, "Lamb of God, who taketh away the sins of the world, give us peace."[33] The thirteenth-century folk messiah known as the "Master of Hungary" likewise pretended to have received a heavenly letter from the hand of the Virgin,[34] and the youthful revolutionary, Stephen of Cloyes, who led the tragic Children's Crusade of 1212, was said to have shown the French king, Philip Augustus, a similar letter as proof of God's approval of his mission.[35] None of these letters has been preserved, if they ever actually existed. From what we know of their contents and uses they seem to have been different from Eustace's sabbatarian letter and to have served simply as exhortations to join particular religious movements. Yet all of these actual or mythical letters indicate the value of such literature for convincing the Christian multitude of the legitimacy of the callings of various self-proclaimed prophets.

The Christ-letter was enormously popular throughout the middle ages, and a number of editions of it have been preserved in unpublished English sources. An exact copy of the letter quoted by Roger of Hoveden appears in British Museum Additional Manuscript 6,716;[36] but the other versions of the letter differ in style or contents from Abbot Eustace's copy. Although the manuscripts almost never provide extrinsic information concerning the origin or use of particular letters, the contexts in which they appear suggest their homiletic value and their connection with the devotional practices of medieval folk religion. For example, copies of the letter are frequently associated in the manuscripts with collections of sermons and saints' lives. B.M. Add. MS. 19,725, which is a tenth- or eleventh-century miscellany consisting of a martyrology, a penitential treatise, a canon of Bede's works, some saints' Lives, and a few medical tracts, also includes a copy of the Christ-letter, probably interpolated by a later writer.[37] The preface mentions its transmittal by the Archangel Michael, its descent upon the altar of St. Peter's Sepulchre in Jerusalem, and its perusal by an assembly of clergy in an unnamed city in Armenia. The text of this version, which differs appreciably from Abbot Eustace's letter, adds to the injunction to honor Sunday the duties of paying tithes, keeping baptismal vows, and attending church regularly. It has been argued that this version of the letter, another copy of which appears in a fourteenth-century continental manuscript, represents the form of the letter used by Aldebert in the eighth century.[38] The Christ-letter's homiletic use is also implied by its inclusion in an eleventh-century manuscript of French origin. This is B.M. Add. MS. 30,853, which, in the context of a collection of sermons, quotes a copy of the letter with a prefatory note and postscript stating that a certain "Bishop Peter of Nîmes" (probably Peter Ermengaud, bishop of Nîmes c. 1080 to 1095) attested to the genuineness of the letter, which claimed to have been found on the altar of the church of St. Baudile in the city of Nîmes.[39] Finally, B.M. Add. MS. 16,587, which is a fourteenth-century German manuscript consisting of a calendar of saints and sermons on Sunday and the saints' days by Gregory, Jerome, Augustine, and Bede, contains a copy of the letter, which, supposedly inscribed on a marble tablet, had descended upon the altar of St. Peter's Sepulchre in Jerusalem.[40]

The Christ-letter's occasional association in the manuscripts with occult or medical tracts implies that it was popularly viewed as having inherent protective or therapeutic properties. Seventeenth-century Icelandic peasants employed it as a talisman;[41] and this use is also suggested by its appearance in B.M. Add. MS. 15,236, which is a late thirteenth- or early fourteenth-century manuscript consisting of several medical and occult works – herbal recipes, charms, tables for astrological divination, guides for the interpretation of dreams, and prophecies.[42] This manuscript quotes a copy of the Christ-letter, which, lacking the usual preface detailing the circumstances of its appearance, begins abruptly with the biblical quotation: "In the sweat of thy face shalt thou eat bread" (Gen. 3:19). In addition to cautioning Christians to keep the Sabbath and the saints' days, it admonishes them to avoid avarice, perjury, sorcery, and usury.

Generally speaking, the character of the manuscripts in which copies of the Christ-letter appear implies that the letter was viewed as a sort of quaint, old-fashioned homily on the observance of Sunday and the saints' days which was sometimes thought to have quasimagical virtues. Its continued popularity and its acceptance by the clergy may have been due to its usefulness for getting people to attend church, where they would be subject to clerical influence and instruction.[43] On the other hand, its apocalyptic quality and puritanical point of view occasionally recommended its use by religious reformers as a means of dramatizing their teachings and authenticating their claims to a special revelation.

The composition of fictitious letters in the names of a variety of historical or mythical personages was, however, fairly common in the middle ages, and not all of the "letters from Christ" identified as such in the catalogs of English and continental manuscript collections are identical with Eustace's sabbatarian letter. For example, several late medieval English manuscripts contain copies of a Christ-letter, usually entitled, *Carta humani generis*, which is very different in origin and intent from the abbot's letter. B.M. Add. MS. 6,716, which preserves an exact copy of Eustace's letter as quoted by Roger of Hoveden, also contains a copy of this "Charter of Mankind."[44] Beginning, "Sciant presentes et futuri et omnes qui sunt in celo et terra," this letter assumes the form of a last will and testament, written in Jesus' "own blood," "sealed by his divinity," "witnessed by Father, Son, and Holy Spirit," and dated "in the year, 5232 After Creation." By virtue of this testament Christ had succeeded to his divine inheritance and had bequeathed the fruits of his sacrifice on Calvary to all mankind. The *Carta humani generis*, or, as it was sometimes titled, the *Carta redemptionis humanae* or *Magna carta de libertatibus mundi*, has survived only in a relatively limited number of Latin copies or versified English translations contained in manuscripts of English origin.[45] Its late medieval English ancestry is implied by its format, legalistic style, and its use of the distinctive common law term, "seisin." Much less popular and widely read than the sabbatarian letter from Christ, it appears to have been simply a pious fraud perpetrated by an anonymous English cleric of the later middle ages.

Likewise, of entirely different origin and intent from Eustace's letter were those epistolary forgeries purporting to come from Christ (or sometimes from the devil), which were produced in response to religious and political controversy during the late middle ages and the Renaissance.[46] These spurious letters, which made no pretense of concealing their contemporary origin or partisan nature, were the work of European authors who used the epistolary style to debate the great issues confronting church and state during the thirteenth, fourteenth, and fifteenth centuries. English examples of this propagandistic literature, which was also very popular on the continent, are the "invective" against King John in the form of a letter from Christ to the pope, the lengthy defense of ecclesiastical reform composed by a certain "Peter of Clairvaux" in the form of a letter from Christ to Pope Innocent VI (1352–62), and another

Christ-letter addressed to the council of Basel – all of which appear in British Museum manuscripts.[47] The diatribe against King John and the vices of English clerical and secular society during his reign was the work of an English monastic, probably a Hospitaller, writing after the king's death. The letter which claims to have been elicited by the prayers of the Virgin and the saints, excoriates the misgovernment of that reign and contains an interesting reference to the preaching of Peter of Pontefract, the "prophet of Wakefield," whom John ordered to be hanged in 1213 for prophesying the king's death.[48] The letter from Christ to Innocent VI is a long theological exposition of the ideal of Christian perfection and the need for clerical reform, which constitutes a reply to another of Peter of Clairvaux's works, preceding it in B.M. Harley MS. 2,667 – a letter from Beelzebub satirizing the faults of the clergy.[49] Finally, the letter to the council of Basel, which is similar to an earlier Christ-letter supposedly sent to the council of Constance, urges the council to undertake the reformation of the papacy and cardinalate as part of its effort to purify the church.[50]

Although Eustace's heavenly letter was merely a variant of a famous medieval forgery, which was known in England more than three centuries before his arrival, nevertheless, Roger of Hoveden's account of the abbot's mission provides important information concerning the letter's circulation in medieval Europe and its relationship to the prophetic and reformist traditions within medieval Christianity. With the exception of the episode involving Aldebert, the story of Eustace of Flay constitutes the most detailed account we have of the pastoral use of the Christ-letter in the middle ages. As portrayed by Roger, Eustace was, like his master Fulk of Neuilly, a Christian moralist and advocate of the crusade, who taught a fundamentalist, apostolic faith based on devotion to God and the saints, regular communion, perfect compliance with scriptural commandments, compassion for the poor, and strict observance of the established times and places of Christian worship. In his sermons, and implicitly in the miracles he worked, the abbot attacked what he saw as the worst consequences of secularism and materialism – the use of Christian shrines and holy days for selfish and servile purposes. And the Christ-letter, which served both as a capsule sermon and as a warrant, pointed the way toward a more perfect righteousness grounded on the reaffirmation of the inviolability of churches and the Christian calendar, periodic abstention from secular pursuits in order to participate in the liturgical practices of the faith, and a sharing of the new prosperity with the poor through regularized almsgiving. Further, the letter publicized the second goal of Fulk's and Eustace's mission – the need to launch a crusade for the liberation of Jerusalem. Its apocalyptic style and its threat of the destruction of indifferent Christians by merciless "pagan peoples" made its message acutely relevant to Europeans on the eve of the fourth crusade.[51]

NOTES

1. Hippolyte Delehaye, "Note sur le légende de la lettre du Christ tombée du ciel," *Bulletin de l'Académie Royale de Belgique: Classe des lettres et des sciences morales et politiques et de la classe des beaux-arts* (1899), 171–213; aso E. Renoir, "Christ (lettre du) tombée au ciel," *Dictionnaire d'archéologie chrétienne et de liturgie*, eds. Fernand Cabrol and Henri Leclercq (15 vols. in 29; Paris, 1924–53), vol. III, pt. 1, pp. 1534–46. For background on the observance of Sunday and the saints' days, see Max Levy, *Der Sabbath in England* (Leipzig, 1933), esp. pp. 54ff; Edith Cooperrider Rodgers, *Discussion of Holidays in the Later Middle Ages* (New York, 1940); Barbara Harvey, "Work and *Festa Ferianda* in Medieval England," *Journal of Ecclesiastical History*, XXIII (1972), 289–308.
2. Delehaye, "Note sur le légende de la lettre du Christ," p. 211.
3. Robert Priebsch, *Letter from Heaven on the Observance of the Lord's Day* (Oxford, 1936), esp. pp. 1–2, 19ff.
4. Jeffrey Burton Russell, *Dissent and Reform in the Early Middle Ages* (Berkeley and Los Angeles, 1965), p. 105; Priebsch, *Letter from Heaven*, pp. 3–5; Delehaye, "Note sur le légende de la lettre du Christ," pp. 175–6.
5. The English text is in British Museum Additional Manuscript 19,725, fols. 87ᵛ–8. See Priebsch, *Letter from Heaven*, pp. 6–7.
6. Priebsch, *Letter from Heaven*, p. 9; Delehaye, "Note sur le légende de la lettre du Christ," p. 186.
7. Priebsch, *Letter from Heaven*, pp. 6–7, and text, pp. 35–7; Etienne Baluze, *Capitularia regum Francorum* (2 vols.; Paris, 1677), II, 1396–99. I have used the 1780 edition of Baluze, which has pagination identical with the original.
8. James F. Kenney, *The Sources for the Early History of Ireland: Ecclesiastical – An Introduction and Guide* (Shannon, 1968), pp. 476–7; also J. G. O'Keeffe, "Cain Domnaig," *Ériu: the Journal of the School of Irish Learning*, vol. II, pt. 2 (1905), 189–214; Donald Maclean, *The Law of the Lord's Day in the Celtic Church* (Edinburgh, 1926).
9. Delehaye, "Note sur le légende de la lettre du Christ," p. 189; Maclean, *Law of the Lord's Day*, pp. 34–5; Priebsch, *Letter from Heaven*, p. 10.
10. Priebsch, *Letter from Heaven*, pp. 15–17.
11. Norman Cohn, *The Pursuit of the Millennium* (2d. ed., New York, 1961), pp. 75–6.
12. *Chronica Magistri Rogeri de Houedene*, ed. William Stubbs [Rolls Series, 51] (4 vols.; London, 1868–1871), IV, 123–4, 167–72; and for Roger's interest in occult literature, references in the Introduction, IV, xii and discussion of the letter of Toledo below.
13. See Walter of Coventry, *Memoriale*, ed. William Stubbs [Rolls Series, 58] (2 vols.; London, 1872–1873), II, 165, 185–8; Roger of Wendover, *Flores Historiarum*, ed. Henry G. Hewlett [Rolls Series, 84] (3 vols.; London, 1886–89), I, 295–301; Ralph of Coggeshall, *Chronicon Anglicanum*, ed. Josephus Stevenson [Rolls Series, 66] (London, 1875), pp. 80–3, 130–4; Matthew Paris, *Chronica Majora*, ed. Henry Richards Luard [Rolls Series, 57] (7 vols.; London, 1872–83), II, 462–6.
14. Cohn, *Pursuit of the Millennium*, p. 76.
15. Milton R. Gutsch, "A Twelfth Century Preacher – Fulk of Neuilly," *The Crusades and Other Historical Essays Presented to Dana C. Munro by*

His Former Students, ed. Louis J. Paetow (New York, 1928), pp. 183–206; A. Charasson, *Un curé plébéien au XII siècle* (Paris, 1905); Edgar H. McNeal and Robert Lee Wolff, "The Fourth Crusade," *A History of the Crusades*, ed. Kenneth M. Setton (2 vols.; Madison, Milwaukee, and London, 1969), II, 157–8.

16. Roger of Hoveden, *Chronica*, IV, 76–77.
17. Cohn, *Pursuit of the Millennium*, p. 76.
18. Ralph of Coggeshall, *Chronicon Anglicanum*, p. 130; Roger of Hoveden, *Chronica*, IV, 76, 123. For Fulk's associates, see Gutsch, "A Twelfth Century Preacher," pp. 202–03; Charasson, *Un curé plébéien*, pp. 78, 105, 118, 123.
19. The biographical data is summarized by J. L. Cate, "The English Mission of Eustace of Flay (1200–1201)," *Études d'histoire dediées a la mémoire de Henri Pirenne par ses anciens élèves* (Brussels, 1937), pp. 69–70, 77.
20. See *Chronica*, IV, 167; and for Roger's faulty chronology, IV, xxviii–xxxi. Cate suggested that Eustace may not have been abbot at the time of his first visit, "The English Mission of Eustace of Flay," p. 74, n. 1.
21. For Fulk's difficulties in Normandy, see Roger of Hoveden, *Chronica*, IV, 77.
22. The letter is printed, *ibid.*, IV, 167–9. English translations of portions of the letter are based on Roger's text and are mine.
23. The actual patriarch from 1194 to 1202 was Aymar the Monk.
24. Roger of Wendover, *Flores Historiarum*, I, 297–8; Matthew Paris, *Chronica Majora*, II, 464; Cate, "The English Mission of Eustace of Flay," pp. 71, n. 2, 73, n. 1.
25. See the reference in the Vita S. Hugonis, *Giraldi Cambrensis Opera*, eds. J. S. Brewer *et al.* [Rolls Series, 21] (8 vols.; London, 1861–91), VII, 121–2; and *The Chronicle of Jocelin of Brakelond concerning the Acts of Samson, Abbot of the Monastery of St. Edmund*, trans. H. E. Butler (New York, 1949), p. 132.
26. Cate, "The English Mission of Eustace of Flay," pp. 79ff.
27. Lester K. Little, "Pride Goes Before Avarice: Social Change and the Vices in Latin Christendom," *American Historical Review*, LXXVI (1971), 16–49.
28. Roger of Hoveden, *Chronica*, II, 272–3.
29. E.g., B.M. Add. MS. 23,390, fol. 93ᵛ; Add. MS. 16,587, fol. 184. Both date from the fourteenth century.
30. See the "Epistola Corumphizae astrologi de conjunctione planetarum," quoted by Roger under the year, 1184, *Chronica*, II, 290–1.
31. For the letter's history, see M. Gaster, "The Letter of Toledo," *Folk-Lore*, XIII (1902), 115–34; W. R. Jones, "Rhetoric and Politics: the Political Uses of the *Ars Dictaminis* in Later Medieval Europe," *Cithara*, IX (1970), 5–6.
32. Cohn, *Pursuit of the Millennium*, p. 42.
33. Norman P. Zacour, "The Children's Crusade," *History of the Crusades*, ed. Setton, II, 329.
34. *Ibid.*, II, 341.
35. Jones, "Rhetoric and Politics," p. 4.
36. B.M. Add. MS. 6,716, fols. 72–3ᵛ, cited by Delehaye, "Note sur le légende de la lettre du Christ," p. 188.
37. Fols. 87ᵛ–88: "Epistola in nomine Trinitatis domini nostri Jhesu Christi qui [sic] de celo in Hierusalem per Michaelem cecidit Archangelum."

38. Priebsch, *Letter from Heaven*, pp. 6–7.
39. Fols. 231–2ᵛ: "Epistola Sancti Salvatoris que directa est a Domino et inventa est super altare Sancti Bauduli in civitate Nimaso."
40. Fols. 184–6: "Epistola domini nostri Jesu Christi descendens de celo super altare Sancti Petri in Jerusalem scripta in tabulis marmoreis." Another copy of this version of the letter, likewise dating from the fourteenth century, appears in B.M. Add. MS. 23,390, fols. 93ᵛ–94ᵛ: "Epistola domini nostri Yhesu Christi descendens de celo super altare Sancti Petri."
41. Delehaye, "Note sur le légende de la lettre du Christ," p. 192.
42. Fols. 92ᵛ–4: "Epistola domini nostri."
43. *Dictionnaire d'archéologie chrétienne*, eds. Cabrol and Leclercq, vol. III, pt. 1, p. 1538.
44. B.M. Add. MS. 6,716, fol. 4.
45. Other copies are in B.M. Add. MS. 21,253, fols. 186–6ᵛ; Harley MS. 1288, fol. 44ᵛ. Additional copies are cited in *Catalogue of Romances in the Department of Manuscripts in the British Museum*, ed. J. A. Herbert (3 vols.; London, 1883–1910), III, 683 (No. 25).
46. See Jones, "Rhetoric and Politics," pp. 8–15; also W. Wattenbach, Über erfundene Briefe in Handeschriften des Mittelalters, besonders Teufels-briefe," *Sitzungsberichte der Königlich Preussischen Akademie der Wissenschaften zu Berlin* (1892), pt. 1, pp. 91–123; and examples cited by W. Koehler, "Himmelsbrief," *Die Religion in Geschichte und Gegenwart*, eds. Hermann Gunkel and Leopold Zscharnack (2d. ed.; 5 vols.; Tübingen, 1927–1931), II, 1902.
47. The invective against King John is in Vespasian E. iii, fols. 171–78ᵛ; the letter attributed to Peter of Clairvaux is in Harley 2,667, fols. 72ᵛ–123ᵛ; and the letter to the council of Basel is in Add. MS. 16,584, fols. 133–8.
48. There are references in the Tewkesbury and Worcester annals to a letter from the Virgin Mary brought to John by an unnamed cleric (*clericello*) in 1205. See *Annales Monastici*, ed. Henry Richards Luard [Rolls Series, 36] (5 vols.; London, 1864–69), I, 58; IV, 393. For references to Peter of Pontefract, see *ibid.*, I, 60; II, 278; III, 34; IV, 56, 57, 401.
49. The letter from Beelzebub is at fols. 72–72ᵛ. Another English example of this genre is the "Epistola Luciferi ad papam et praelatos," dating from Richard II's reign and once in the possession of Thomas Hendyman, Chancellor of Oxford, c. 1395–1400, in Cleopatra B. I, fols. 183ᵛ–6. Two seventeenth-century antipapalist tracts in the form of letters from the devil are the letter from the devil to Pope Urban VII, c. 1625, in Add. MS. 22,587, fols. 20ᵛ–1, and the letter sent to Rome by an infernal spirit and the next day conveyed to England by the pope's command, dated September 7, 1640, in Harley 5108, fols. 138–44ᵛ.
50. The letter to the council of Constance is cited by Delehaye, "Note sur le légende de la lettre du Christ," p. 173; *Dictionnaire d'archéologie chrétienne*, eds. Cabrol and Leclercq, vol. III, pt. 1, p. 1535.
51. The author expresses his gratitude to the Trustees of the British Museum for permission to consult manuscripts in their custody and to the Central University Research Fund of the University of New Hampshire for assistance in completing this study.

William of Malmesbury and Some Other Western Writers on Islam

RODNEY M. THOMSON

In his book *Western Views of Islam in the Middle Ages*, R. W. Southern distinguished between an "Age of Ignorance," extending to the early twelfth century, and the "Century of Reason and Hope" which succeeded it.[1] Typical of views popularly current in the earlier period are those expressed in the *Song of Roland*, in which the Saracens are polytheists and idolaters, Mohammed being one of their several gods.[2] However, from c. 1120, notable advances were made in western knowledge of the Islamic religion and of its prophet-founder. Among several reasons for this, the Crusades and travels associated with or made possible by them may be singled out as especially important. So also were the increasing and amicable contacts between Eastern and European scholars in frontier-areas such as Spain and Sicily.

And yet the Westerner who, according to Southern, first presented a reasonably accurate account of Islam and Mohammed, was a monk who never traveled outside England, the historian William of Malmesbury (c. 1095–c. 1143). Remarkably, as Southern puts it, "[he] . . . was the first . . . to distinguish clearly between the idolatry and pagan superstitions of the Slavs and the monotheism of Islam, and to emphasize against all current popular thought that Islam held Mahomet not as God but as His prophet."[3] In support of this, Southern quotes a passage from William's *Gesta Regum*, written before 1125:

[Henricus III] erat imperator . . . bellicosissimus, quippe qui etiam Vindelicos et Leuticios subegerit, ceterosque populos Sueuis conterminos, qui usque ad hanc diem soli omnium mortalium paganas superstitiones anhelant; nam Saraceni et Turchi Deum Creatorem colunt, Mahomet non Deum sed eius prophetam aestimantes.[4]

The purpose of this paper is to draw attention for the first time to other passages, found in William's unprinted works, which enlarge and refine our knowledge of his views on this subject; in combination they illustrate the intensity of his interest (prompting the question why), and his insistence that the popular tradition was wrong. They also enable some account to be given of the sources of his new and surprising knowledge.

The first passage, a brief one, is found in William's *Commentary on*

179

Lamentations, written c. 1136.[5] Similar to the *Gesta Regum* extract already quoted, it runs thus:

Denique quamuis Christianorum et Iudeorum et Sarracenorum secte habeant de Filio compugnantes sententias, omnes tamen Deum patrem Creatorem rerum et credunt corde et confitentur ore.[6]

This is an interesting statement on two grounds: in the first place, it indicates that William's knowledge of the Islamic religion was even more precise than the *Gesta Regum* passage permitted one to assume. In the second, this accurate knowledge is accompanied by an unusually sympathetic attitude. Though tacitly so, William actually categorizes Christians, Jews, and Moslems together as "secte," in this passage; in the *Gesta Regum* extract he more explicitly distinguishes them as a group from the inferior "pagani." The Moslems and Jews are by implication heretics rather than members of entirely different religious systems to Christianity. The same term was used, and the same view held, by Peter the Venerable in his *Liber contra Sectam Saracenorum,* written in the late 1140s.[7] But William could express an accommodating attitude even to pagans, as witness the following extract from the same commentary:

Vnde Aristotiles pulchre *atque haut scio an inferius aliquo Christiano* precepit, ut uoluptatum non principium sed finem attendamus.[8]

William was therefore prepared to look for points of contact between Christianity and other religions, both in theology and, in the case especially of the ancients, in ethics.[9] The latter attitude was shared by some other litterateurs and humanists of William's time, notably by Hildebert of Le Mans,[10] whose verse William read and admired.[11]

The second passage is much longer, and it is on this that I wish to concentrate discussion, beginning with the manuscript in which it is found. Bodleian MS Arch. Seld. B. 16 has been associated with William at least since Stubbs' time.[12] Mostly in William's own hand, it contains a compendium of material designed to form a continuous history of the Roman emperors. The main contents, in order of appearance, are Dares Phrygius, Orosius, Eutropius, Jordanes, Paul the Deacon, what purports to be a digest of Aimoin of Fleury's *Historia Francorum,* and the *Breviarium Alarici.*[13] To most of these William has provided his habitual introductory comments and interpolations, and the sections not in his hand have been annotated by him. The portion claiming our attention is the "digest of Aimoin." It opens with an introduction as follows:

Precedentium gesta imperatorum Iordanes episcopus et Paulus diaconus texuerunt. Sequentium acta Haimo monachus Floriacensis ex diuersis auctoribus collegit. Eius ergo semper sensum aliquando uerba ponemus, omissis quecumque de Longabardis, Francis, Gothis immiscuit. Earum enim gentium gesta alias propriis libris leguntur.[14]

The reader acquainted with Aimoin's work will raise his eyebrows at this passage, for the *Historia Francorum* has very little to say about the Eastern emperors at all, and concentrates, as its title suggests, on the history of Merovingian Gaul, breaking off at A.D. 652.[15] Yet William's lengthy account continues to the reign of Louis the Pious, with some scrappy additions and regnal lists to his own time. In fact a careful examination of it soon shows that it has nothing to do with Aimoin; it is rather a summary of Hugh of Fleury's *Historia Ecclesiastica*, in the second edition of 1110.[16] This edition concluded with the reign of Louis the Pious, so that the regnal lists which follow are William's own addition. I have discussed the possible reasons for William's error elsewhere.[17] As to the date of the manuscript, although the latest king in the regnal lists is Louis VI, crowned in 1131, an earlier passage indicates that William was writing about the time of his death:

Sicilia Sarracenis paruit usque abhinc xl. annos, quando eam Normanni subiecerunt, anno Dominicae Incarnationis millesimo centesimo minus xiii.[18]

This passage was therefore written in the year 1137. It occurs shortly after the section devoted to the reign of the emperor Heraclius. It was at this point in his narrative that Hugh of Fleury inserted a long account of the career of Mohammed, noticed by Dr. Daniel as the first appearance in the West of the "Khorasan" version.[19] This account William has abbreviated, at the same time making some additions of his own. So that a proper comparison can be made, I print Hugh's version opposite William's. William's additions to Hugh's account are italicized.

Hugh of Fleury

Hac praeterea tempestate Saraceni, qui et Turci dicuntur, Machomet pseudopropheta eis ducatum praebente, a suis sedibus exierunt, et imperium Heraclii grauiter deuastare coeperunt. Porro iste Machomet, Saracenorum et Arabum princeps et pseudopropheta, fuit de genere Ismael filii Abrahae. Qui cum in primaeua aetate sua esset mercator, pergebat frequenter cum camelis suis ad Aegyptum et Palaestinam, et conuersabatur cum Iudeis et Christianis, a quibus tam Nouum quam Vetus Testamentum didicit; sed et magus perfectissimus effectus est; et cum hac illacque discurreret, contigit ut Chorozaniam ingrederetur prouinciam. Cuius prouinciae domina Cadiga

William of Malmesbury

Nec minus Turchi Muameth pseudopropheta duce imperium Romanum populantur. Hic Muameth Ismahelita genere in arte negotiationis iuuentam suam triuit, et cum mercatoribus Iudeis et Christianis conuersatus, utrorumque legem adprime addidicit. Itaque discursu mercaturae cuidam mulieri Cadigam nomine que Corozaniae prouinciae principabatur, notior factus, magicis prestigiis quorum peritus erat, quod ipse esset Messias quem Iudei expectant, facile persuasit. Qua opinione muliercula decepta, in eius coniugium concessit. *Nec dubitandum est multis eum effecisse miraculis, ut tot fidei suae populos conciliaret, cum usque hodie omnes illae nationes eum non Deum* nominabatur; quae cum diuersa species, quas secum Machomet attulerat, miraretur, coepit ei praefata mulier familiarius adhaerere. Quam Machomet incantationum suarum praestrictam phantasmate, coepit astu paulatim in errorem inducere, dicens ei quod ipse esset Messias, quem esse uenturum adhuc Iudaei expectant. Suffragabantur uerbis eius tam incantationum praestigiae quam calliditatis eius ingenium copiosum; qua opinione non solum potens mulier decepta est, sed et omnes Iudaei, ad quos fama eius pertingere poterat, ad eum cum Saracenis cateruatim confluebant, attoniti tanta nouitate rei; quibus coepit nouas leges fingere, et eis tradere, adhibens ipsis legibus testimonia de utroque Testamento. Quas leges Ismaelitae appellant suas, eumque suum legislatorem esse fatentur. Praefata quoque mulier, uidens hominem Iudaeorum et Saracenorum pariter contubernio uallatum, existimabat in illo diuinam latere maiestatem; et cum esset uidua, assumpsit eum sibi maritum; sicque Machomet totius prouinciae illius obtinuit principatum. Demum uero Arabes ei adhaerentes, regnum Persidis infestare coeperunt, ac demum orientalis imperii fines usque Alexandriam, contra Heraclium inuadere. Posthaec uero Machomet coepit cadere frequenter epileptica passione; quod Cadiga cernens oppido tristabatur, eo quod nupsisset impurissimo homini et epileptico; quam ille placare desiderans, demulcebat eam, dicens: quia Gabrielem Archangelum loquentem mecum contemplor, et non ferens splendorem uultus eius, utpote carnalis homo, deficio, et cado. Credidit ergo mulier, et omnes Arabes, et Ismaelitae, quod ex ore Archangeli Gabrielis, illas susciperet leges, quas suis discipulis dabat, eo quod Gabriel Archangelus saepe a Deo mittatur hominibus sanctis.[21]

ut quidam putant sed ut summum Dei prophetam colant, utanturque legibus quas ipse composuit, adhibens ex utroque Testamento uerisimilia testimonia. Tunc ergo confluentibus ad eum Iudeis et Sarracenis et Arabibus (*quo nomine uocantur communiter Idumei et Moabitae et Ammonitae*), quia miraculis suis animos eorum dementauerat (*Iudei quippe sicut Apostolus ait signa querunt* [I Cor. 1:22]), illis ergo fretus et regnum presidis et orientale imperium Heraclii usque Alexandriam infestare cepit. Is cum frequenter epilemptica passione caderet, idque immodicae mentis mulieri permolestum esset, dicebat ille non se infirmari, sed a sensibus corporis abduci, ut liberius cum Gabrihele loqueretur Archangelo, qui sibi leges illas quas ceteris promulgaret, asserebat e caelo. *Recepta est haec opinio apud gentes barbaras, et adhuc credunt leges illas esse angelicas.*[20]

Hugh's account is a mixture of little-known fact and current, well-established fiction.[22] Obligingly, he tells his readers what his main source for it was:

Verum multa, quae secuntur, ab Anastasii Romani bibliothecarii libro decerpsi, quem . . . de Greco transtulit in Latinum . . . Prefatus autem Anastasius suis temporibus ea, quae in Greca continebantur historia ab Octauiano Augusto usque ad Michaelem, qui Nicephoro successit, rationabili prosecutus oratione Latino transtulit eloquio, in quo opere nobis multa quae hactenus nesciebamus, aperuit, *ibique de Muhamet pseudopropheta pauca quidem locutus est, sed quibus temporibus fuerit lucide designauit.*[23]

Hugh seems to imply that before he read Anastasius' *Historia Tripartita*, he did not really know when Mohammed lived; he also appears to suggest that he had access to other information about him. A comparison of his treatment of Mohammed's life with Anastasius' indicates that this is so. Since Anastasius' account is lengthy, and readily accessible in De Boor's edition, I will not print it here *in extenso*, but merely summarize the chief points of agreement and difference between it and Hugh's.[24] Hugh's account is shorter than Anastasius', and it is to his credit that he has completely omitted some of the more fabulous tales told in his main source, such as Khadija's friendship with the adulterous pseudomonk, the conversion of ten Jews, and Mohammed's preaching of the erotic delights of paradise. Hugh has retained from Anastasius the term "pseudopropheta" applied to Mohammed, his Ishmaelite ancestry, his mercantile profession and conversation with Jews and Christians, his marriage, his assumption of a messianic role, his epileptic fits and explanation of them. All else is added, and even in his presentation of those facts which he shares with Anastasius, Hugh departs markedly from his predecessor's confused sequence of events. Thus Hugh, more correctly, has Mohammed meet with the Christians and Jews, accept a version of their law and proclaim himself Messiah, before marrying Khadija. Khadija herself he describes not as a rich widow, but, again more accurately, as a person of authority in Khorasan. All the detail found in Anastasius but omitted by Hugh comes into the category of legend; conversely, nearly all of Hugh's additions are factual – these include Mohammed's early conversations with Jews and Christians and interest in their scriptures, his going to Khorasan, and the origin of the Koran, containing elements of the Old and New Testaments. The major exception is the mention of Mohammed's magical powers and epileptic fits, part of the *koinê* of western writers about Islam in Hugh's day, and his vague and overstated account of Mohammed's campaigns. Oddly, in a separate passage, Hugh places the date of Mohammed's death about a decade too late, although Anastasius should have set him right about this.[25] Nonetheless, thanks to his main source, Hugh's dating of Mohammed is streets ahead of that proposed by most other contemporary authors.

Where did Hugh obtain his information correcting and supplementing Anastasius? It is not possible to say precisely. Much of his additional material is not found in any known earlier source, Eastern or Western. He may have spoken with travelers or crusaders who returned from the East;

an oral rather than written tradition seems to lie behind the new details.[26]

The relationship between William of Malmesbury's account and Hugh's is similar to Hugh's with Anastasius'. William has abbreviated heavily, again mostly to the advantage of his version. He omits principally two kinds of material: mere rhetorical verbiage, of which Hugh is inordinately fond and which serves only to pad out his narrative and slow it down; and the marvelous element, which, although still present in William's version, is much reduced as a prime explanation of Mohammed's actions and successes. Mohammed's interpretation of his epileptic fits is not only seen as a ploy to calm his wife, but, less simplistically, as related to the prophet's earlier-developed religious ideas and magical powers – powers whose efficacy William does not doubt.

William makes three small additions to Hugh (the italicized passages in the passage quoted earlier), the second of which we may at once dismiss as illustrative only of William's book-learning.[27] The first is an explanation by William of the tremendous number of believers in Islam in his own time, nothing short of miraculous. William was impressed and worried by this fact. He enlarges on it in his *Commentary on Lamentations:*

(Glossing Lam. 1:14 – Vigilauit iugum iniquitatum mearum . . . ; infirmata est uirtus mea.) Hi mores sepe Christianos exercitus gentilibus fecerunt cedere, ut etiam abhinc plus ducentis annis, Thurci et Sarraceni dominacione sua illa premerent loca quae fuerant Dei natiuitatis et passionis conscia. Hi mores ad quantulos nos redegerunt, qui eramus quondam gens etsi non multa, at certe multis eruditione et affabilitate preferenda. Profecto illud in nobis uidetur impletum quod psalmista Iudeos denotauit dicens: Disperge illos in uirtute tua, et destrue eos protector meus Domine (Ps. 58:12).[28]

The spread of Islam plainly puzzled William, as did its past victories over Christianity. In his own account of the Council of Clermont in 1095, William reports Pope Urban II as lamenting Christian territorial losses to Islam and the comparatively small number of Christians in the world.[29] In his Selden Collection he saw Mohammed's miracles as important to the expansion of Islam; in his Commentary he sees in it God's judgment on the unfaithful Christians.

The third of William's additions again refers to contemporary Islam, and the belief in the heavenly origin of the Koran. This is the only *specific* piece of information which he adds, and it is of course correct. There is no need to suppose that William was dependent on a written source for this detail. Together with the other minor modifications to Hugh's account it could have resulted from his interviews with returned crusaders, presumably the same men who supplied him with scraps of information about the first Crusade, recorded in the *Gesta Regum.*[30]

One must ask whether the statements about Islam contained in William's *Gesta Regum* and *Commentary on Lamentations* are dependent on his knowledge of Hugh of Fleury. He knew Hugh by 1137, about the time when he was writing the Commentary; he would have needed to know him before 1125 if Hugh was the source for the *Gesta Regum* passage. There is no proof of this, and in any case William had access to other sources of information about Mohammed: he was, as mentioned, in contact with returned crusaders, and he possessed Arabic writings in translation.[31]

There remains the intriguing question as to the reason for his interest in Islam. After all, the long passage on Mohammed occurs in the midst of the *gesta* of the Roman emperors, to which it is not highly relevant, at least in such detail. The shorter passages from the *Gesta Regum* and *Lamentations Commentary* are also gratuitous pieces of information, so far as the main themes of each work are concerned. His interest was not overtly polemical; Hugh's account is much more of a "smear" than William's. True, William does mention Mohammed's use of magical deception, but on the whole his account is temperate and unrhetorical. I think that his interest in Mohammed is largely to be explained in terms of his historical sense. He seems to have recognized that in Mohammed's career lay the origins of an important religion and significant historical developments involving very large numbers of people; these developments, by giving rise to the crusades, had impinged upon the Western Europe of William's day, and to a historian of his quality, demanded an explanation. In support of this I note the sentence in his description of Mohammed's career in which he defends the genuineness of the prophet's magical or miraculous powers by adducing the very large number of his followers in William's own time. I also note that from this point on, in his abbreviation of Hugh's chronicle, which purports to be a history of the Roman emperors, William devotes a disproportionate amount of space to the expansion of Islam. Doubtless the long account of the first Crusade which William wrote into the earlier *Gesta Regum* – again departing from his main theme – prompted him to ask questions about the nature and origins of Islam, a religion of tremendous motivating power. Mohammed, he soon saw, was himself the explanation, and he also saw that the earlier accounts of him available and current in the West were unsatisfactory. As his explicit criticisms of them show, he thought it important that they should be corrected, and he certainly succeeded in improving on them.

This exploration of the treatment of Mohammed's career by some Western writers from the tenth century to the second quarter of the twelfth century illustrates the importance of establishing the sources of information available to such men, and the relationships between their various accounts. In this connection it draws attention to a flaw in Dr. Daniel's fine study. Organized on topical lines, rather than on chronological, as is Southern's shorter essay, the work does not enable one to map the temporal development of Western knowledge of Islam; it presents a static rather than a dynamic picture. It also fails to trace connections between the accounts of Western writers. Thus, for instance, a passage on Mohammed quoted from Vincent of Beauvais was lifted verbatim by Vincent from Hugh of Fleury.[32] This exploration also calls in question the neatness of Southern's division between the ages of ignorance and reason. Anastasian the Librarian knew nearly as much about Mohammed as did William of Malmesbury; he knew much more than the poet of the *Song of Roland*. Conversely, William clearly implies that the commonest assumptions about Islam by Westerners of his own day were quite false. Although accurate knowledge of Islam spread more widely and quickly in the crusading era, distinctions clearly have to be drawn between the amount and the quality of information possessed by the educated elite and the illiterate masses in medieval Europe at any one time, as well as between the "average" levels of knowledge which existed at different periods. Any future study of this fascinating and important subject should be particularly sensitive to these problems.

NOTES

1. R. W. Southern, *Western Views of Islam in the Middle Ages* (Oxford, 1962); these are the titles of the first two chapters.
2. W. W. Comfort, "The Saracens in the French Epic," *Publications of the Modern Language Association of America*, 55 (1940), 628–59.
3. Southern, pp. 34–5.
4. Ed. W. Stubbs (Rolls Series, London, 2 vols., 1887–1889), I, p. 230.
5. Oxford, Bodleian Library, MS Bodl. 868. See H. Farmer, "William of Malmesbury's Commentary on Lamentations," *Studia Monastica*, 4 (1962), 289; R. W. Hunt, "English Learning in the Late Twelfth Century," in R. W. Southern ed., *Essays in Medieval History* (London, 1968), p. 117 and n. 3, p. 118. Hunt's date for Robert's mention of William (1138 or later) is to be slightly corrected (to 1137 or later) by reference to D. Knowles, C. N. L. Brooke and V. London, *The Heads of Religious Houses* (Cambridge, 1972), p. 79.
6. MS Bodl. 868, f. 78ᵛ.
7. J. Kritzeck, *Peter the Venerable and Islam* (Princeton, 1964), pp. 141–9.
8. MS Bodl. 868, f. 58ᵛ. I have not been able to identify the source of William's quotation.
9. Cf. the view expressed in the prologue to his own *Polyhistor*, translated by M. R. James, *Two Ancient English Scholars* (Glasgow, 1931), pp. 26–7.
10. P. von Moos, *Hildebert von Lavardin* (Stuttgart, 1965), pp. 94–116, 240–89.
11. *Gesta Regum*, II, pp. 402–3.
12. *Ibid.*, I, pp. cxxx–cxl; described in F. Madan, H. Craster et al., *A Summary Catalogue of Western Manuscripts in the Bodleian Library*, vol. 2 pt. 1 (Oxford, 1922), p. 619.
13. *Ibid.*, and James, *Two Ancient English Scholars*, pp. 14, 17.
14. MS Arch. Seld. B. 16, f. 135; printed by Stubbs, *Gesta Regum*, I, p. cxxxiv.
15. J.-P. Migne, *Pat. Lat.* 139, cols. 617–798.
16. Ed. B. Rottendorff, *Hugonis Floriacensis Monachi Benedictini Chronicon*

(Münster, 1638); cf. A. Vidier, *L'Historiographie à Saint-Benoît-sur-Loire et Les Miracles de Saint-Benoît* (Paris, 1965), pp. 76–9.

17. In an article entitled "The Reading of William of Malmesbury," forth-coming in *Revue Bénédictine*, 85 (1975).

18. MS Arch. Seld. B. 16, f. 137.

19. Rottendorff, pp. 149–50; N. Daniel, *Islam and the West* (Edinburgh, 1960), pp. 12, 324 n. 11.

20. MS Arch. Seld. B. 16, f. 136ᵛ.

21. Rottendorff, pp. 149–50.

22. To the fictional class belong the references to Mohammed's use of magic and his epilepsy (Southern, pp. 30–1; Daniel, pp. 27–8). Some of the true facts were known to earlier and other contemporary writers, such as Mohammed's marriage, his contacts with Christians and Jews, and his early career as a merchant (Southern, pp. 29 and n. 26, 30–1; Daniel, pp. 80–90). For a few other matters Hugh seems to be our earliest western authority.

23. *Mon. Germ. Hist., Script.* IX, p. 357.

24. *Theophanis Chronographia*, ed. C. de Boor (Leipzig, 2 vols., 1883–1885), II, pp. 208–10. It should be noted that Hugh was not the only, nor the first Western writer to be influenced by Anastasius' account of Mohammed's career. Anastasius' words are reproduced almost verbatim by Landolf Sagax in his *Historia Miscella*, written in southern Italy shortly before 1023; *Landolfi Sagacis Historia Miscella*, ed. A. Crivellucci (*Fonti per la Storia d'Italia*, Rome, 2 vols., 1913), II, pp. 132–4.

25. Rottendorff, p. 153; De Boor, II, p. 208.

26. Daniel, p. 342 n. 9; Southern, p. 30 n. 26, p. 31 n. 28.

27. I do not know the source of William's identification of the Arabs with the ancient Idumaeans, Moabites and Ammonites, but suspect that it was a written one, perhaps a biblical commentary of the Carolingian period or later.

28. MS Bodl. 868, f. 34ᵛ.

29. *Gesta Regum*, II, pp. 393–8.

30. *Ibid.*, II, pp. cxviii–cxxvii.

31. William's interest in Arabic scientific writings is documented in my forth-coming article mentioned above.

32. Daniel, p. 27 and p. 327 n. 45.

Literary Criticism in
William Godwin's Life of Chaucer

PAUL M. CLOGAN

Of the nineteen lives or biographies of Chaucer written during the period from Tyrwhitt's 1775 edition of the *Canterbury Tales* to Sir Nicholas H. Nicholas' *Life of Chaucer* in 1845, William Godwin's *Life of Chaucer* was the most ambitious and influential.[1] Eleanor Hammond was the first to classify the Lives of Chaucer into the "Legend," from the work of John Leland to 1845, and the "Appeal to Fact," from Nicholas to the life-records of the Chaucer Society and after.[2] Although Godwin's *Life,* published in 1803, produced many actual documents, it is indeed classified as belonging to the period of the "Legend," for it records more fiction than fact. The age in which Godwin wrote was not as concerned as the Victorian period with factual information in literary lives or in philological inquiries. The knowledge of Chaucer in the early nineteenth century was based upon tradition and acceptance of the spurious works as belonging to the Chaucer canon. Writing at the end of the Victorian era, Thomas Lounsbury, who called Godwin's *Life* "an extraordinary specimen of biography," is too harsh in his criticism of Godwin and his lack of information: "It is perhaps the earliest though unhappily not the latest or even the largest illustration of that species of biography in which the lack of information about the man who is its alleged subject is counterbalanced by long disquisitions about anything or everything he shared in or saw, or may have shared in or seen."[3]

Godwin was deeply interested in the life, times, and literature of Chaucer, and had been reading Tyrwhitt's second edition of the *Canterbury Tales* published in 1798.[4] The immediate reasons that led the "radical" philosopher, essayist, and former novelist to undertake a biography of the poet are not clear. We do know that his playwriting attempts had met with failure and that his financial operations were in a dangerous state. Since Tyrwhitt had produced only an eight-page life of Chaucer based upon extant facts, Godwin perhaps considered the possibility of writing a more thorough and extensive Life, while hoping, perhaps, to benefit financially from its publication. Indeed, Godwin's *Life* was a financial success. One thousand copies of the two-volume quarto edition of 1803 were immediately sold, and in the following year a four-volume ottavo edition appeared.[5] Yet Godwin's profit from the undertaking amounted to only six hundred pounds, and his own biographer reports that "he was very much dissatisfied."[6]

Although he was able to gather and use a few life-records in addition to those known to Tyrwhitt, Godwin's purpose for writing a two-volume life of over one thousand quarto pages was not to produce all known documentary references to the poet or materials concerning his ancestors, his wife, and his descendants. In his Preface, Godwin indicates that the first object of the *Life* is to erect a monument to Chaucer's name. He hoped to develop a general audience, composed of not scholars or antiquaries, but new readers who might be stimulated to study and appreciate Chaucer and his language. Godwin makes it clear that he is not writing for scholars or antiquaries, men of "cold tempers and sterile imaginations."[7] A full and complete life of the poet should, according to Godwin, picture the manners, opinions, arts, and literature of the age in which the poet lived. The biographer believed that man is the creature of the circumstances in which he is placed, and he tried to portray Chaucer, his life and personality, by describing his environment and age – "To delineate the state of England, such as Chaucer saw it, in every point of view of which it can be delineated, is the subject of this book."[8]

To delineate Chaucer's environment and to picture Chaucer the man, Godwin devotes sections and even chapters to the medieval church, fourteenth-century London, the feudal system, and customs of knighthood, hunting, and hawking. Godwin's approach to his subject was influenced by eighteenth-century medievalists and biographers. The increasing interest in the primitive English past had produced such works as Percy's *Reliques of Ancient English Poetry* (1765), the Rowley poems of Chatterton, and the Ossianic poems of Macpherson. Dr Johnson's *Lives of the English Poets* (1779–1781) and Boswell's *Life of Samuel Johnson* (1791) were designed to show in density of detail the life of the writer, and to present the writer as a public figure, not simply as a creator or craftsman. Moreover, Godwin did not have the biographical information which was available to Dr Johnson or the advantage of seeing his living subject before him. He had the double task of sketching the poet's life and the age in which he lived. Godwin's approach to the *Life* was somewhat similar to Hippolyte Taine's stress on race, moment, and milieu as the environmental causes of literature (*History of English Literature,* 1864). To understand the literature and ultimately, the man, it is necessary to study and to understand the environmental causes which shape the creator and his creation. The biographer sees in the writings of the poet indications of an extraordinary mind, and this leads him to reflect upon the personality of the poet as seen in his writings and finally to connect the poet to his race, moment, and milieu, exhibiting the poet as he was seen and influenced by his fourteenth-century English environment.

It has been noted that in the *Life* Godwin "saw the age of Chaucer through the spectacles of Romanticism."[9] While it is true that Godwin sketches the courts of love, wars, the rise and fall of monarchs as well as the "Romish religion," his purpose was not to stress the fantastic or unusual but to see Chaucer the man in the dynamic world of fourteenth-century England. Godwin believed that "the wonder and the degree of power displayed in any monument of literature will often be enhanced, when we come to be acquainted with the circumstances under which it was erected."[10] In addition to the essential background information, a significant part of the *Life* includes historical criticism of Chaucer's poetry with emphasis on the man as reflected through his work. Like later Romantic critics, in particular Hazlitt and Coleridge, Godwin's criticism of Chaucer's poetry sought to portray the mind and character of the poet in his works, to discuss creative imagination, natural genius, and the nature of great literature.[11] These concerns and interests became the characteristics of Romantic criticism of Chaucer in the nineteenth century, and Godwin's *Life* played no small part in their development.

Godwin considers Chaucer a man of great intelligence and learning because he attended three universities: Cambridge, Oxford, and Paris. This belief was perhaps based upon a supposition originally expressed by Leland and Bale that Chaucer had a university career.[12] The biographer finds evidence of Chaucer's attendance at Cambridge University in the *Court of Love*, lines 912–3, in which the narrator reveals himself as a Cambridge student.[13] In his discussion of the *Court of Love*, which was still included in the Chaucer canon in the early nineteenth century, Godwin is impressed by its "natural structure and easy flow of language" but criticizes it "as deficient in powers of description, as in intricacy of plot of variety of incidents."[14] He further notes that imagery and description were not the chief literary characteristics of the poet's mind, but pointed out that no writer "seizes more powerfully the manners, the humours and the sentiments of mankind or delineates them more vigorously."[15] It is to Godwin's credit that at the end of the discussion of the *Court of Love* he calls for a true and correct edition of all Chaucer's works. Tyrwhitt's edition of the *Canterbury Tales* had shown what a good edition could do for a writer, and Godwin points out the necessity of a true and correct edition of the rest of Chaucer's works, a fuller and more accurate one than those of Speght (1598, 1602) and Urry (1721). Godwin further argues that Chaucer's language was neither obsolete nor obscure and his versification, though hard to read aloud, was not inharmonious. "All that repels us in the language," according to Godwin, "is merely superficial appearance and first impression."[16]

In his literary criticism of Chaucer's poetry, Godwin gives much attention to the discussion of *Troilus and Criseyde*, and he compares it with the versions of Boccaccio, Henryson, and Shakespeare. The biographer considers *Troilus* an early work, probably written at Oxford and finished before 1350. It is a translation, not of Boccaccio's *Il Filostrato*, but of some lost twelfth-century Latin work.[17] He is critical of the length of the poem which is "merely a love-tale" and not an epic.[18] The plot is thin with few incidents, excitement, or suspense and not enough of "vicissitudes of fortune, awakening curiosity and holding expectation in suspense."[19] Moreover, "the catastrophe is unsatisfactory and offensive." In a "love-tale," the poet

should soothe our minds with the fidelity and disinterestedness of the mutual attachment of the parties, and, if he presents us with a tragical conclusion, it should not be one which arises out of the total unworthiness of either.[20]

Godwin points out many "base and vulgar lines," such as Criseyde's statement: "Soche arguments ne be not worthe a bene" (III, 1167). He also finds lines vulgarized by brutality of sentiment, such as the narrator's comment on Criseyde's conduct: "But whether that she children hadde or none, / I rede it nought, therefore I late it goon" (I, 132–3). The biographer finds particularly offensive the long section in Book IV, in which "upward of one hundred verses upon predestination are put into the mouth of Troilus."[21] In the *Filostrato*, Godwin notes that Boccaccio did not interrupt the movement of the story with irrelevant discussions on predestination, and he concludes that "what is commonly called taste had made a much greater progress" in Italy than in England in the fourteenth century.[22]

On the other hand, Godwin admires many beautiful passages in *Troilus* which reveal "nice and refined observations of the workings of human sensibility."[23] *Troilus* is a good poem, Godwin argues, because it has "intrinsic and unchangeable pretensions" and it occupies an important place "in the scale and series of literary history."[24] Chaucer in *Troilus* revived and refined the English language from its languid state:

the English tongue had long remained in a languid and almost perishing state, overlaid and suffocated by the insolent disdain and remorseless tyranny of the Norman ravagers and dividers of our soil.... With Chaucer it seemed to spring like Minerva from the head of Jove, at once accoutered and complete.[25]

Godwin expresses what became the standard critical view of *Troilus* in the early nineteenth century when he states that the poem "contained nothing but what was natural" and "presents real life and human sentiments, and suffers the reader to dwell upon and expand the operations of feeling and passion."[26]

Godwin exhibits Chaucer's artistry in *Troilus* by comparing it to Henryson's *Testament of Cresseid* and Shakespeare's *Troilus and Cressida*. The famous ending of Henryson's narrative, in which Cresseid is punished by leprosy and is shown as a beggar giving alms to Troilus, presents what Godwin calls an inherent problem in the story. On the one hand, Godwin maintains that Henryson's grim ending displays excessive use of poetic justice; yet on the other hand, he argues that "though virtue may be shown unfortunate, vice should not be dismissed triumphant."[27] In the end, he finds the fate of Cresseid in Henryson's *Testament* too "savage and heart-appalling a retribution," and he concludes that Henryson's narrative cannot measure up to "the magic sweetness and softness of Chaucer."[28] When he compares Chaucer's *Troilus* to Shakespeare's *Troilus and Cressida*, Godwin contrasts the slowness and stateliness of Chaucer's narrative, which he says "has the stately march of a Dutch burgomaster as he appears in a procession,"[29] to the vitality and sublimity of Shakespeare's play. Because the playwright's characters seem more human and alive than those of Chaucer, the biographer ranks Shakespeare's play as superior to Chaucer's poem. He maintains that Shakespeare removed from the characters "the classic stiffness of their gait," and supplied them instead with attributes "which might render them completely beings of the same species with ourselves."[30] Yet in the final analysis, Godwin finds that his poet surpasses Shakespeare in one respect: "the characters of Chaucer are much more respectable and loveworthy than the correspondent personages in Shakespear[sic],"[31] and as a result Godwin asserts that Shakespeare's play can never strongly hold our affections and interest.

It is interesting to note that in his review of the *Life of Chaucer*, published in the *Edinburgh Review* of 1804, Sir Walter Scott singled out for special praise Godwin's discussion of *Troilus* which he said had "considerable merit" and was "the production of a man who had read poetry with taste and feeling."[32] Charles Lamb, in a letter to Godwin of 10 November 1803, expressed special delight in Godwin's discussion of *Troilus and Cressida* and Shakespeare and called it "some of the most exquisite criticism" that he had ever read.[33]

Godwin is indeed touched and pleased by the "Knight's Tale." According to him, it was written between 1350 and 1358 and is probably an abridgement of an earlier and longer work. Although he knows of the similar story of Palamon and Arcite by Boccaccio, the biographer is uncertain whether Chaucer's tale is indebted to the *Teseida*. Objecting to Dryden's ridiculous and excessive praise of the poem, Godwin considers the "Knight's Tale" "full of novelty and surprise," "every where alive," "the most interesting turns of fortune," and remarks that it displays the most "powerful portrait of chivalry that was perhaps ever delineated."[34] For him, the "Knight's Tale" has "every thing in splendour and in action that can most conspicuously paint out the scenes of the narrative to the eye of the reader."[35]

The biographer is especially interested in Chaucer's connection with the court of Edward III and the reasons he entered the king's household in 1358. He rejects Tyrwhitt's supposition that the king may not have known of the poet's literary talents, and argues that Edward III knew of

Chaucer's fame and sought him out to improve and cultivate the mind of his son John of Gaunt. In this connection, Godwin finds new evidence to support the theory that the *Parliament of Fowls* is an allegory of the courtship and marriage of John of Gaunt with Blanche of Lancaster. He maintains that "it is not improbable that it was penned at the request of the lover, for the purpose of softening the obduracy of his mistress's resistance."[36] Godwin admires the loftiness of the opening section of the *Parliament*, the fanciful and elevated picture of the Garden and Temple of Venus, and the fanciful "Parliament" itself which displays Chaucer's remarkable ability in characterizing the different birds. Yet as an allegory of the courtship of John of Gaunt and Blanche, Godwin considers the work as a whole unsuccessful. There is "something meagre and unnatural in this sort of allegory, where Chaucer introduces the lovers he means to compliment, under the personage of birds."[37]

The allegory of the *Book of the Duchess*, which is called chiefly historical, also disturbs Godwin, for he finds in the poem passages "which mark in no common degree the crudeness of taste of the times in which Chaucer wrote."[38] He points out as an example of such crudeness the allegory of the Black Knight playing a game of chess with Fortune. A chess game, to Godwin, is an appropriate way of expressing the grief which John of Gaunt feels at the loss of his duchess.

For the *House of Fame*, Godwin has much admiration:

It is full of imagination; a beauty congenial to, and not to be dispensed with in, a performance of this class. It abounds in passages of a philosophical cast, as might well be expected from a mind like Chaucer's, in the full maturity of its faculties. And it is interspersed...with traits of human nature and strokes of humour, excellences not most obviously to be looked for in a composition the subject of which is supernatural.[39]

Godwin is impressed by the rock of ice, the whirling of the House of Tydinges, and the two trumpets of Aeolus; the philosophy of sound contributes to the excitement of the *House of Fame* which is composed in "the finest style of allegorical delineation":

They have that fresh and wholesome hue, and that muscular and elastic character, which are peculiarly the inheritance of great minds. No elaborateness, no artifice, no affectation. It is the signature of Chaucer's imagination, that he dwells in generals, and by a single happy trait sets fire to his reader's fancy, and conjures up in him the feeling and state of mind which would have been present to the objects of which his author treats.[40]

Godwin the philosopher is indeed interested in the scientific and philosophical aspects of this love-vision as well as the extraordinary conversational powers of the eagle. He is so impressed by the liveliness and fancifulness of the *House of Fame* that he makes no mention of the fragmentary condition of the poem.

Perhaps the most important chapter in Godwin's *Life* is the last chapter on the character of the poet in which the chief traits of his character, his manners, habits, and the qualities of his mind are examined. The biographer sees Chaucer as a placid and gentle character:

The customary cheerfulness and serenity of the mind of Chaucer is particularly conspicuous in his delineations of nature. They all take their hue from the mind of the beholder, and are gay, animated and fresh.[41]

Although Godwin views the *Canterbury Tales* as Chaucer's chief claim to fame, he emphasizes the value and importance of Chaucer's minor works where the reader sees the poet's "love of rural scenery, his fondness for study, the cheerfulness of his temper, his weaknesses and his strength, and the anecdotes of his life."[42] These characteristics of Chaucer are to be found especially in the *House of Fame* and the *Parliament of Fowls*.

Limited by his publisher from writing a longer work, Godwin was unable to provide detailed criticisms of the *Canterbury Tales*, but he does present brief comments on the work as a whole and on selected tales. He describes the *Canterbury Tales* as "one of the most extraordinary monuments of human genius." He is impressed by the "variety of character" in the "General Prologue," the "splendour" of the "Knight's Tale," the "fancy" of the "Squire's Tale," and the fine satire of the "Summoner's Tale." He considers the "Clerk's Tale" "the most pathetic that was ever written," and the "Nun's Priest's Tale" the best fable ever written. He especially praises the poet's "power of humour, of delineating characters, and of giving vivacity and richness to comic incidents."[43] However, the biographer notes that Chaucer "was, perhaps, deficient in decorum," but he adds that his lack of decorum "was more a reflection of the age than on the poet."[44] In this regard, Godwin describes the "Miller's Tale" and the "Reeve's Tale" as "filthy, vulgar and licentious" and infers that the "Merchant's Tale" and the "Wife of Bath's Prologue" "are in an eminent degree liable to the last of these accusations."[45] Yet he recognizes "that Chaucer never appears more natural, his style never flows more easily, and his vein is never more unaffected and copious, than on these occasions."[46] Discussing the Tales as a group, Godwin credits them with absolute and intrinsic merit and finds this achievement all the more outstanding:

in a remote and semi-barbarous age, that Chaucer had to a certain degree to create a language, or to restore to credit a language which had been sunk into vulgarity and contempt by being considered as a language of slaves, that history and knowledge of the past ages existed only in unconnected fragments, and that his writings, stupendous as we find them, are associated, as to the period of their production, with the first half-assured lispings of civilization and the muse, the astonishment and awe with which we regard the great father of English poetry must be exceedingly increased....[47]

Godwin's *Life of Chaucer* was indeed the most ambitious and influential biography of the poet written during the Romantic era. While it is true that he followed many of the legendary traditions concerning Chaucer and his works, Godwin in the *Life* presented the essential qualities of Chaucer's poetry for the early nineteenth century:

Splendour of narrative, richness of fancy, pathetic simplicity of incident and feeling, a powerful style in delineating character and manners, and an animated vein of comic humour.[48]

It was not until the Victorian age and after the work of Nicholas, Furnivall, and the Chaucer Society that a factual biography of the poet could be produced. Lounsbury's harsh criticism of Godwin's *Life* contributes little to our understanding of what Godwin was trying to do. The biographer was a great admirer of Chaucer and deeply interested in the manners, opinions, arts, and literature of fourteenth-century England. He paid close attention to the text of a poem under discussion, quoting or citing lines and passages from Chaucer and other poets and critics to support and illustrate his analysis. Sir Walter Scott admired him as "a man who had read poetry with taste and feeling," and Godwin was perhaps the first critic of Chaucer to praise the style of his fabliaux despite their lack of decorum. In many ways, Godwin's criticisms were in advance of his time. His discussion of the variety of character exhibited in the "General Prologue," the fanciful in the "Squire's Tale" and the *Parliament of Fowls*, the pathos of the "Clerk's Tale," the comic humour of the "Nun's Priest's Tale" as well as the tediousness of the somber lines on predestination in *Troilus*, contributed to the establishment of the Romantic tone of criticism and commentary on Chaucer. In his analyses of the poetry, the biographer displays the Romantic interest in the man behind the poetry. There is the strong tendency to relate the author's work to the poet's life and to find biographical allusion in a detail of characterization or plot. His literary criticism is influenced by the biographer's desire to exhibit the poet's life by way of references to his writings. The discussion of the *Parliament of Fowls* and the *Book of the Duchess* exhibit Godwin's keen interest in characterization, and he maintains that in the "General Prologue" the poet furnishes the reader with "a copious and extensive review of the private life of the fourteenth century in England."[49] Godwin discovers in Chaucer's characters real life situations.

The success of Godwin's two-volume *Life of Chaucer* is seen in the printing of a second edition of the *Life* in four volumes the next year. It is significant that interest in Chaucer's poetry should be strong enough that readers should want a full-scale biography of the poet. Historical and practical in his approach, Godwin's literary criticism of Chaucer's poetry contributed to the Romantic conception of Chaucer the man, and in a wider sense his *Life* provides an insight into the history of medievalism or the idea of the Middle Ages in early nineteenth-century England.

NOTES

1. *Life of Chaucer, the Early English Poet: including Memoirs of his Near Friend and Kinsman, John of Gaunt, Duke of Lancaster: with Sketches of the Manners, Opinions, Arts and Literature of England in the Fourteenth Century.* 2 vols. (London, 1803). Second edition, 4 vols. (London, 1804). All references and citations are to the second edition, hereafter referred to as *Life.* For a convenient list of Chaucer criticism and allusion, see Caroline F. E. Spurgeon, *Five Hundred Years of Chaucer Criticism and Allusion, 1357–1900,* 3 vols. (Cambridge, 1925). On the significance of Chaucer's apocryphal works in the Romantic era, see Francis W. Bonner, "Chaucer's Reputation During the Romantic Period," *Furman Studies,* 34 (1951), 1–21. I am indebted to J. Davis for information and help.
2. *Chaucer: A Bibliographical Manual* (New York, 1908), p. 1. For a discussion of the nine editions of Chaucer's works produced during this period, see Hammond, pp. 134–40. On the modernizations of Chaucer, see Charles Muscatine, *The Book of Geoffrey Chaucer: An Account of the Publication of Geoffrey Chaucer's Works from the Fifteenth Century to Modern Times* (San Francisco, 1963), p. 50.
3. *Studies in Chaucer,* 3 vols. (New York, 1892), I, 191–2. Lounsbury presents a very brief account of Chaucer's reputation during the Romantic period in Vol. III, "Chaucer in Literary History."
4. Ford K. Brown, *The Life of William Godwin* (London, 1926), p. 214.
5. Ibid., p. 220.
6. Ibid.
7. *Life,* I, p. ix.
8. Ibid., p. vii.
9. Thomas P. Peardon, *The Transition in English Historical Writing, 1760–1830* (New York, 1933), p. 247.
10. *Life,* IV, p. 199.
11. William Hazlitt, *Lectures on the English Poets* (1818) in *The Complete Works of William Hazlitt,* ed. P. P. Howe, 21 vols. (London, 1930-1934), V, p. 20; Coleridge, *Table Talk,* 15 March 1834, in *Coleridge Miscellaneous Criticism,* ed. Thomas M. Raysor (Cambridge, Mass., 1936), p. 433.
12. See Hammond, *Chaucer: A Bibliographical Manual,* pp. 1–13. For a recent study using fresh archeological evidence and newly discovered old records in Oxford and Cambridge, see J. A. W. Bennett, *Chaucer at Oxford and at Cambridge* (Toronto, 1974).
13. See Walter W. Skeat, ed. *Chaucerian and Other Pieces,* Vol. VII (1897) of *The Complete Works of Geoffrey Chaucer,* 7 vols. (Oxford, 1894-1897), p. 433.
14. *Life,* I, pp. 375, 377.
15. Ibid., p. 377.
16. Ibid., p. 395.
17. Ibid., p. 435.
18. Ibid., pp. 471–72.
19. Ibid., p. 472.
20. Ibid.
21. Ibid., pp. 483–4.
22. Ibid., p. 485.
23. Ibid., p. 474.

24. Ibid., p. 475.
25. Ibid., p. 476.
26. Ibid., p. 477.
27. Ibid., pp. 488–9.
28. Ibid., pp. 494–5.
29. Ibid., p. 502.
30. Ibid., p. 512.
31. Ibid., p. 513.
32. Review of Godwin's *Life* in the *Edinburgh Review*, III (January, 1804), 445.
33. *The Works of Charles and Mary Lamb*, ed. E. V. Lucas, 7 Vols. (London, 1903–1905), VI, p. 282.
34. *Life*, II, p. 75.
35. Ibid., pp. 75–6.
36. Ibid., pp. 168–9.
37. Ibid., p. 180.
38. Ibid., pp. 356, 362.
39. *Life*, III, p. 2.
40. Ibid., p. 34.
41. *Life*, IV, p. 176.
42. Ibid., p. 184.
43. Ibid., p. 186.
44. Ibid.
45. Ibid., p. 187.
46. Ibid.
47. Ibid., p. 200.
48. *Life*, I, pp. i–ii.
49. *Life*, IV, p. 186.

Collected Works of Erasmus: *Volume One*
A Review Article

DOUGLAS BUSH

The Correspondence of Erasmus: Letters 1 to 141, 1484 to 1500. Translated by
R. A. B. Mynors and D. F. S. Thomson, annotated by Wallace K. Ferguson.
(*Collected Works of Erasmus*, 1.) Toronto: University of Toronto Press,
1974. Pp. xxviii, 368; 12 illustrations, map. $25.00.

This volume, the first of perhaps forty, inaugurates one of the most massive
and important scholarly enterprises of our time – *The Collected Works of
Erasmus*. This enterprise reflects the greatest credit upon the humanistic zeal
and courage of the Canada Council, the University of Toronto Press, and
the many individuals concerned. The Editorial Board comprises a Coordinating
Editor, Professor Beatrice M. Corrigan (succeeding R. J. Schoeck, who moved
in 1971 to the Folger Shakespeare Library); two Literary Editors, Sir Roger
Mynors of Oxford and Professor Thomson of Toronto, who are translating
the first six volumes; and two Historical Editors, Professors Ferguson and
J. K. McConica, who are annotating respectively the first and second pairs
of volumes. An Executive Committee comprises some of these scholars, Professor P. G. Bietenholz (who is to annotate volumes 5 and 6), and officers of
the University of Toronto Press. An Advisory Committee consists of eighteen
scholars, mainly American, English, and European.
   The declared aim of the edition "is to make available an accurate, readable
English text of Erasmus' correspondence and his other principal writings"
(p. v). The first twenty volumes will contain "more than three thousand
letters, of which some sixteen hundred were written by Erasmus, the remainder
by a representative cross-section of educated European society" (Ferguson,
p. ix, n. 3). The other twenty volumes will be given to Erasmus' "other
principal writings." Publication has been expected to extend over twenty
years or so.
   The careful planning of the work is amply evident in this first volume. It
contains a succinct Introduction (ix–xxiii) in which Professor Ferguson
surveys Erasmus' whole career as mirrored in his letters, noting regretfully
that these are more or less scanty for some important phases. Further, there are
two Notes by the editors and translators on their texts, aims, and procedure;
a "Map showing the principal places mentioned in volume 1"; a fully annotated translation of Letters 1–141; and an excursus (pp. 311–47) by Professor
J. H. Munro on "Money and Coinage of the Age of Erasmus: An historical
and analytical glossary . . . ," which – supplemented by his monetary footnotes to the letters – is valuable not only in regard to the generally needy
Erasmus' concern with money but for readers of all literature and history of
the period. Finally, the volume includes a Table of Correspondents, Bibliography, Abbreviations, Short Title Forms for Erasmus' Works, and an Index.

The volume is handsomely designed and produced, with finely readable type on uncrowded pages, and has a dozen illustrations.

Professor Ferguson quotes Professor Myron Gilmore's dictum that the correspondence of Erasmus is "perhaps the greatest single source for the intellectual history of his age." The letters of 1484–1500, exchanged between him and an ever-widening circle of humanistic friends (and some other people), carry him from the age of 18–21 (the date of his birth remains a question), through early discouragements and uncertainties of direction, to ripe maturity and clarity of purpose on the threshold of his great career. We first see him at the Augustinian monastery of Steyn near Gouda, emotionally (or rhetorically) disturbed as a young monkish friend grows unresponsive. We follow as he begins his intermittent service with the niggardly bishop of Cambrai, later moving to Paris, where the theological sterilities of the Collège de Montaigu are somewhat mitigated by his gaining acquaintance with the eminent Robert Gaguin and other humanists. On the strength of his letters and mostly unpublished writings (including verse), Erasmus grows in repute among his epistolary friends, and he continually rejoices in or urges devotion to literature. Compelled to teach for subsistence, Erasmus found a deliverer in the best-known of his pupils, the young Lord Mountjoy, who, returning to England in 1499, took his tutor with him. This first English visit expanded and enriched the mind and soul of a monk of unfulfilled powers who was no longer young. What was to become lasting friendship with Colet, More, and others, made England a center of humanism no less inspiring than the Italy which had been Erasmus' goal.

Back in Paris in 1500, he published the first small edition of the *Adagia*, which were intended to distill the sane, pithy wisdom of the ancients for modern benefit. Erasmus' higher life-work was animated by the study of Greek, to which he was now giving his "entire attention," and probably by Colet's spiritual Christianity, so far above the Scotist quiddities he had always despised. He was determined henceforth to devote himself "entirely to sacred literature," a cherished ambition. He had "long had a burning desire to write a commentary on the letters" of the greatly humanistic but neglected Father, Jerome, and thus make him read far and wide (Erasmus' edition was to appear in 1516, the year his Greek New Testament, which upset so many reactionary theologians, appeared).

While Erasmus had looked forward to a career in theology, his real commitment to religion came with his maturity; and his preoccupation with literary and stylistic matters (which counted strongly in his early esteem for Jerome and Valla) had to ripen into something much richer and deeper. The result was that he became the Christian humanist *par excellence*. In that powerful role he won the ear, if not quite of all educated Europe, at least of all men of good will – while sufficiently disturbing others. The deepening and the fusion of these literary and religious strains constitute the most important thread of interest, in or between the lines, in these letters of 1484–1500. Other elements are perhaps more obvious, and some belong to the distinct genre of the humanistic epistle (a genre on which a later volume of this work will have an excursus). Among such elements are flattery of a patron, possible patron, or a possibly useful friend; a diatribe against an enemy; or, in the absence of literary reviews, an essay intended to be passed around or perhaps incorporated in a book. We may regret that such a man should at times gild begging with flattery or self-praise, but we know that scholars, like poets and artists, could not live and work without patronage; Professor Ferguson remarks (p. 267) that "The importunate tone of his begging letters for the next year or so [1500 f.] reflects a growing confidence in the importance of his work. . . ." What matters is that Erasmus became the kind of man who could later crystallize his vision and mission in that famous phrase, "Sancte Socrates, ora pro nobis," and in the complementary phrase, less arresting but no less pregnant, "Christi philosophia" (*Opera*, 1703–6, I, 683D-E, VI, 63D).

The translators' foreordained text is that of P. S. Allen's great edition (1906 f.); their rare divergences are recorded (but not some rare and slight divergences in dating). From the start, the new translation supersedes the good work of F. M. Nichols who omitted many passages he found lacking in personal interest, and whose three volumes (1901, 1904, 1918) covered the period through 1518 only. This translation promises to fulfill our high expectations of learned authority and attractive readability. The translators anticipate a reader's feeling somewhat embarrassed by the artificial flourishes of humanistic rhetoric, but they wisely counsel patience: "it is not long before we get to the real thing." There may be occasional labored bits, such as "His gratitude and his way of remembering such acts will impress you" (Ep. 3, p. 5, li. 47; Allen, I, 76, li. 42: "senties hominem et gratum et memorem"); Nichols I, 43) is shorter and simpler: "You will find him grateful, and he will not forget it." And one might note an instance of the refining of homely vigor: a certain young poet is so drunk with poetic inspiration "ut nihil expuat, nihil emungat nisi versus" (Ep. 29, Allen, p. 120, li. 29), which is rendered: "he exudes verses at every pore" (p. 54, li. 32). The normal blend of fidelity and urbane ease sometimes permits a colloquialism which bridges time and quickens our sense of the living man. The words "neque enim id est literas condere sed colligere" (Ep. 15, Allen, p. 89, li. 37), rendered literally by Nichols (I, 51) as "That is not composing a letter, but merely putting letters together", becomes "That is not literary composition but mere scissors-and-paste" (p. 21, li. 40). In Ep. 29, "tanti facinoris impunitatem" (Allen, p. 120, li. 25) takes the racier form of "get away with a crime like this" (p. 53, li. 27). Willem Hermans' remark about a tricky person, that his "doli mihi subolebant" (Ep. 34, Allen, p. 130, li. 6), gains in metaphorical concreteness: "made me smell a rat" (p. 65, li. 8). Well-bred guests "do not crash in uninvited" Ep. 61, p. 129, li. 163); Allen, p. 185, li. 153–4: "inuocati sese non ingerunt." Erasmus' "do manus, ex harena cedo" is turned into "I throw in the towel, climb out of the ring" (Ep. 102, p. 192, li. 2; Allen, p. 237, li. 2). Since no references are given for the translations into verse of the many quotations from Latin poetry, chiefly classical (and a cursory search has not turned up sources), it may be assumed that, though often unmodern in style, they are the work of the translators; some of them are remarkably neat (e.g., pp. 36, 42).

Professor Ferguson's biographical headnotes (on Erasmus' many correspondents, et al.) and footnotes depend heavily, as they must, on Allen's very thorough researches, but, while giving all that anyone wants or needs to know, they are happily less full and formidable. For quotations from Latin poetry Allen commonly supplied references, and for most of those he missed Professor Ferguson fills the gaps; he also adds miscellaneous notes. A few more allusions might have been identified, e.g.: the tying of straw to the horns of a dangerous bull (Ep. 58, p. 118, li. 79; Horace, *Sat.* 1.4.34); Timon (ibid., p. 119, li. 101–3), who is linked only with Shakespeare's play, recalls Plutarch's *Mark Antony* and Lucian's *Timon* (which, to be sure, are cited in editions of Shakespeare); the elaborate picture of Somnus and Morpheus (Ep. 61, p. 125, li. 16–28) seems to draw on Ovid, *Metam.* xi.592 f.; "the ancient proverb, 'while I breathe, I shall hope' " (Ep. 123, p. 250, li. 34; Allen, p. 285, li. 31: "vetus adagium, dum spirabimus, sperabimus,") has various roots: Terence, *Heaut.* 981: "modo liceat vivere, est spes"; cf. *Adagia* II.iii.12: "Ægroto dum anima est, spes est" (Cicero, *Ad Atticum* 9.10); ibid., IV.iv.63: "Spes servat afflictos."

In all the 400 pages I have observed only three misprints: "fine" for "finer" (p. 91, li. 143); "is" for "it" (p. 213, li. 42); and "Pythogoras" (p. 366). The index is commendably precise in citing authors' works under their names. But many names in the notes are not indexed, so that one can miss, e.g., under Hendrik van Bergen, bishop of Cambrai, the earliest references to Erasmus' relations with him (pp. 63, 71, 75, 82, 97). The citation of p. 3 for St. Jerome is a slip. Aeschines and Socrates are three times mentioned together in the text (pp. 57 [twice], 280), but only Aeschines appears in the index. "Timon, Sceptic philosopher" hardly fits the note on p. 110. While several dozen mythological and fictional characters are, properly enough, omitted, two are included: Epimetheus (but not Pandora) and Midas; Ennius' Neoptolemus is a special case and rightly included.

If these and some earlier items mainly fulfill a reviewer's obligatory function of nit-picking, some may be of use for later printings. Altogether, when we think of the rows of Erasmian works reposing in libraries and of the building, in these unpropitious times, of this truly monumental translation, we – and the builders – may echo Kipling's cathedral mason (perhaps without profaning the upper-case "Thy"): "One stone the more swings into place / In that dread Temple of Thy worth" – though we shall not all be on hand to welcome the completed structure.

Some Oblique Light: Three
Studies in Reformation History
A Review Article

ARTHUR J. SLAVIN

Dermot Fenlon. *Heresy and Obedience in Tridentine Italy: Cardinal Pole and the Counter Reformation.* Cambridge: At The University Press, 1972. Pp. xiii, 300. $19.50.

William E. Wilkie. *The Cardinal Protectors of England: Rome and the Tudors Before the Reformation.* London: Cambridge University Press, 1974. Pp. ix, 262. $14.50.

Brendan Bradshaw. *The Dissolution of the Religious Orders in Ireland under Henry VIII.* London: Cambridge University Press, 1974. Pp. xi, 276. $16.50.

Each of the books under review throws some new light on the English Reformation. Each also points out new facets of the work of Professor G. R. Elton, or of the many *opera* which taken together now constitute our most powerful interpretation of the crucial events of the 1530s, and the "revolution" in English government and society experienced under the drive of Henry VIII's will and the genius of his minister Thomas Cromwell. Sometimes the light cast serves to clarify and make more firm a position held by Professor Elton in one of his many important books: *The Tudor Revolution in Government* (1953); *England under the Tudors* (1955); *The Tudor Constitution* (1960); *Policy and Police* (1972); *Reform and Renewal* (1973); or in the two volumes of collected papers now reprinted as *Studies in Tudor and Stuart Politics and Government* (1974).

It is important to note at the outset, therefore, that each of the books under review also casts some doubt on one or more positions held by Professor Elton. This is less a discomfort to his reputation than it is a very strong tribute to a scholar's fidelity to his Muse: Each of the books reviewed originated in a Cambridge doctoral thesis done under Professor Elton's supervision. So far are we from the ambience of what has recently been called an "Establishment" interpretation, that it is the supposed maker of that interpretation who is guiding younger scholars to challenge it and make important revisions. (See *AHR*, LXXIX [1974], 1546-7, where Professor Hurstfield taxes me for the maintenance of Elton's theses, in reviewing my *The Precarious Balance* [New York: Knopf, 1973].)

Dr Fenlon's work is on its face remote from Henrician England. His study focuses on the continental movements of humanism and reform in an effort to explain why Pole split with Henry VIII – his cousin and one of the two men he most revered in the world (the other being the Pope) – and what was the nature of Pole's religious conviction touching the supreme question of justification. Hence Dr Fenlon's sights are set not on Pole's English friends but on the members of the Viterbo Circle who gathered around him in his role as a curial reformer and later Legate to the Council of Trent. His target is the group of *spirituali* who supported Lutheran ideas about the economy of salvation and sought to head off a definition of doctrine certain to end the prospect of restoring unity in the Church.

Dr Fenlon, following in the path broken by Cantimori, Hughes, Jedin, Lortz, and Paschini, argues that Pole was the very soul of the movement to make a compromise. But he differs from other historians who have dealt with Pole and his circle from the Cardinal's appointment on the commission to reform the Church in 1537 through the period of hope at Regensburg in 1541 and the utter defeat dealt to the compromisers by *zelanti* like Carafa at Trent in 1546. Dr Fenlon argues convincingly, basing his thoughts on a wide variety of manuscript sources and published materials, that Pole accepted both Luther's scripturalism and the radical rejection of the efficacy of works central to Protestant thought. Calvin justly called Pole a Nicodemist, and men like Vergerio were correct to say that the Cardinal betrayed the cause by not directly declaring himself against the draft decrees on justification made at Trent in 1546. This failure was less the result of cowardice than of a deeper trait of personality, however. Pole was a man unsuited for political life and too gentle to maneuver in a world filled with the likes of Carafa, Loyola and Salmeron. The Cardinal of England also lacked the will to become himself a divider of the Church; in his mind the papal tradition itself, the *magisterium*, was a surer guide to truth than personal conclusions drawn from biblical study.

There are some parts of Dr Fenlon's book bearing directly on England and on the work of Professor Elton. Pole had a view of dissent quite similar to that held by Cromwell. Pole allowed to every man the *private* expression of heterodox beliefs. Public utterance of heresy deserved persecution. The Cardinal therefore helps to fill in a line of continuity in the English Reformation, despite his Marian reputation for intolerance. On Fenlon's account Pole is the middle point in connecting Cromwell to Lord Burghley who advised Elizabeth I to demand external conformity only of her subjects and to avoid altogether cutting windows into men's souls. Professor Elton grasped that point in 1955 (*England under the Tudors*, pp. 215–22), despite the historiographic traditions in which Pole appeared either as a Catholic saint or the vilest persecutor of the Protestant martyrs.

Dr Fenlon also throws some light on the report of Pole given by Thomas Starkey in his justly famous *Dialogue*. There, Pole's former secretary and friend depicted the future Cardinal as an upholder of Lutheran ideas in some things. He also showed Pole as a careful watcher of "time and place" in setting forth ideas. Pole was far more restrained than his English supporter at Trent, the humanist Richard Pate who had been under Cromwell's patronage from 1534 to 1540. Pate took a strong public stand for the Lutheran exposition of justification in 1546, although he had fled from England after the fall of Cromwell because he was "plainly Catholic" in religion and anxious to relieve his anxiety over serving Henry VIII (p. 156). Now this is an interesting finding, because it adds support to those like Professor Elton (and myself: see *Thomas Cromwell on Church and Commonwealth* [1969]) who have depicted Cromwell as a Protestant in some things but above all else as a man dedicated to unity in the Commonweal. Pole and Cromwell are usually presented as antitheses, but it is perhaps more accurate to see in both men a more tolerant insight into the problems of reform than one hopes to find in zealots of any persuasion.

Dr Wilkie's Cardinal Protectors lacked the depths of piety and concern for the regeneration of the Church found by recent historians in a wide variety of reformers. They were for the most part Italian curialists interested in serving many masters and thus in advancing families and fortunes. They often embraced conflicting interests, and Dr Wilkie finds in the fabric of their political careers an important alternative explanation to the stock efforts to make sense of Clement VII's failure to grasp the meaning of the Divorce in 1529. The Pope is usually depicted as either a weak and vacillating man or simply as the captive of the Emperor in the wake of the Sack of 1527 and the smashing defeat administered to the Italians at Landriano in 1529 (*England under the Tudors* [1955], pp. 117–9). But Dr Wilkie has severely undermined such arguments.

He does so by dispensing with the necessity for them. Both the legate Campeggio, who doubled as England's Protector at Rome, and Clement VII were in ambiguous situations. The Pope had himself been England's Protector as the Cardinal Guilio de'Medici, from the death of Bainbridge in 1514 until his own elevation to Peter's throne, when Campeggio succeeded him in the lesser office. Neither had given particularly distinguished help to Henry VIII in critical matters in contrast to the handling of routine papal provisions and patronage affairs. De'Medici had been Cardinal Protector of France while holding the English protectorship. This had caused him to throw influence to Francis I in settling the dispute over the bishopric of Tournai in 1517–1518. De'Medici had also benefitted the French in the more important contest to control the provision to St. Andrews, when Henry VIII tried to follow up the triumph at Flodden by gaining control over the Scottish Church. Dr Wilkie calls these "dress rehearsals" for the role de'Medici would play as Pope in the Divorce (p. 96).

Campeggio's career advanced with Imperial support for nearly twenty years before the Divorce crisis. Like his predecessors Piccolomini and Castellesi, he had been legate to Germany and also Cardinal Protector of the Germans, while filling many special commissions from 1511 down through the efforts to resolve the religious crisis in the 1520s. Campeggio also thoroughly disliked Wolsey, perhaps because he had been humiliated by the Englishman in 1518 while in London to negotiate an alliance of the Christian princes against the Turks.

It thus was less the accidents of campaigns in Italy than the inherent ambiguity of roles played by the Pope and the Legate as Italian politicians which doomed the Divorce. Campeggio and Clement VII had stronger ties to France and to the Empire than to England. They were also disposed to be driven by the stronger force in a crisis, as they had more than demonstrated in the matter of Tournai and St. Andrews. Wolsey and Henry VIII had a great capacity for self-delusion in 1529, as Dr Wilkie points out (pp. 181ff), if they supposed the record of the Protectors was a thing indifferent. It was only with the advent of Cromwell that a sharper understanding of the interests of the Cardinal Protectors began to shape policy on the principle of independence from Rome (pp. 210ff).

As Wilkie demonstrates (pp. 63–80 and 161–80), the failure of Henry VIII to establish control over the Scottish Church after Flodden was matched in Ireland by a significant failure to dominate the Irish Church, except in the Pale and the old "loyal" Anglo-Irish territories before 1533. This was to have a great impact on Cromwell's attempts to make headway toward greater control over Ireland after 1535, when the minister applied a remedy in the form of monastic suppression. Dr Bradshaw reaches this important question in his

book, while also providing a detailed account of the more conventional issues
associated with studies of the Dissolution in England: the state of the religious,
the development of policy, the process of secularization and its social and
economic results. For it is his intention to seek in the Dissolution in Ireland
some help in understanding the origins of the present state of nationalist, con-
fessional, and even racial strife there.

Dr Bradshaw begins by reminding us that the suppression in England had
no intrinsic link to reformation there and was not the result of applying a
Machiavellian scheme devised by Cromwell. The English program grew up in
phases: the piecemeal approach of 1534–1535 associated with the oaths of
supremacy; the broader effort at retrenchment for good social and religious
reasons in 1536; and the wholesale policy of induced surrender in the aftermath
of the Pilgrimage of Grace, as the Crown needed to reduce a political danger
and also to secure financing for the threatened war against France, Scotland,
and the Empire.

Against that background, Dr Bradshaw shows how similar circumstances
affected the suppression in Ireland after the revolt of the Kildares in 1535 and
the setting up of the nativist Geraldine League shortly before Cromwell's fall
in 1540. He demonstrates also Cromwell's flexibility in setting forward a
policy, as he grappled with Irish parliamentary opposition from the old Anglo-
Irish administrative cadres and the lawyers who already had the initiative in
exploiting the monastic lands. Cromwell needed the spoils to buttress the loyal
Irish and Anglo-Irish against the threat beyond the Pale and the loyal territories. But his goal, one continued after 1540 by his friend and agent Antony
St. Leger, was not to dispossess the native Irish on racialist lines or even to
settle vast plantations of New English. It was rather to secure the march areas
under Crown influence and to provide suitable rewards for loyalists of any
heritage.

There were many forces inhibiting the accomplishment of these ends, however. One was the good reputation of the friars in Ireland, where in the fifteenth century the Observant Movement had become popular – not elitist as
in England. The older orders of regular monks and nuns had not the same
safety on popular bases, but there were forces working to protect them as
well. In the territories of the chiefs where Gaelic folk culture was strong, for
example, ancestor cults made the monastic churchyard sacred in a double sense;
and this made attacks on the monasteries difficult in some areas. Against this
was the force of self-interest, of course, as Cromwell well knew. The Irish
lords and gentry were as avid for land as any Englishmen, and an effort to
tie chiefs in Ormond and elsewhere enjoyed some success on that basis. Thus
Cromwell pursued in Ireland a policy of buffering the loyal territories from
the native Irish rebels as he tried to fashion a basis for an effective centraliza-
tion of government in Ireland. There is thus in Dr Bradshaw's account powerful
support for some of the central theses of Professor Elton's "Tudor revolution." There is also support for the view of Cromwell which does not see him
as a fanatic, harsh and repressive man. For Dr Bradshaw produces solid evidence of the moderate approach of Cromwell's men to the Irish (pp. 106ff).

Yet Cromwell seemed to lose touch with the realities of the Irish situation
also in 1539, and thus appears to be less than a master politician. He did not
seem to understand the popularity of the Observants or the ethnic basis of it:
the Gaelic monks set over against Anglo-Irish or New English provincials
and administrators. Any effort at a general suppression and redistribution must
necessarily force a choice on the Anglo-Irish in what might prove a struggle

for survival. There was already a struggle between some Cromwellian New English and the loyalists among the Anglo-Irish. There certainly was a war going on against both groups from nativist quarters.

In such circumstances the suppression hardly reached beyond the Pale, the loyal Southern Shires, and into some chieftancies. In the Anglo-Norman sovereign territories and most of the Gaelic areas neither suppression nor any other reformist campaign had much effect, particularly the attack on images spun off on the model of the English effort in 1538.

After Cromwell's death the situation had thus become one in which some newly reconciled Irish, the New English and the older Anglo-Irish might have come together in a single administrative elite sharing the duties of government and monastic lands. For there had been a modest degree of success in confiscation and secularization *without regard to ethnic origins*. And the efforts of Archbishop George Browne at radical reform had been halted even while Cromwell lived. There was little mourning at the passing of the monks; and the Observant friars were not the basis of any nativist movement where they survived. Dr Bradshaw is at pains to stress these things, because there are many myths in Irish history, not the least of them being that the early efforts at reformation created the discrimination fundamental to the later success of Counter Reformation and nationalist politics rooted in resentment of religious intolerance and racialist ideas. Nothing could be more removed from the truth. Cromwell had pursued a policy of "killing Rome with kindness" (p. 200). He opposed mass colonization and dispossession. He withdrew support from radical reformers and made no effort to suppress religious ideas of any *popular appeal*. He was quite content to let monasticism crumble on its own merits. In fact it was only the espousal of policies of racial and religious intolerance under Elizabethan and Stuart notions of mass "plantation" that degraded the Irish and forced the Anglo-Irish into an alliance against the still newer New English, setting the stage for exploitation, expropriation, Counter Reformation religious orders, and the call to battle in behalf of race and faith.

Dr Bradshaw has filled a major *lacuna* in Reformation history with grace and economy. His book is brilliant where those by Dr Fenlon and Dr Wilkie are merely very good. And it puts one in a state of hope – that none of the present writers adopts a polemical stance, either with regard to the substance of their own work or the achievements of Professor Elton.

Political and Social Thought in
Fourteenth-Century England: Two Recent Studies
A Review Article

MICHAEL ALTSCHUL

John Barnie. *War in Medieval English Society: Social Values in the Hundred Years' War, 1337–99*. Ithaca: Cornell University Press, 1974. Pp. xiv, 204. $10.00.

Arthur Stephen McGrade. *The Political Thought of William of Ockham: Personal and Institutional Principles* (Cambridge Studies in Medieval Life and Thought, Third Series, volume 7). New York and London: Cambridge University Press, 1974. Pp. xiv, 269. $18.50.

These two studies are devoted to aspects of the thought and values of prominent Englishmen in the fourteenth century. Professor McGrade's work is a major contribution to our understanding of William of Ockham, the greatest English intellectual of the late Middle Ages, although there is nothing specifically "English" about his thought. Dr Barnie's book, more impressionistic in treatment and slighter in texture, surveys contemporary literature to gauge attitudes toward English involvement in the Hundred Years' War. Students of late medieval society and culture will find much of value and interest in both works.

Barnie argues that England was a society dominated by actual or potential warfare, and that the literature of the age provides the evidence needed for an understanding of the moral and social values generated in this atmosphere. He presents a series of brief, judicious evaluations of a number of works, drawn from an impressive range of genres, including the poems of Laurence Minot and Gower, Thomas Gray's *Scalacronica*, the chronicles of Knighton and Walsingham, and of course Froissart. Barnie contrasts an early age of enthusiasm for the war under Edward III with a later sense of disillusionment, attributed either to war-weariness per se or to disappointment with those in power for failing to exercise the leadership necessary to recapture the heroic days of military success. He argues that the chivalric virtues nurtured by Edward III and the Black Prince were genuine and purposeful; among the higher nobility, there truly existed a cosmopolitan culture, priding itself on valor. On more popular levels, xenophobic sentiments directed against the French or Scots were transformed into a genuine sense of national consciousness.

Barnie recognizes that social history cannot be written exclusively from literature, but by the same token insists that literary evidence cannot be ignored. This, however, is where his own work is marked by certain deficiencies. The literary works used cannot tell us about "popular" values except in a limited, highly qualified fashion. Did the *Scalacronica* truly reflect the ideas and aspirations of a significant group with practical influence in their local communities or in parliament? Governmental records need to be explored here, but they are not. Moreover, the question may forever be moot because of the difficulties in ascertaining the exact audience for this kind of writing. Similar problems confront the interpretation of every literary source adduced here, from Froissart to the anonymous authors of scraps of political poems. Barnie is also guilty of a serious *non sequitur* in his chapter on "patriotism": it *must* have been popular and developing, thus if the literature failed to reflect it, this was caused by limiting rhetorical conventions and by the lack of an adequate political vocabulary. Surely this sort of reasoning will not do. The personal encomia directed at Edward III must be taken at face value as precisely that, not as unfortunately truncated shorthand for England as a unique national entity and identity. The absense of such sentiments in literature cannot be taken as proof of their existence!

Despite these shortcomings, this study has much to commend it. Historians do need to broaden and deepen their traditional concerns with the political-economic aspects of the war by coming to grips with the moral and intellectual implications of contemporary literature. Barnie has made a useful and largely plausible contribution in this regard. Perhaps of no less importance, he has provided historians with an object lesson in graceful, interesting writing.

With William of Ockham, one immediately enters an entirely different mental world. McGrade's book is difficult and complex, but is written with sympathy, engagement, and conviction. The work is squarely based on Ockham's later writings, stemming from his exile at the court of Ludwig of Bavaria, in particular the *Dialogus*, the *Breviloquium*, and the *Octo Quaestiones*. Impelled by his conviction that the popes were heretical in their judgment on Franciscan poverty, Ockham was led to reexamine the relations between office and person, both in ecclesiastical and in secular government. His ideas represented a fresh and significant evaluation of the nature and purposes of both polities in a Christian world. The key to his thought is his essentially nonpolitical vision of Christian human order, the notion of freedom tempered by corporate solidarity, and the norms of right reason. Ockham's theory called for a depoliticized Church, with the papacy reduced to a pastoral role based on *ministerium*, in contrast to the curialists' emphasis on juristic *dominium*. Except in the specific case of a heretical pope, however, Ockham had no fundamental quarrel with the notion of hierarchy, provided Church rulers recognized that the quality of governance ultimately depended on the quality of the members it was designed to serve. By the same token, secular government (the Empire) was stripped of sacral characteristics, and construed in largely negative terms, as an instrument for, but not the object of, human fulfillment. Thus, Ockham's political writings were neither systematic nor undertaken in any positive spirit. His preoccupations were the theological conceptions of liberty and the relations between reason, law, and volition. Precisely because of this indifference to traditional concerns with the forms of government, Ockham fruitfully reopened and refocused debate on the ultimate quality of governance.

Seen in this light, little remains of the standard view of Ockham as a radical laicist, or as a proponent of anarchic subjectivism. Just as his theology and logic have come to be viewed as positive, rather than destructive contributions to medieval thought, so also now with his political and social ideas. McGrade rightly stresses that Ockham was an *homme engagé;* not, however, as an implacable foe of all papal authority or as an automatic apologist for imperial independence, but as a Franciscan visionary with abiding convictions about Christian virtue and freedom. Ockham emerges as a constructive, albeit non-systematic, political thinker, worthy both of his own age (the age of Marsiglio, Dante, and the great papal monarchists) and of the larger tradition of Christian writing on the nature and purpose of human community. This book, too, is a major and constructive contribution to medieval scholarship. Anyone concerned with late medieval society and values must, in one way or another, ultimately confront Ockham; in so doing, he must consult, and learn from, McGrade.

Toronto Medieval Latin Texts:
Three New Editions
A Review Article

DANIEL J. SHEERIN

Michael Winterbottom, ed. *Three Lives of English Saints.* Toronto: Pontifical
  Institute of Mediæval Studies, 1972. Pp. 94. $2.75 paper.
H. C. Kim, ed. *The Gospel of Nicodemus: Gesta Salvatoris.* Toronto: Pon-
  tifical Institute of Mediæval Studies, 1973. Pp. 54. $2.75 paper.
Janet Martin, ed. *Peter the Venerable: Selected Letters.* Toronto: Pontifical
  Institute of Mediæval Studies, 1974. Pp. 107. $2.75 paper.

The purpose and nature of this series have been described in a Preface by its
General Editor, A. G. Rigg (vol. I, pp. i–ii). The primary intention is "to
provide editions suitable for university courses and curricula, at a price within
the range of most students' resources." This purpose is suggestive of that of
the old "in usum scholarum" volumes of the MGH, but there the resemblence
ends. The need for this enterprise has arisen because "Many Medieval Latin
texts are available only in expensive scholarly editions, equipped with full
textual apparatus but with little or no annotation for the student; even more
are out of print, available only in libraries; many interesting texts still remain
unedited." We are informed, moreover, that the editions in this series will
commonly be based on one manuscript, with emendations made "only where
the text fails to make sense, not in order to restore the author's original
version." What is proposed is a "scribal version" of the text. This is defined as
"a version that was acceptable to its scribe and was read and understood by
medieval readers." The obvious perils of this method are to be avoided
through the discrimination of the individual editor, that is, his *codex unicus*
should be a *codex optimus*, representative of a tradition "as little removed
from the original as possible" or representative of a local variant of a text or
of a "widely influential version." This method has certain virtues, the greatest
of which must be economy of production. The scribal version may present
us with a fixed redaction of a text, the document as copied and read in one
place and at one time, a witness to one stage in the text's tradition. In the case
of a true *codex unicus* such a procedure may be necessary. In cases in which
a multiplicity of witnesses exist, the isolation of the text of one witness is
of interest to the specialist, but one must wonder whether this approach is best
suited to the *editio princeps* of a text or to the needs of the university student.
Happily, the editors of the present volumes have provided us with more critical information than the general guidelines would suggest.
   The first volume in the series contains Aelfric's Life of St. Ethelwold (BHL
2646), Wulfstan of Winchester's Life of St. Ethelwold (BHL 2647), and Abbo
of Fleury's Life of St. Edmund (BHL 2393). The Aelfric Life is based on its
only witness, B.n. lat. 5362, ff. 74ʳ–81ʳ. This text has been twice printed, by
J. Stevenson in R. S. 2 (1858), and by the Bollandists in their catalogue of

hagiographical MSS in the Bibliothèque Nationale. Winterbottom collects the emendations of the previous editors in his "Textual Notes" (p. 89). The only good reason for the editing anew of this document must be that which Winterbottom professes (p. 2): "Both [*sc.* Aelfric's and Wulfstan's lives] are reprinted here because of the instructive contrast in style and because they illustrate so well the attitude of medieval writers to the task of hagiography." The text of the Wulfstan Life, the first publication of this version, is based on B.M. MS Cotton Tib. D.iv, vol. 2, ff. 272ᵛ–281ᵛ. Readings lost from this MS, damaged in the Cottonian fire, have been restored from B.M. Cotton Nero E.i. Selected readings from Nero E.i and other witnesses are given in the Textual Notes. Abbo's Life of St. Edmund is based on Cotton Tib. B.ii, ff. 2ʳ–19ᵛ, with some help from two contemporary witnesses. In the case both of Wulfstan and Abbo, Winterbottom provides much information which would aid in the preparation of a critical edition. One fears, however, that such an undertaking will be put off indefinitely due to the appearance of Winterbottom's work. The introduction provides a bare minimum of information about the works and their authors; the explanatory notes on lexicography, syntax, sources and analogues, and historical matters are sound, if occasionally oversimplified and somewhat sparse. The Glossary (pp. 93–5) is more limited, both in the number of entries and in the amount of lexicographical data presented, than one might expect. Winterbottom's discussion of style (pp. 3, 6) is of real, but limited help (on the Anglo-Latin of the period see M. Lapidge, "Three Latin Poems from Æthelwold's School at Winchester," *Anglo-Saxon England* I, pp. 85–137, the works cited there, and Lapidge's forthcoming edition of Lantfred's *Translatio et miracula S. Swithuni*). Perhaps the most telling and just criticism of this volume, and of the series in general, would proceed from the reader's comparison of it to G. I. Needham's *Aelfric: Three Lives of English Saints* (N.Y., 1966) in Methuen's Old English Library, an inexpensive but very satisfactory school edition whose utility extends far beyond the classroom.

The second volume is an edition of the Late Latin version of the document traditionally referred to as the *Gospel of Nicodemus*. It is based on Einsiedeln Stiftsbibliothek MS 326 (*s.* x) with some help from Bodl. MS Laud Misc. 79 (*s.* xii), and is an improvement on the *textus receptus* (C. Tischendorf, *Evangelia Apocrypha*, 2nd ed., Leipzig, 1876). The Editor draws much of his introduction from the article of G. C. O'Cealleigh, "Dating the Commentaries of Nicodemus," *Harvard Theological Review*, 56 (1963), pp. 21–58. But neither O'Cealleigh (it was beyond his intention) nor the editor makes any effort to date the composition of the Late Latin version. Kim's approach to the philological features of the document ("The language of the MS is generally Medieval Latin with some interesting Vulgar Latin elements," p. 9), offers no help from that discipline toward dating the work. The introduction (pp. 1–10) is sketchy and, at times, naive (*e.g.* the remark on language cited above, the failure to suggest a date for the composition of the work, the failure to discuss the many nonscriptural sources for Christ's *descensus*). The notes are useful, but fewer than such a text requires. The bibliography (p. 11) is quite limited; the Editor would have been well-advised to refer to A. Grillmeier's article "Höllenabstieg Christi, Höllenfahrt Christi" in LThK V, 450–5, and the materials cited there.

The third volume is the best, and, within the limitations of this series, an unqualified success. The work is independent of G. Constable's edition of Peter the Venerable's letters (Cambridge, Mass., 1967). It contains seventeen carefully chosen letters, fourteen by Peter, one each by St. Bernard, Peter of Poitiers, and a physician Bartholomew. The letters are drawn from their appropriate sources with variants listed in the Textual Notes (pp. 99–101). The introduction, in light of the massive materials available in Constable's edition, is quite adequate. It provides a good sketch of Peter's experience and ideas, well illustrated from the letters in the selection. The notes are supplemented by a Glossary (pp. 102–17), and these are adequate for undergraduate instruction, since the difficulties of the language and style of the letters can be dealt with in the limited format of the series.

The series has achieved some of the goals set for it. Certain criticisms and suggestions might be made. The choice of texts in the series so far leaves something to be desired. Only volume III would recommend itself to the instructor of Medieval Latin survey courses, and even so, a larger selection containing a greater number of twelfth-century letter writers would recommend itself even more. Volume I would be useful in a course on the Anglo-Saxon monastic revival or on hagiography in general, but in the second case a more carefully chosen variety of lives would be preferable. Volume II will prove to be of even more limited use. Given the inadequacy of the anthologies of Medieval Latin currently available, the Toronto series is a step in the right direction. One might suggest a choice of documents of more general interest with already established texts (the usual procedure in school editions), the use of more elaborate introductions, and an increased number of notes which would provide for the student more information and a greater familiarity with the tools of Medieval Latin scholarship.

Review Notices

James J. Murphy. *Rhetoric in the Middle Ages: A History of Rhetorical Theory from St. Augustine to the Renaissance.* Berkeley and Los Angeles: Universiy of California Press, 1974. pp. 409. $15.75.

Professor Murphy's book fills a long-standing need. Charles Baldwin's *Medieval Rhetoric and Poetic* (New York, 1928; reprinted 1959), although serviceable, pays little attention to those historical matters that are the major contribution of Murphy's book – the origins of the medieval arts of discourse, and the cultural context of their development.

Murphy starts with a useful tour through the well-known strands of classical tradition and of the period of transition (Augustine, Boethius' *De differentiis topicis,* and the *rhetores minores*). His own contribution to the subject really begins with his discussion of the survival of the classical tradition in the Middle Ages. Significant exceptions to this survival were Cicero's mature and humanistic *De oratore,* and Quintilian's *Institutio oratoria.* The latter work was available only in *florilegia* or in the *mutili,* and even in these forms was generally ignored except for a brief revival in the twelfth century. Aristotle's *Rhetoric* was not widely known; and Murphy convincingly argues that the Middle Ages associated this work with ethics or political science rather than with rhetoric.

Murphy finds, as early as Rabanus Maurus, a pragmatic, eclectic approach to surviving classical texts, an approach which was to lead to the fragmentation of rhetoric into the *ars dictaminis, ars poetica,* and *ars predicandi,* each formulated to meet specific new needs. This fragmentation continues until Poggio's triumphant discovery of the complete text of Quintilian in 1416.

Murphy argues that rhetoric can hardly be said to have a place in the medieval curriculum. In the classical period, grammar had encroached on some of the functions of rhetoric, such as the elucidation of figurative language and the study of poetry; this tendency continued in the Middle Ages. Grammar and the growingly popular dialectic divided the field: the existence of a *trivium* is "largely a myth" (p. 105).

Murphy's discussion of medieval grammar is useful but admittedly incomplete, since not enough source material has been made available for study. An important element of Murphy's treatment lies in his continued insistence that the medieval arts of poetry must be understood as belonging to grammar and not to rhetoric. The surviving arts of poetry were produced during a rather brief period (c. 1175–post 1229); all of their authors, including Geoffrey of Vinsauf, were teachers of grammar. Murphy insists that their work cannot properly be understood except as part of a new, pragmatic "perceptive grammar" which contained doctrines that are "quasi-rhetorical" (p. 142).

The chapter on the *ars dictaminis* is a clear and comprehensive study of this tangled subject. Murphy gives a full account of the contents of the major treatises, often in outline or summary form. He includes a reproduction of a table of phrases (to be combined into a letter) from Lawrence of Aquilegia's *Practica*, a work which Murphy justifiably describes as a "rhetorical dead end unparalleled in the history of the arts of discourse" (p. 261). Although Murphy feels that the *ars dictaminis* answered a practical need, and ends this chapter with a plea for further study, he leaves the impression that this art of necessity led to "ultimate sterility" (p. 266).

Murphy seems more enthusiastic about the art of preaching, which he traces from Biblical times to the development of the medieval thematic sermon and the *artes predicandi*. Again, his method is to give detailed accounts of the contents of individual works. One of the most interesting of these is Thomas Chabham's *Summa de arte predicandi* (early thirteenth century). Murphy has rescued this important treatise from virtually total neglect. This early treatise attempts to draw connections among preaching, rhetoric, and poetics. Murphy's treatment of this document is absorbing and thorough, yet not detailed enough for me, at any rate, to decide whether this attempt at synthesis was genuinely any more successful than a similar attempt in John of Garland's *Parisiana poetria*.

The book contains a few lapses. Walafrid Strabo is put forward as the author of the *Glossa ordinaria* (p. 297). There are typos (Aquinas' "passive translation project," p. 90) and slips in Latin (e.g. Hugh "Primatis," p. 157). The summary of Matthew of Vendôme (pp. 164–7) seems at times based on mistranslation and is somewhat misleading. Further, since medieval debate about the relation among the arts of the *trivium* "had little to do with the actual use of preceptive doctrines" (p. 193), and since "quibbling about these terms [viz. *rhetorical* and *grammatical*] has limited usefulness to us in our attempts to understand what Geoffrey [of Vinsauf] and his fellows were about" (p. 173), then *why* is it essential to think of the arts of poetry as being basically grammatical? There is so much in the book that everyone will find something with which to disagree; but Murphy's study is indispensable.

Ernest Gallo
University of Massachusetts

Chazan, Robert, *Medieval Jewry in Northern France: A Political and Social History* (The Johns Hopkins University Studies in Historical and Political Science, Ninety-First Series, 2). Baltimore and London: The Johns Hopkins University Press, 1973. Pp. ix, 238. $12.50.

The Jews of northern France, becoming perceptible as a class in eleventh-century sources, flourished in the general revival of economic opportunity in the twelfth century. Professor Chazan finds little evidence of the atrocities perpetrated in German lands at the time of the First Crusade, and provides a restrained account of the growth of popular Christian hostility. He stresses the personal characteristics of the successive Capetian kings (and of other rulers) in explanation of the shifting fortunes of the Jews; indeed, it is a virtue of his study that he conceives of the Jewish experience as integral to the political history of France. Regarding the thirteenth century, he clarifies the indecisiveness of royal policy on money-lending after Philip Augustus, as well as the pivotal and tragic significance of the reign of Louis IX; and he brings out the political and fiscal opportunism by which Philip IV alternately favored and jolted the modest revival after 1270 prior to wielding the final blow in 1306.

On most of these matters, Professor Chazan's judgments are well-proportioned and reliable. But specialist historians will find little original argumentation and a disturbing lack of intensive analysis. The problem of propriety in Jews, of singular interest for the Capetian homelands, is hardly broached, nor is the distinction between serfdom and subjection (cf. p. 139) always kept clear. The contrast between the pious Louis IX and his "worldly' grandson is not only overstated but inconsistent with the preceding assessment of Louis' reign. The concept of "northern French Jewry" slips out of control in the discussion of the later thirteenth century, where the author relies heavily on Saige's documentation for Languedoc, without allowing explicitly for the likelihood that the bonds between northern and southern Jewries were tightening as both alike fell victim to an expansionist Capetian state. It is precisely because the implications of the designation *procurator communitatis Judeorum regni nostri* are not clear, that they deserve investigation. There are signs of haste in the documentation: an *arrêt* of the (Norman) Exchequer is misread (p. 156), Achille Luchaire is confused with Auguste Longnon (pp. 30, 40), while the study of the accounts of Provins, ruthlessly reduced to one sentence (p. 159), omits the page references to Prou and d'Auriac.

Nevertheless, the book will be useful, especially to readers lacking Latin or Hebrew, for the sources are amply quoted in translation. Specialists are likely to regret that sources are also *cited* in translation, but they will welcome the references to much recent secondary work on problems for which Hebrew materials are extant. One can only echo the author's regret that, with the passing of the great age of French Jewish culture after 1200, direct testimonies like the *responsa* fade out. This history of the medieval Jews becomes increasingly and excessively the story of an oppressed society as told by its oppressors.

Thomas N. Bisson
University of California,
Berkeley

Edward A. Armstrong. *Saint Francis, Nature Mystic: The Derivation and Significance of the Nature Stories in the Franciscan Legend* (Hermeneutics: Studies in the History of Religions, 2). Berkeley, Los Angeles, and London: University of California Press, 1973. Pp. 270, 19 plates. $12.00.

The image of Francis of Assisi as lover of birds and beasts and Mother Nature herself is almost as traditional as apple pie. What the image makers generally overlooked, however, was that St. Francis' love for nature was rooted beyond nature. The present study reminds the reader forcefully that Francis loved all creatures, whether animate or inanimate, rational or nonrational, and called them brothers and sisters, because he was overwhelmed by the awareness of the presence of God whom he loved as creator and father of all.

In the first chapter of the book the author describes Francis as that rare kind of person who can be labeled a "Christian nature mystic." Subsequent chapters investigate in a critical but interesting way the legends which deal with St. Francis' relationship to specific categories of creatures, such as birds, the animals of household and farm, fish, furred beasts, etc. Particularly well done are the analyses of the "Wolf of Gubbio" (pp. 199–217) and the "Canticle of Brother Sun" (pp. 218–43). Because the author has a very good acquaintance with the early Franciscan sources, he often is able to use the animal stories very effectively to gain valid insights into the mind of St. Francis, and also into the biographers' outlook and even into the intellectual climate of that era.

The author does not treat the Franciscan legends as if they arose in a vacuum. He views them, rather, within the wider context of the history of culture and literature. Indeed, the author makes a convincing case for the possible dependence of these legends on earlier sources, especially Irish ideas and literature and even Indian tales. The author's knowledge of folklore is extensive and quite amazing. Over and over he treats the reader to fascinating tales and tidbits of lore, for example, that the ancients considered bees to be "messengers of the gods" and "carriers of souls to the hereafter" (p. 149, n. 9).

The only notable difficulty with the book is that the author does not sufficiently evaluate the primary sources he uses. He quotes the *Mirror of Perfection* and the *Fioretti* as if they held the same importance and reliability for the history of St. Francis as do the biographies written by Thomas of Celano and St. Bonaventure. The character, origin, and purpose of the first two writings are significantly different from those of the last two. It would have been very helpful to expand the biograpihcal note (p. 253) to include such an evaluation of sources and to place the note at the beginning of the book.

A number of lesser distractions should also be mentioned. The author reflects the opinion of Sabatier that as early as the middle of the thirteenth century there were serious internal divisions within the Franciscan Order (pp. 116, 253). This assumption has been rejected by such scholars as M. Bihl, K. Esser, and S. Clasen, who point out these divisions occurred only at the end of the century. To avoid confusion, the *Regula Prima* (p. 22) should be referred to as the *Regula non bullata* or the *Rule of 1221*. The theme that Francis "married" Lady Poverty (pp. 24, 239) is a relatively late development; the earliest sources (e.g. the *Sacrum Commercium*) portray Francis as a "knight" in the "service" of "Lady" Poverty, who is always the "bride" of the "Lord," namely Jesus Christ. It would be more correct to state that Gregory IX declared St. Francis' Testament "not binding" rather than "invalid" (p. 29). Finally, the phrase *praeparatio evangelium* (p. 38) should probably read *praeparatio ad evangelium* or *praeparatio evangelii*.

The present book certainly helps the modern reader to understand the historical Francis of Assisi, a fascinating and simple human being. It can also help the reader to appreciate the saint's relevance for the man of today, searching for meaning in life and trying to understand his relationship to the universe in which he lives. Here are some striking words which the author writes about St. Francis: "Enthralled by the beauty and mystery of Creation, he believed and showed that love of God, love of man, and love of nature were not only compatible with one another but the natural, divinely purposed state of humanity" (p. 242).

Duane V. Lapsanski
St. Bonaventure University

Marcelle Thiébaux. *The Stag of Love: The Chase in Medieval Literature.*
Ithaca and London: Cornell University Press, 1974. Pp. 249; 19 illustrations.
$13.50.

The subtitle, "The Chase in Medieval Literature," states in a phrase the
general subject matter of this fine book; the title, *The Stag of Love,* drawn
from an allegorical poem, *Li dis dou cerf amoreus,* hints that the topic will
become particularized and that the chase will be studied as a literary motif, as
a metaphor or a symbolic chase of one kind or another, and finally as an amatory allegory. Like a stag the topic is pursued wherever it goes – across wide
landscapes of English, French, and German writings. Some landmarks will be
familiar; some places will no doubt be strange and perhaps forbidding; but if
the reader is a good hunter not easily discouraged by the difficulties of the
trail, he is likely to be rewarded in ways he never foresaw.

The author lays out the book in four large sections, actually four chapters
and an epilogue, with their subdivisions. Since the medieval hunt or chase with
dogs is no longer a familiar sport today, in the first chapter necessary preliminary information is presented under the headings "Hunting Practice and
Ceremony," "The Iconography of the Stag," and "The Hunt as a Literary
Structure." It is pointed out that what we know about medieval hunting is
largely a reconstruction from literary sources and cynegetic handbooks, which
themselves tended to be "literary" and idealized. To this must be added the
symbolic iconography of the stag in art and literature. The handbooks tended
to become elaborate in prescribing ceremonial decorum, attitudes, and proper
dress as well as equipment, procedures, and correct terminology to be used in
the pursuit, capture, and breaking of different kinds of game. Perhaps they
present a notion of what the hunt ought to be in all details rather than what it
usually was. In any case the poet had such materials to draw upon when he
chose to use hunting metaphors, or the chase as a structure, or a symbol, or a
starting point even though his personal experience with hunting was limited.
Whether he used his knowledge of the hunt in a conventional or an original
manner depended on the poet.

Dr Thiébaux considers the sacred chase, the mortal chase, and the instructive chase in the second chapter and reserves the love chase for the final
chapters. Aelfric's *Passion of St. Eustace* is studied as an example of the sacred
chase, and then "Siegfried's Death" in the *Nibelungenlied* as an example of the
mortal chase, for Siegfried is the great hunter who himself becomes the quarry
and is slain. *Sir Gawain and the Green Knight* as an example of the instructive chase is analyzed at greater length because of its complexity. The medieval
attitude toward the hunt as a sport which keeps its practitioners away from
harmful moral temptations and problems, in contrast to sleeping late and lying
in bed, is behind the intricate relationships among events at Bertilak's castle and
their relationship to the test at the Green Chapel. Sir Gawain is instructed in
virtue and courage – not in hunting techniques.

Love, human and divine, is a major theme of romances and lyrics from the
twelfth century on, and the amatory hunt often is used as a metaphor or a
controlling symbol. Writers were heirs to a stock of images and uses of the
love chase from Classical writers such as Ovid; allegorical interpretations of
the hart from scriptural commentaries had their influence; and contemporary
aristocratic interest in the hunt provided motivation. Through a considerable
forest of possible material Dr Thiébaux traces a path by selecting a small number of poems by important poets for close analysis where the symbolism of

the sacred, the mortal, and the instructional chase fuse with each other and with the human love chase. The *Erec* of Chrétien de Troyes, *The Book of the Duchess* of Chaucer, and the *Tristan* of Gottfried are given most attention. The insights to be gained from these analyses I believe are rewarding.

Chapter IV with its epilogue carries the investigation into medieval allegories of the love chase. The hunt becomes the pursuit of a woman, explicitly stated or implied. Hounds are given names of attributes of the hunter, and things belonging to the stag or associated with it are allegorized as attributes of the beloved. Stages in the chase designate stages in the love affair; there are noble hunters who observe the rules and bad hunters who do not; and the stag may ruse, take to the water, be caught, or escape. *Die Jagd* of Hadamar von Laber, the major allegory of the love chase in the fourteenth century, is examined in greater detail than the allegories before or after it. Although Dr Thiébaux controls with remarkable skill large quantities of minute detail from the allegories of the love chase, I believe that this section of the book will have less interest for the reader because allegories of the love chase seem even more remote than the medieval hunt itself.

Paul E. Beichner, C.S.C.
University of Notre Dame

Books Received

This list was compiled from books received between 1 May 1974 and 28 March 1975. The publishers and the editorial board would appreciate your mentioning *Medievalia et Humanistica* when ordering.

Alan of Lille. *Anticlaudianus or the Good and Perfect Man,* trans. and notes by James J. Sheridan. Toronto: Pontifical Institute of Mediæval Studies, 1973. Pp. 251. $5.50.

Alexander, Sidney. *Lions and Foxes: Men and Ideas of the Italian Renaissance.* New York: Macmillan, 1974. Pp. xiii, 375. $12.95.

Armstrong, Edward A. *Saint Francis: Nature Mystic. The Derivation and Significance of the Nature Stories in the Franciscan Legend.* Berkeley, Los Angeles, and London: University of California Press, 1973. Pp. 275. $12.00.

Azzopardi, John. *Handlist of the Episcopal and Pro-Vicarial Archives (Curia Episcopalis Melitensis) at the Malta Cathedral Museum.* Collegeville: St. John's University, 1975. Pp. 54. $4.00 paper.

Barnie, John. *War in Medieval English Society, Social Values and the Hundred Years War, 1337–1399.* New York: Cornell University Press, 1974. Pp. xiii, 204. $10.00.

Bennett, J. A. W. *Chaucer at Oxford and at Cambridge.* Toronto: University of Toronto Press, 1974. Pp. 131. $7.50.

Bernardo, Aldo S. *Petrarch, Laura, and the "Triumphs."* Albany: State University of New York Press, 1974. Pp. xi, 234. $15.00.

Boccaccio, Giovanni. *The Book of Theseus: Teseida delle Nozze d'Emilia,* trans. by Bernadette M. McCoy. New York: Medieval Text Assoc., 1974. Pp. vii, 352. $6.95 paper.

Boyd, Morrison C. *Elizabethan Music and Musical Criticism.* Philadelphia: University of Pennsylvania Press, 1974. Pp. xi, 363. $3.95 paper.

Bradshaw, Brendan. *The Dissolution of the Religious Orders in Ireland under Henry VIII.* New York and London: Cambridge University Press, 1974. Pp. xi, 276. $16.50.

Bromwich, Rachel. *Medieval Celtic Literature: A Select Bibliography* (Toronto Medieval Bibliographies 5). Toronto: University of Toronto Press, 1974. Pp. 109. $3.95 paper.

Browning, Robert. *Byzantium and Bulgaria: A Compartive Study across the Early Medieval Frontier.* Berkeley and Los Angeles: University of California Press, 1975. Pp. 232. $11.50.

Brundage, James A. *Richard Lion Heart, a Biography.* New York: Charles Scribner's Sons, 1974. Pp. ix, 278. $10.00.

Burford, E. J. *The Orrible Synne, a Look at London Lechery from Roman to Cromwellian Times.* London: Calder & Boyars, 1973. Pp. 256. $12.00.

Clemoes, Peter, ed. *Anglo-Saxon England 3.* New York and London: Cambridge University Press, 1974. Pp. x, 270. $22.50.

Cullen, Patrick. *Infernal Triad: The Flesh, the World, and the Devil in Spenser and Milton.* Princeton: Princeton University Press, 1975. Pp. xxxvi, 265. $13.50.

Dronke, Peter. *Fabula: Explorations into the Uses of Myth in Medieval Platonism* (Mittellateinische Studien und Texte, IX). Leiden und Köln: E. J. Brill, 1974. Pp. 200, 3 plates. 58 gilders.

Erasmus, Desiderius. *Collected Works of Erasmus, Volume 1: The Correspondence of Erasmus, Letters 1 to 141 (1484 to 1500),* trans. by R. A. B. Mynors and D. F. S. Thomson, annot. by W. K. Ferguson. Toronto: University of Toronto Press, 1974. Pp. xxviii, 368. $25.00.

Fenlon, Dermot. *Heresy and Obedience in Tridentine Italy: Cardinal Pole and the Counter Reformation.* New York and London: Cambridge University Press, 1972. Pp. xiii, 300. $19.50.

Ferguson, Mary A. *Bibliography of English Translations from Medieval Sources, 1942–1968.* New York: Columbia University Press, 1974. Pp. x, 274. $15.00.

Fish, Stanley E. *Self-Consuming Artifacts: The Experience of Seventeenth-Century Literature.* 1973; rpt. Berkeley and London: University of California Press, 1975. Pp. xiv, 432. $3.95 paper.

Gildea, Joseph, O. S. A., ed. *L'Hystoire Job: An Old French Verse Adaptation of 'Compendium in Job' by Peter of Blois.* I: Texts. Villanova: St. Thomas Press, 1974. Pp. xxiv, 286. $15.00 paper.

Guido da Pisa. *Expositiones et glose super Comedium Dantis.* Ed. Vincenzo Cioffari. Albany: State University of New York Press, 1974. Pp. lxi, 724. $40.00.

Handler, Andrew. *The Zirids of Granada.* Coral Gables: University of Miami Press, 1974. Pp. xii, 208. $10.00.

Hughes, Andrew. *Medieval Music: The Sixth Liberal Art.* Toronto: University of Toronto Press, 1974. Pp. xii, 326. $20.00.

Kenney, E. J. *The Classical Text.* Berkeley, Los Angeles, and London: University of California Press, 1975. Pp. xi, 174. $8.95.

Kinsman, Robert S., ed. *The Darker Vision of the Renaissance: Beyond the Fields of Reason.* Berkeley, Los Angeles, and London: University of California Press, 1975. Pp. vi, 320. $14.00.

McGrade, Arthur Stephen. *The Political Thought of William of Ockham: Personal and Institutional Principles.* New York and London: Cambridge University Press, 1974. Pp. xiii, 269. $18.50.

Mills, Maldwyn, ed. *Six Middle English Romances.* Totowa, N. J.: Rowman and Littlefield, 1973. Pp. xxxiii, 224. $7.50, $3.50 paper.

Miskimin, Alice S. *The Renaissance Chaucer.* New Haven and London: Yale University Press, 1975. Pp. xii, 315. $15.00.

Morewedge, Rosmarie T., ed. *The Role of Woman in the Middle Ages* (Papers of the Sixth Annual Conference of the Center for Medieval and Early Renaissance Studies). Albany: State University of New York Press, 1975. Pp. 195. $12.50.

Mostra Bibliografica Ariostea: Nel V Centenario della Nascita di Ludovico Ariosto. Roma: Biblioteca Statale Angelica, 1974. Pp. 63.

Mullins, Edwin. *The Pilgrimage to Santiago.* New York: Taplinger, 1974. Pp. xiii, 222. $12.95.

Murphy, James J. *Rhetoric in the Middle Ages: A History of Rhetorical*

Theory from St. Augustine to the Renaissance. Berkeley, Los Angeles, and London: University of California Press, 1974. Pp. xiv, 395. $15.75.

Le Mystère de la Passion Nostre Seigneur, du manuscrit 1131 de la Bibliothèque Sainte-Geneviève. Édité avec une introduction et des notes par Graham A. Runnalls. Genève: Librairie Droz, 1974. Pp. 305.

Nelson, Alan H. *The Medieval English Stage, Corpus Christi Pageants and Plays.* Chicago: University of Chicago Press, 1974. Pp. xiv, 274. $12.50.

Novelle Cinque: Tales from the Veneto, Illustrated with Facsimiles from the 16th Century Manuscript. Trans., ed., and annot. by George H. Bumgardner. Barre, Mass.: Imprint Society, 1974. Pp. 144. $45.00.

O'Callaghan, Joseph F. *A History of Medieval Spain.* Ithaca and London: Cornell University Press, 1975. Pp. 729. $25.00.

Place, Edwin B. and Herbert C. Behm, trans. *Amadis of Gaul, Books I and II: A Novel of Chivalry of the 14th Century Presumably First Written in Spanish.* Lexington: University Press of Kentucky, 1974. Pp. 685. $15.00.

Plante, Julian G., Ph.D. *Checklist of Manuscripts Microfilmed for the Monastic Microfilm Library, Saint John's University, Collegeville, Minnesota, Vol. I, part 2.* Collegeville, Minn.: St. John's University, 1974. Pp. v, 296. $5.00.

The Poetry of Llywarch Hen. Ed. and trans. Patrick K. Ford. Berkeley, Los Angeles, and London: University of California Press, 1974. Pp. xvii, 145. $8.95.

Raftis, J. Ambrose. *Warboys.* Toronto: Pontifical Institute of Mediaeval Studies, 1974. Pp. x, 267. $15.00.

Ranum, Orest, ed. *National Consciousness, History, and Political Culture in Early-Modern Europe.* Baltimore and London: Johns Hopkins University Press, 1975. Pp. x, 177. $10.00.

Reeves, Robert Nicholas, III. *The Ridiculous to the Delightful: Comic Characters in Sidney's New Arcadia.* Cambridge, Mass.: Harvard University Press, 1974. Pp. 53. $2.50 paper.

Rochon, A. *Les Ecrivains et Le Pouvoir en Italie à L'Epoque de la Renaissance* (Le Volume 3 des publications du Centre de Recherche sur la Renaissance Italienne). Paris: Université de la Sorbonne Nouvelle, 1974. Pp. 325. 50 francs.

Rowland, Beryl, ed. *Chaucer and Middle English Studies in Honour of Rossell Hope Robbins.* Kent, Ohio: Kent State University Press, 1974. Pp. 424. $15.00.

Sanderlin, David. *The Mediaeval Statutes of the College of Autun at the University of Paris* (No. XIII of Texts and Studies in the History of Mediaeval Education). Notre Dame, Ind.: Mediaeval Institute, 1971. Pp. 117.

Sayles, George O. *The King's Parliament of England* (Historical Controversies: A Norton Series). New York: Norton, 1974. Pp. xi, 164. $7.95, $2.95 paper.

Searle, Eleanor. *Lordship and Community, Battle Abbey and its Banlieu, 1066–1538.* Toronto: Pontifical Institute of Mediaeval Studies, 1974. Pp. 469. $20.00.

Smalley, Beryl. *Historians in the Middle Ages.* New York: Charles Scribner's Sons, 1975. 99 illustrations, 10 in color. Pp. 202. $12.50.

Stevens, John. *Medieval Romance: Themes and Approaches.* London: Hutchinson University Library, 1973. Pp. 255. $10.00.

Swarzenski, Hanns. *Monuments of Romanesque Art: The Art of Church*

Treasures in North-Western Europe. 2nd ed. Chicago: University of Chicago Press, 1974. Pp. 102, 238 plates. $8.95 paper.

Taylor, Jerome and Alan H. Nelson, eds. *Medieval English Drama: Essays Critical and Contextual* (Patterns of Literary Criticism, 11). Chicago: University of Chicago Press, 1972. Pp. vii, 351. $14.00.

Thiébaux, Marcelle. *The Stag of Love: The Chase in Medieval Literature.* Ithaca and London: Cornell University Press, 1974. Pp. 249, 19 illustrations. $13.50.

Thundyil, Zacharias P. *Covenant in Anglo-Saxon Thought.* Delhi: The Macmillan Co. of India, 1972. Pp. viii, 241.

Trithemius, Johannes. *In Praise of Scribes (De Laude Scriptorum).* Ed. Klaus Arnold. Lawrence, Kansas: The Coronado Press, 1974. Pp. xv, 111. $6.50.

Ullman, Walter. *The Future of Medieval History: An Inaugural Lecture.* Cambridge: at the University Press, 1973. $1.45 paper.

——. *Law and Politics in the Middle Ages: An Introduction to the Sources of Medieval Political Ideas.* Ithaca: Cornell University Press, 1975. Pp. 320. $15.00.

Wakefield, Walter L. *Heresy, Crusade and Inquisition in Southern France, 1100–1250.* Berkeley and Los Angeles: University of California Press, 1974. Pp. 295. $14.50.

Watson, George, ed. *The New Cambridge Bibliography of English Literature.* Vol. I: 600–1660. Cambridge: At the University Press, 1974. Pp. xxxii, 2491. $49.50.

Webster, Bruce. *Scotland from the Eleventh Century to 1603.* Ithaca: Cornell University Press, 1975. Pp. 239. $12.50.

Weitzmann, Kurt. *Illustrated Manuscripts at St. Catherine's Monastery on Mount Sinai.* Collegeville, Minn.: St. John's University Press, 1973. Pp. 34, 32 plates. $2.00 paper.

Wilkie, William E. *The Cardinal Protectors of England: Rome and the Tudors before the Reformation.* New York: Cambridge University Press, 1974. Pp. viii, 262. $14.50.

Woolf, Rosemary. *The English Mystery Plays.* Berkeley, Los Angeles, and London: University of California Press, 1972. Pp. 437. $16.00.

Yates, Frances A. *The Art of Memory.* Chicago: University of Chicago Press, 1974. Pp. xiv, 400. $5.95 paper.